FAITHFUL
GENERATIONS

FAITHFUL GENERATIONS

Effective Ministry Across Generational Lines

John R. Mabry

 Morehouse Publishing
NEW YORK · HARRISBURG · DENVER

Unless otherwise noted, the Scripture quotations contained herein are from the New Revised Standard Version Bible, copyright © 1989 by the Division of Christian Education of the National Council of Churches of Christ in the U.S.A. Used by permission. All rights reserved.

Some sections on Faith Styles are adapted from *Faith Styles: Ways People Believe* (Morehouse, 2006) by John R. Mabry.

Excerpts taken from *The Millennials* by Thom S. Rainer and Jess W. Rainer © 2011 B&H Publishing Group, used by permission.

Excerpts taken from *Souls in Transition: The Religious and Spiritual Lives of Emerging Adults* by Smith & Snell (2009) 952 pp. 20, 25, 36–37, 45, 68, 71–72, 74, 146, 152–153, 164, 202. By permission of Oxford University Press, USA.

Morehouse Publishing, 4775 Linglestown Road, Harrisburg, PA 17112

Morehouse Publishing, 445 Fifth Avenue, New York, NY 10016

Morehouse Publishing is an imprint of Church Publishing Incorporated.

www.churchpublishing.org

Cover design by Laurie Klein Westhafer

Typeset by Denise Hoff

Library of Congress Cataloging-in-Publication Data
Mabry, John R.
  Faithful generations : effective ministry across generational lines / John R. Mabry.
      pages cm
  Includes bibliographical references.
  ISBN 978-0-8192-2820-8 (pbk.) -- ISBN 978-0-8192-2821-5 (ebook)   1. Church work. 2. Intergenerational relations--Religious aspects--Christianity. I. Title.
  BV4470.M33 2013
  259.084--dc23
                    2012045753

Printed in the United States of America

OTHER BOOKS
by JOHN R. MABRY

Growing Into God:
A Beginner's Guide to Christian Mysticism

Salvation of the True Rock:
The Sufi Poetry of Najat Ozkaya

Sermons That Connect:
A Beginner's Guide to Crafting
and Delivering Powerful, Excellent Sermons

The Kingdom:
A Berkeley Blackfriars Novel

People of Faith:
An Interfaith Companion
to the Revised Common Lectionary

The Monster God:
Coming to Terms with the Dark Side of Divinity

Noticing the Divine:
An Introduction to Interfaith Spiritual Guidance

Faith Styles:
Ways People Believe

The Way of Thomas:
Nine Insights for Enlightened Living
from the Secret Sayings of Jesus

God Has One Eye:
The Mystics of the World's Religions

God is a Great Underground River:
Articles, Essays, and Homilies
on Interfaith Spirituality

I Believe in a God Who is Growing:
Process Perspectives on the Creed,
the Sacraments, and the Christian Life

Who Are the Independent Catholics?
(with John P. Plummer)

Crisis and Communion:
The Re-Mythologization of the Eucharist

Heretics, Mystics & Misfits

God As Nature Sees God:
A Christian Reading of the Tao Te Ching

DEDICATION

To the "old guard" at Grace North Church:

John and Marguerite Azer

Leslie Blavins

Bob and Val Bloemink

Russell & Mardell Corning

Pat Crossman

Robert and Elizabeth
  Develbiss

Ken Durling

Richard and Kate Ferry

Keith and Laura Fisher

Wilson and Hazel Flick

Basil Guy

Janeen Jones

Richard and Lindzi
  Mapplebeckpalmer,
  Lilli & Richard

Jim and Harriet McCullom

Tom and Virginia McKone,
  Justin & Stephen

Harriet Peters

Phyllis Schafer,
  Ann Brooks & Nick

Katherine Schenck

David and Mary Shanley

Harvey and Skippy Short

Royal and Charlotte Thompson

Ed and Alma Vanek

John Wheat

Laura White

Helga and John Wilson

Francora Wuesthoff

Thank you for welcoming me,
calling me, and loving me
as your associate pastor all those years ago,
in spite of my pony tail. And my earrings.
And the fact that I called
everyone "dude," even the ladies.

CONTENTS

INTRODUCTION

WHEN I WAS first called as associate pastor to my current parish, I experienced a profound culture shock. But it had nothing to do with ethnic or geographic dislocation—it was entirely a product of generational unfamiliarity. I was in my early thirties, and fit in well with my liberal Berkeley peers. But the church that called me was composed almost entirely of octogenarians. They looked at my earrings suspiciously, and I tried not to react negatively to their overwhelmingly Republican leanings.

Over time, we grew to love each other deeply. They discovered that they might actually learn something from this whippersnapper, and I found that beneath their gruff, pull-yourself-up-by-your-bootstraps exteriors were tender and caring souls with a very different way of viewing the world from my own. Pretty much everything I had learned about ministry up to that point went out the window, as I began to feel into what *these particular people* expected and needed from a pastor.

What I discovered was that ministering to this generation was a bit like moving to a wild and unexplored place. I became an anthropologist of sorts, discerning the mythology, ritual system, and societal quirks of the native population from observation and imitation. It was a different world, and more than once I uttered a seemingly innocuous observation that blew into a dustup before I realized what I'd said.

I learned to navigate this exotic world, and in my nearly twenty years in congregational ministry and ten years practicing and training spiritual directors, I have since found that every generation is likewise unique, with its own generational culture, language, and spiritual needs. What works for one generation most assuredly does not work for another, and a great deal of misunderstanding and conflict in our spiritual communities is born of the fact that so few people are aware of this truth.

In this book I will discuss each of the five adult generations today, noting their cultural distinctiveness, their unique spirituality, and spiritual needs. It is my hope that spiritual directors, ministers, and other helping professionals—and those training for these fields—will find it a helpful starting point for discussion and preparation for working with different generations.

Indebtedness

I am deeply indebted to Dr. Howard Rice for first introducing me to the idea of inter-generational ministry. His 1998 interview in *Presence: An International Journal of Spiritual Direction*, "Generational Issues in Direction," was profound for me, and helped me make some much-needed connections in my own ministry.

It was during his lecture at the 1998 Spiritual Directors International Conference in Burlingame, California, that the light bulb went on regarding my own generation, Generation X. I realized (and stated, during the Q&A after the lecture) that far from not having a generational myth, my generation was strongly guided by a story that they unconsciously know: the Gnostic myth.

This made sense of the fact that I had been, for several years, drawn to Gnostic scriptures as my nightly bedtime reading, and the many Gnostic themes emerging from Gen X culture.[1] Like pieces of the puzzle, I realized why it was so compelling, and explored these connections in my 1999 *Presence* article, "The Gnostic Generation."[2] I continued to explore the significance of this theme, through my book *The Way of Thomas*,[3] and, musically, through my band Metaphor's rock opera, *Starfooted*, based on the Gnostic myth.[4]

Howard Rice's work was based on the research of sociologists William Strauss and Neil Howe, whose groundbreaking book *Generations*[5] introduced generational theory and research to a wide audience when it was first published in 1991. I am grateful to Rice for steering me to Strauss and Howe's work, and this book is more deeply indebted to their research than to any other single source. I quote from them frequently, and the entire edifice of this current work is constructed upon theirs—although in an extremely simplified and abbreviated form. If you don't buy their theories, there will be little of value for you, here. If, however, you find their ideas compelling, I highly recommend *Generations*, where you can examine their theories in their fullness and complexity.

Finally, I am grateful to my students at the Chaplaincy Institute and Sophia University (formerly the Institute of Transpersonal Psychology) for their kind and enthusiastic input as I taught this material over the past several years. It is only because time and again they approached me after class and said, "you *must* find a wider audience for this—it helped me so much" that I have continued to work on it. I want to say to them: Thank you, and thank you for your many and invaluable suggestions.

Context and Limitations

When I teach this material, I always tell my students that everything I am about to say is a fiction.[6] Anytime we talk about people in a generalized or universal way, we are talking in fictional terms. Individual exceptions to each of these generational portraits are legion, and everyone knows someone who does not fit into the stereotypes depicted below. But generalizations are tools—often useful ones—and hopefully you will find these fictions helpful in your ministries, as they do describe vast cross-sections of the generations discussed.

It is important to note that Strauss and Howe were writing specifically about generations in an American context, and Howard Rice was likewise speaking about spiritual direction in the United States. Like them, my work has been largely based in the United States, although I believe that most of what I say will also accurately reflect generations in most (so-called) First World contexts. Certainly those in Canada and Europe who have encountered my work have resonated with it. In addition, some of the research I relied upon regarding the Millennial Generation was done in England and Australia, yet I find it to be an accurate reflection of young people in the United States as well.

Those who are well read on generational theory will note that there are a lot of variations regarding where different researchers and theorists actually say a generation begins and ends. For example, some theorists (such as Thom and Jess Rainer)[7] place the Baby Boomer's cutoff date at 1964, meaning that Generation X begins at 1965. Strauss and Howe, however, cut the Boomers off at 1960, and begin Generation X at 1961.

I follow Strauss and Howe on this, because while those who prefer a later date are looking at actual birth records (when did the Baby Boom actually *stop*?), the generational culture actually shifted with the earlier date. Most people born in 1962 or 1963 do not *act* like Boomers, they act like Xers and their attitudes are Xer. They *are* Xers (birth rates be damned!). The dates I have chosen relate to the general time when, according to a consensus of theorists (and in my experience) a generational culture shifts.

Given this, there are individuals on the cusp who "slide around" a bit. Some "cuspers" are obviously more identified with adjacent generations. For example, survey respondent Teri was born in 1961, but her comments are in every way Boomeresque. Note that such cases only "overlap" a neighboring generation by a year or two, and are rare—the largest gap I encountered in my research is one person born three years before the beginning of her generation of affinity.

Further, from my own observation, I have noticed that people who are from very conservative religious traditions—although they may share many or even most important aspects of their generational cohort—seem to exhibit a generational ghosting, or lag. For instance, Silents who are extremely religious skew towards many G.I. attributes. Religiously conservative Boomers may present as Silents, while fundamentalist Xers may exhibit an idealism more characteristic of Boomers. This is a very curious phenomenon deserving of further study, but is beyond the scope of this work.

A final limitation needs to be mentioned. One thing this book will not teach you to do is minister. I assume that my reader is already a trained professional in his or her field: pastor, chaplain, spiritual director, social worker, therapist, or the like. Whatever your area of ministry, I assume you already have the skills to do it well. This book serves only to identify possible generational blind spots—areas of ministry that many people overlook because they are not aware of the profound discontinuity between generational cultures. Professionalism and responsible ministry practices are assumed throughout.

Method

Although I employ the tools of sociology, and draw upon the work of many respected sociologists, I want to be very clear that I am *not* a sociologist. I am a pastor, writing as a pastor *to* pastors, as well as to other people in ministry. My method cannot be construed as scientific in any way, nor can the responses I received really be taken to be representative. They are, however, truly random.

Some of the quotations in this book come from previously published sources (those sociologists mentioned above) but the vast majority of them come from surveys. I sent out requests to literally thousands of people, asking them to fill out surveys. Via Facebook posts, online bulletin boards, email lists, friends, acquaintances, and strangers—whomever I could ask, I asked. I kept asking until I got about twenty completed surveys from each generational cohort. Again, there was no attempt to be systematic here. My respondents are mostly Americans, but they are from every part of the country, represent a broad economic spectrum, and a variety of religions. As for racial diversity, I didn't ask, and I have absolutely no idea—email is color-blind.

G.I.s presented a unique problem, in that so few of them are online. To collect their stories, I hired research assistants in various parts of the country to go into retirement communities, strike up conversations, and walk people through the survey questions. I am indebted to them for their ingenuity, resourcefulness, and dedication to the project. I am particularly grateful to Marta Dabis, Eileen M. Harrington, Elizabeth Ingenthron, and James McClellan for their help with the Silent and G.I. interviews. Thanks also to Ashley Jett, Samantha Lussier, Jen Owens, and Jadelynn Stahl for their help collecting surveys from Millennials.

I have constructed the chapters following the same basic pattern. In a few cases, the sections are handled in a slightly different order. This is simply because the flow of the material seemed to suggest a slightly different arrangement. I suppose I could have "forced" the material into absolute consistency, but it seemed pointless to go against the grain in such a way, just to enforce an arbitrary uniformity. Instead, I followed my instincts and allowed them each to "breathe" a little.

Attentive readers will notice some redundancy within chapters. I have tried my best to present a linear explanation of the generations, but spirituality is holistic, not compartmental. Everything is connected to everything else, and in describing one aspect of a generation, I will often repeat a detail already mentioned as pertinent to another aspect. I ask the reader to see this not as a flaw in the writing, but as indicative of the complexity and wholeness I am trying (in my flawed and limited way) to describe.

Objectivity

Not long ago I got an email from someone complaining about the unequal length of chapters in my book *Faith Styles: Ways People Believe*. While each chapter was exactly as long as it needed to be in order to say what I needed to say, this person felt I was playing favorites and being unfair to some styles, giving some short shrift. When I told my wife about this, she laughed and said, "Someone should inform him that the carcass of the Myth of Objectivity stopped kicking years ago." (My wife teaches moral theology to seminarians, but she really ought to be writing for David Letterman.)

In fact, it is impossible to do pastoral ministry outside of a subjective, affective frame of reference. It's equally impossible to write authentically about theology or spirituality "objectively." In this book I am "out and proud" about my subjectivity. While the 100+ random surveys and interviews that I compiled for this book provided invaluable information and often some course-correction for my ideas, I write mostly from my own perspective, having done ministry among people of different generations for over twenty years, in various roles including pastor, chaplain, teacher, and spiritual director.

Some chapters are longer not because I think some generations more important than others, but because I simply had more to say, and for this I make no apology. For instance, more ink is devoted to the Millennials than any other generation. I am hoping this will be welcome, since Millennials are the largest generation alive, are a mystery to many of us, and are conspicuously absent from our spiritual communities. But I also had more to say about them because there is so much information available from the many studies that have been done on Millennial spirituality in the past several years.

Useful Models

In each chapter, I employ a couple of models to help readers understand the generations at hand, specifically in how they relate to one another, and in the distinct ways in which they hold faith.

According to Strauss and Howe, generations in America move in a predictable cycle:[8] a Civic generation (responsible builders) is usually followed by an Adaptive generation (compassionate reformers), which is followed by an Idealistic generation (radical visionaries), followed by a Reactive generation (disillusioned pragmatists).[9] Reactive generations are usually followed by another Civic generation, and the cycle begins again. Fortunately, the first of our five living adult generations is a Civic generation, which makes this cycle easy to see and discuss.

To help people grasp various ways in which people—even in the same faith tradition—approach their spirituality differently, I have made reference to my previous book, *Faith Styles*. This is a spiritual assessment system developed from the research and insights of James Fowler, Scott Peck, and Jurgen Schwing.

In it I present six "styles" of faith: *Traditional Believers* (who approach religion from a conservative, literal orientation), *Liberal Believers* (progressives who view religion more metaphorically), *Spiritual Eclectics* (who pick and choose their beliefs from a variety of traditional and contemporary sources), *Religious Agnostics* (those who are skeptical about religious truth claims but nevertheless avail themselves of the benefits of spiritual community), *Ethical Humanists* (secular atheists and agnostics who possess an orientation of awe toward the universe and feel a connection to Life as a truly sacred force), and *Jack Believers* (those who believe the Traditional Believer paradigms but cannot or will not live up to the moral codes required by those faiths, thereby finding themselves outside of their traditions' circles of grace).

While each generation has people of all six Faith Styles, most generations have an affinity for one or another of them, and I found it useful to draw out the parallels between them.

Final Thoughts

The final section of each chapter offers advice for each generation, offering spiritual guidance to the generation at hand—for example, "Millennials Ministering to Silents." I suggest not just reading the generation pertinent to you, dear reader, as the other sections may yield insights for you as well. If nothing else, they may help you understand why those of other generations may have had difficulty in their attempts to minister to this particular generation.

I am aware that sometimes these ministry suggestions read like newspaper astrology predictions. *Sigh* . . . . Please remember that these are vast overgeneralizations, but that there is indeed some useful truth in there. Please take what is helpful to you and merrily dismiss the rest. After all, my moon may have been in Neptune the day I wrote it.

Finally, I feel compelled to say that I hope you will take these profiles with a grain of salt. Truly, there is something to upset everyone in these pages—none of the generational portraits are entirely flattering. Out of kindness, I have relegated some of my snarkier asides to the endnotes.[10] Remember that there is nothing objective about the material I am presenting. I am an Xer, and I write as an Xer, and as you probably know (or are soon to discover) Xers can be insufferably sarcastic. I would say, "I'm sorry," but I'm not.

It is my sincere prayer, however, that the material in this book—unscientific and subjective though it may be—will resonate with others' experiences, and will help people minister and offer spiritual guidance more effectively to people of all generations.

CHAPTER ONE

THE "BUILDERS" —THE G.I. GENERATION

When Myrtle came for her monthly spiritual direction session, she was visibly agitated. Her director, a Sister of Mercy named Margaret, made her a cup of chamomile tea, and held her hand until a quiet descended on the room. "What's happening, Myrtle?" she said, with a reassuring smile.

"My granddaughter Jackie is saying she's . . . not getting married in the Church," Myrtle began haltingly. "She says she wants to get married outside, in a park, and her priest won't do it. And her fiancé isn't Catholic!"

"I can understand why you're disappointed. A wedding in church is so beautiful. But it's not that unusual these days for a couple to want to do something different."

"But it's not right!" Myrtle looked up at her, with real grief in her eyes. "What will happen to her?"

"To your granddaughter? What do you mean?"

"If her marriage isn't blessed, how will it survive? How can she start off something so important by offending God? How will they make it without God's help?"

MYRTLE'S GENERATION IS one firmly grounded in tradition, in conformity to a collective ideal, and to authority which one questions at one's peril. Far from being backwards or limiting, this formula has worked magic for them—our oldest generation has undoubtedly also been our most potent, influential, and effective. Their courage is unmatched in any living generation, their sacrifices unrivaled, their achievements unsurpassed. Tom Brokaw called them "the Greatest Generation," and few dare challenge this. And little wonder. Anyone who ever *has* challenged this confident, can-do generation has wound up on the losing side of the scuffle. In their prime, none dared oppose them—before them tyrants fell, fascism failed, and communism crumbled. Just who are these sure-footed scrappers, and how did they get that way?

Birth Years and Place in the Cycle

Born between 1901 and 1924, the first wave of this generation grew up in the shadow of the Great War, and the entire generation gave their all during the Second World War. They are the most uniformed generation in American history, and for this reason, sociologists refer to them as the G.I. Generation. "G.I." stands for "general issue" or "government issue," as in "G.I. Joe." They began their uniformed careers early, as the first boy scouts, campfire girls, and girl scouts.[1] Later, during the Great Depression, many of them wore the green of the Civilian Conservation Corps. And as they entered full adulthood, fully one half of them enlisted in the military—a greater percentage than any generation in history.[2] As G.I. Carol, from Green Springs, Ohio, told me, "We've been at war with somebody practically my whole life."

Raised by Idealists (the Missionary generation, born 1860–1882) and Reactives (the Lost Generation, born 1883–1900), G.I.s were the next Civic generation in the four-fold cycle that Strauss and Howe outlined in their book *Generations*. They were told by their missionary parents that they were special, that they could be great. This might have simply been wishful thinking on the part of idealistic parents had world events not conspired against them, thrusting tragedy and poverty onto their unready shoulders. Yet far from shaking these confident youngsters, these events gave the G.I.s an opportunity to step up and prove their greatness.

And step up they did. They also went the extra mile. Civic generations are builders, and the G.I.s did not disappoint on this score. For in spite of apparently insuperable obstacles, through sacrifice and hard work, they built the infrastructure of our modern society with their own calloused hands, including roads, freeways, buildings, banks, churches, and service organizations of all kinds. Everything we have come to think of as "America" today began with them.

Formative Events

Growing up during the transitional period between the horse-and-buggy and the modern world, our oldest living generation learned to both adapt well to change and to revere tradition and stability. Immigrants from all over the world were learning that they could cherish their ethnic heritage and at the same time take pride in an emerging "American" identity.

Katherine, originally from Greeley, Colorado, recalls her childhood this way: "World War One had just finished. My dad didn't fight—he had myopia. He had a lot to do, trying to support our family. Automobiles came in. When I was young, we just had a horse and buggy. Then my father bought a Model T. We were surrounded by immigrants—we had a Slavic family on one side, and Scots on the other . . . . Because of WWI, Germans were in disgrace in this country. They weren't part of the Kaiser, they were good people. They had trouble graduating." Marian, originally from Chicago, Illinois, remembers, "What was hard for me was that my parents were from Poland, so they never spoke English. I did not speak English until I went to school. I was taught by Polish Catholic nuns."

The boom following the First World War provided G.I.s with a brief flirtation with frivolity. But "the roaring twenties" was quickly and permanently squelched by the grim reality of the Great Depression. Louis, from Mississippi told me, "I was shaped by the Great Depression," but as harsh as it was for their parents, most people I talked to looked back on this part of their early life with fondness. Ellie, from Wilmington, Illinois, said, "I remember we went through the Depression, but my mother was clever enough to find things. So, we always had enough to eat. We didn't realize that we were poor. I do remember my father being without work, and writing letters to try to find work." Similarly, Katherine said, "We had poverty, but my mother made the best of it. We moved to California at the height of the Depression—went 6,000 miles.

We had a wonderful time!" Mildred, from Louisville, KY, also remembers this time as happy. "My father was a Methodist minister, and he didn't make much money. We never had much money, so I didn't know there was a Depression."

Yet, despite their cherished memories of this time, it definitely left its mark on them. As Tom Brokaw noted, "They were mature beyond their years, tempered by what they had been through . . . ."[3]

By the time the Second World War hit, their resourcefulness and resilience were well in place, and they were ready for another challenge. The nation pulled together, sacrificed together, and worked together toward the single goal of defeating fascism and preserving freedom. Most G.I. men went into the military to serve overseas, and many G.I. women went to work at home, pulling on the gloves the men had left behind and keeping the factories and industries going. Nancy, from Peekskill, New York, recalls, "When World War II came along I left with two of my girl friends and we went to New Jersey, and we got a job making navy Hell Cats. So I was a Rosie the Riveter. Even though the war was still going on we always seemed to have a good time."

Marian also claims her "Rosie" status: "World War II was devastating because the youth were going into the service and we were left behind. We weren't accustomed to fighting. We females were not accepted that much. When the seven men raised the flag at Mount Suribachi we had a ceremony in Chicago. That was the same day my daughter popped a new tooth. I was Rosie the Riveter—I was pregnant and doing armatures for B12s."

The fighting took its toll on G.I. men. Many of them suffered from post-traumatic stress disorder, although there wasn't a name for it at the time. Some coped by talking about it, but usually only with others who had "been there." Others were tight-lipped, as if ignoring what had happened would deny its power or damaging effects. When Louis told me curtly, "I went into World War II. I came out whole," I had to wonder just how "whole" he really was.

After the war, G.I. women went back to the kitchen and the men went back to work—after taking advantage of the G.I. bill and getting a good education. At the time, the G.I.s were the most universally educated generation in American history.[4] Armed with bachelor's degrees and jobs provided by a booming post-war business sector, G.I.s married and moved out to the suburbs to begin "the good life." Tract houses began springing up all over the American landscape, along with supermarkets, restaurants, and churches.

Television arrived, providing G.I.s with a visual, homogeneous model of the ideal American family, exemplified by "Ozzie and Harriet" and "Father Knows Best"—an image that they embraced and emulated whole-heartedly. Strauss and Howe called theirs "the most conformist culture of the twentieth century."[5] Theirs was a clean-cut America built on unimpeachable morals and traditional values, with well-defined gender roles and a clear line of hierarchical authority. G.I. fathers saw themselves as the breadwinners and head of the family, and strove to run their households with the same efficiency that had worked so well for them in the military. Unfortunately, this "efficiency" sowed the seeds of resentment and rebellion that would cause the greatest generation gap of the twentieth century, between them and their own children, the Boomers.

Perhaps due to a primal fear of appearing weak, G.I.s rejected the more androgynous values of their Idealistic parents, and embraced an exaggerated masculinity that many of them still posses. This is especially true of men, but even women are not immune. G.I. parents were told that excessive affection would make their children weak and dependent, and as a result, many Silent and Boomer children were raised in home environments that were picture perfect on the outside, but often felt harsh and unloving on the inside.

I remember my mother talking about something my father's mother said once. An Oklahoma dustbowl immigrant to California, my grandmother said, "I regret that we didn't touch our children more. But we didn't know. This is what we were told, and we believed it." Consequently, my own Silent father—tender-hearted as he is—grew up without much physical affection, and is still uncomfortable with it today.

Experience of the World and What They Are Seeking

When I asked Bert, originally from Moorcroft, Wyoming, about his primary experience of the world as he was growing up, he told me, "Crisis, I think, would be the best answer to that. The crisis is because we as people have allowed this to happen to us. It's all part of the world." I wasn't surprised at this answer, since crisis has been the constant companion of the G.I. generation since their infancy. Most were born into a world in crisis as the First World War raged across Europe. Then, after a brief respite during the 1920s, this generation shouldered another crisis—the Great Depression. The greatest crisis was the Second World War, followed by the ominous dread of the Cold War.

And yet, beyond a shadow of a doubt, they met each crisis with resolve. As Tom Brokaw said of his conversations with G.I.s, "One after another they volunteered how in their families and in their communities they were expected to be responsible for their behavior, how honesty was assumed to be the rule, not the exception. They also talked matter-of-factly about a sense of duty to their country, a sentiment not much in fashion anymore."[6] As Wesley Ko told Brokaw, "In the war I learned to be self-sufficient. I matured. I learned to be a leader. When my business failed, I was able to move on."[7]

The Great Depression had made them ultra-responsible, possessed of a hyper-vigilant frugality that became an indelible part of their personality. As Tom Brokaw would note later, "They seem to have everything they need, but they still count their pennies as if the bottom may drop out tomorrow."[8]

This sense of the world in crisis has so shaped their generational character, that those of us who were formed in later, more gentle times often have a hard time relating. G.I.s seem perpetually on edge, even paranoid, especially when discussing national security. This is a very important aspect of their personality, however, that we should take note of. When I asked G.I.s what their generation sought more than anything else, many of them were concerned with this issue. Carl, from Berkeley, California, gave me a one-word answer: "Security." Dorothy, from Walnut Creek,

California, agreed, but expanded on this a bit: "Security. We wanted financial security and national security. I think we did well on the security of the country—I guess we were successful." Cairin, from Baltimore, Maryland, told me her generation was determined to "defend the country, the American Dream."

It could be that the G.I. paranoia that led to a stockpile of nuclear arms during the Cold War actually saved the world, repugnant as the strategy might seem to later generations. The greatest leaders of the G.I. generation—Lyndon Johnson, Richard Nixon, Ronald Reagan, and the first George Bush—seemed obsessed with national security, and although they made the occasional misstep, they did, as Dorothy noted, navigate the tricky waters of their times successfully.[9]

Yet this generation's reputation among later generations as "warmongers" is unfair. The slogan, "peace through strength," reveals that, paradoxically, their war efforts served a larger end: security and peace, not just for Americans, but for all people. As Ken put it, "We were all working toward peace, and toward victory, whether in uniform or not." Although the strategy worked, the G.I. notion that their efforts would lead to a lasting peace seems to them naïve, now. Ellie told me, "I used to think there would come a day when we were smart enough that we didn't have any more war, but I guess that is never going to happen. I've decided that must be man's nature because we can't seem to ever go very many years at peace."

National security was not their only concern, however. G.I.s were vigilant about security in every aspect of life. As they approached retirement, G.I.s lowered the retirement age to sixty-two, and boosted the level of Social Security benefits substantially. Strauss and Howe report that "from 1965 to 1989—as G.I.s reached age sixty-five—federal benefits per elderly person have risen fifteen times more rapidly than wages (300% versus less than 20%, in inflation-adjusted dollars)."[10]

In 1965 G.I.s established Medicare to provide medical security for themselves, gaining "more than others from deficit-laden financing schemes that pushed costs far into the future," according to Strauss and Howe.[11] Strauss and Howe go on to note that, "The

1990 deficit reduction law imposed a 1991 maximum of $41 in extra Medicare charges per G.I. beneficiary, and up to $2,137 in extra Medicare taxes per younger worker."

G.I.s seek, more than any other ideal, security, and will stop at almost nothing to guarantee it. Yes, they sacrificed, but short-sightedly shored up the security of their twilight years by mort-gaging the future of their grandchildren, ensuring that we, too, will sacrifice as they did—whether we choose it or not.

Disposition

G.I.s possess a curious mixture of wariness and hope. They've seen enough trouble to be suspicious, knowing that at any moment a shoe might drop and plunge them and theirs into crisis once again. It's kind of a mild, generation-wide Post Traumatic Stress Disorder that has actually served them quite well, their occasional cantankerousness aside.

Lloyd, who hails originally form Butte, Montana, told me, "In general, I'm an optimist!" and that sums up his cohort pretty well, too. They are universally cautious. They are pretty good judges of character, and if there is a whiff of subterfuge about you, their hackles raise and the questioning will begin. On the other hand, if you have gained their trust, they are fiercely loyal, and will defend their friends against all comers—true in both interpersonal and international arenas.

But the hope is real, too. G.I.s have seen the worst of the worst. They know from experience that hard work, loyalty, and honesty can see the world through the worst of times. They are realists, sure, but optimistic realists—they are not blind to the obstacles we face, but they are confident that, pulling together, there's nothing we can't meet and overcome.

In a Word and a Song

When I asked G.I.s for a motto or a phrase that summed up their generation's outlook on life, I did not get a clear consensus. Still, several answers were insightful. Dorothy suggested, "Waste not, want not," which reflects the frugality gained by the G.I. generation during the Great Depression. Earl, from Denver, Colorado, suggested "Pick yourself up by your bootstraps," which sums up the G.I. philosophy of self-determination and personal responsibility.

A couple of people suggested, "Do unto others as you would have them do unto you," which seems like sage advice for any generation, but didn't seem to be especially applicable to G.I.s, whose bull-in-a-china-shop approach to diplomacy (on both personal and national levels) seems incongruent with Jesus' words. Strauss and Howe quoted a *U.S. News and World Report* story that called them "fearless but not reckless," which has the ring of truth to it, even if it is not a household phrase.

The other night, my wife was watching an old Frank Capra movie, *State of the Union* (1948), in which a Republican politico named Kay Thorndyke (played magnificently by Angela Lansbury) says, "Life is war—don't count the casualties." Certainly not all G.I.s would agree with this statement—but it reveals a strain of opinion shared by many in that cohort.

As for a song that sums up this generation, again there were many diverse suggestions. Many people simply named artists they enjoyed when they were young adults—Glen Miller and Frank Sinatra made multiple appearances. But G.I.s had trouble naming a particular song that had meaning for them. Charlie, originally from Southern California, suggested "Time Was" by Jimmy Dorsey. He said the "music had a theme, had some meaning to it, it was about falling in love, getting married, getting a job," definitely important themes for post-war G.I.s. Many suggested hymns—albeit different hymns. The one that has the most resonance with G.I. themes was suggested by Katherine, "Trust and Obey"—a good two-word summary of the G.I. philosophy of life.

Probably the difficulty in settling upon a song is that, in the G.I. era, popular music wasn't particularly interested in philosophizing—it was pure escape. Add to this the fact that G.I.s, as a group, are not particularly introspective (or at least, they have trouble articulating their inner life—more on this later), and it is not surprising that their music is rarely political or confessional. (Plenty patriotic, yes, but not provocatively political, as music in the 1960s was to be).

MY WAY
by Paul Anka

And now the end is near
And so I face the final curtain
My friend I'll say it clear
I'll state my case of which I'm certain

I've lived a life that's full
I traveled each and every highway
And more, much more than this
I did it my way

Regrets I've had a few
But then again too few to mention
I did what I had to do
And saw it through without exemption

I planned each charted course
Each careful step along the byway
And more, much more than this
I did it my way

Yes there were times I'm sure you knew
When I bit off more than I could chew
But through it all when there was doubt
I ate it up and spit it out, I faced it all
And I stood tall and did it my way

I've loved, I've laughed and cried
I've had my fill, my share of losing
And now as tears subside
I find it all so amusing

To think I did all that
And may I say not in a shy way
Oh no, oh no, not me
I did it my way

For what is a man what has he got
If not himself then he has not
To say the things he truly feels
And not the words of one who kneels
The record shows I took the blows
And did it my way
Yes it was my way

One significant exception to the unconfessional nature of G.I. popular music is the one song that appeared on more than one list, and it seems to me that this song, better than all the rest, sums up the G.I. mindset. That song is Frank Sinatra's "My Way."

The song was released in 1969, just as the first wave G.I.s were retiring and being confronted with their own impending mortality (off the battle-field, that is). The English lyrics were by a Silent entertainer, Paul Anka, but in interviews he has stated that he wrote it specifically for Frank Sinatra. He said, "At one o'clock in the morning, I sat down at an old IBM electric typewriter and said, 'If Frank were writing this, what would he say?'"[12]

Frank recorded it, and it was so popular that it became one of the most covered songs in history. It certainly hit a nerve, and comes the closest of any song to being a G.I. anthem. This is testified to by a *Guardian* article which reveals that, in the United Kingdom at least, "My Way" is played more than any other song at the funerals of the G.I. generation.[13]

The song is lyrically rich and uncharacteristically introspective for G.I.s, but perhaps this is appropriate given it's theme of a final life-review. It's popularity among G.I.s tells us a lot about their perspective—their lives were full and eventful, they made hard choices, but most of them were good ones. They are unapologetic about their accomplishments, they are honest about their sacrifices and losses. And they were *right*, dammit. Who are we to quibble?

Generational Project

Like all Civic generations, G.I.s are builders—their generational project is *constructive*. In every arena of human endeavor, they are people who created things, who built them up, who left something behind where before there was nothing. This is especially evident in the realm of commerce. G.I.s were uniformly better off than their parents, and as elders they enjoyed the lowest poverty level in the twentieth century.[14] G.I.s created businesses where there were none before, providing jobs and opportunities for later generations. They built institutions that continue to be the bedrock of the American economy, such as banks, insurance companies, chain stores, and small businesses of all kinds. As Ken, from St. Louis, Missouri, described his generation, "we were achievers."

In social circles, G.I.s were builders as well, founding or expanding sporting clubs, churches, enthusiast groups of all kinds, and service organizations such as Elks, Odd Fellows, and the like. As Cairin told me, "We valued building America and making it a better place to live. We valued education. We valued defending and protecting freedom and churches."

G.I.s are not loners, and while they might pose as rugged individualists, they are in fact communitarians through and through. They know the value of community, they know from experience that we accomplish more together than apart, and they have always leaped to help community efforts, or to encourage anything that would promote community involvement.

They were pioneers in medicine and science, advancing those fields out of proportion to their generational numbers. As of 1989, G.I.s had won two-thirds of all Nobel prizes. G.I.s have also excelled in the arts, preferring escapist entertainment to challenging intellectual or deconstructive efforts (which they tend to dismiss as "highbrow" or anti-establishment).

G.I.s see their duty to God and one another in terms of keeping their country and their loved ones safe, and leaving behind a better America than the one they were given. This they certainly have done, and even if they accomplished all that they did with an exaggerated swagger and a chip on their shoulders, they did it nevertheless with love.

How G.I.s Perceive Themselves

Universally, G.I.s give themselves high marks. They are proud of what they did with their lives, what they accomplished as a generation. As Betty, originally from Ohio, said, "I think our generation has been very successful—John Glen, NASA. Most of us had the opportunity, did get educated, and when we got into our professions we tried to do the best. I really think our generation was rather unique."

G.I.s recognize that it was a synthesis of their intrinsic makeup and the necessity of the times that really made them great, though. As Carol told me, "We had something that determined what we would do by having the war. A lot of my good friends were drafted. One of the things about World War II, we knew why we were fighting, we carried it out, we did finish it. I think it had a lot of influence on what we did after, maybe getting all the good we can from life was important." Bert, too, pointed to the times: "I think the goals were to see the world didn't wreck itself . . . I think with the Lord's help that our generation has done an awful lot to move us along."

Other generations may not have done so well, had they faced the same hardships. Their greatness was latent, but G.I.s did not cower, they did not quail—they strapped on their boots and marched into the thick of danger. Even back home, the G.I.s were not whiners. Lloyd said, "During WWII, the people really were *in* that war. The speed limit was 35 mph, gas was rationed, food was rationed. Everyone really worked toward the end result." Mildred agreed, saying, "Everybody was sharing the goal and the hardships. We had rationing. You couldn't get enough gasoline to go where you wanted to—so you just wouldn't go. People were drafted but they had to go, which is a lot different from now, and I think that was more of a unifying force."

What was it about the G.I.s that enabled them to meet the

crises they did? Betty said, "We had a lot of self discipline." Earl added, "We were honest, hardworking. We had a lot a drive. There were a lot of discouragements along the way, but we were very self-sufficient."

The G.I.s are proud of their accomplishments, and of their character. Words like "duty," "responsibility," and "honor" mean a lot to them. They are saddened by the fact that, for later generations, these qualities seem to have less and less importance. Tom Brokaw noted, "The idea of personal responsibility is such a defining characteristic of the World War II generation that when the rules changed later, these men and women were appalled."[15] Charlie said to me, "We had a sense of morality . . . . We believed in values." As one G.I. told Brokaw, "My generation . . . did what we needed to do and had values and morals that seem not as important nowadays, at least to some people."[16]

Katherine echoed this theme. She told me, "We took life more seriously than people do now. We were more concerned about each other. Churches were more concerned about mission. We wanted a better world, and we worked to get it." A note of pride can be detected as she adds, "I was at the organizing meeting for the United Nations."

G.I.s see themselves not only as effective and potent people, but also as kind and friendly. Ellie said, "I think we're all pretty nice people. I think everybody probably likes where they are. All the people that I grew up with were good people."

How G.I.s are Perceived

Not all generations agree with this assessment. The generation closest to the G.I.s, the Silents, look upon them with awe. Silents view G.I.s as the big brothers and sisters that steered the ship of state with firm hands, who always had a plan, who didn't suffer fools or layabouts. Violet, a Silent from Clayton, Missouri, told me, "The older generation before me was the hardest-working generation. I think they were the hardest working out of all the generations. I think most of them were happy in their work. They didn't look for handouts except for when the Depression hit, when pretty much everyone had to have help. I think our generation looked back at that generation as old fashioned." Silent Nick, from Berkeley, California, said of them, "The older generation just wanted you to work harder, and liked you if you did. It was a production-evaluation, that was my experience of it."

G.I.s don't fare so well with later generations, however. Although G.I.s have seen themselves as friendly and responsible, subsequent generations—most especially their own children—have viewed them as harsh, strict disciplinarians. Kelly, a Boomer from Phoenix, Oregon, told me, "My father's world was definitely racist, homophobic, and sexist. If I had to choose a generation to align myself with, it wouldn't be with 'The Greatest Generation.' True, they were forged in a crucible that inspires respect and amazement, but what emerged is uncompromising in ways that don't always promote the general good. My mother would be appalled [to hear me say this]. She told me that she and her generation were perfect, while me and mine were undoubtedly flawed." Kelly's opinion is not at all unusual among Boomers.

Xers knew G.I.s as kindly grandparents, but that doesn't get them completely off the hook with this generation. Xer Ken from Berkeley, California, told me, "Older generations didn't prepare well for this moment in time; they leveraged everything on present power and present status, without thinking about those that would come after, and how those generations would be able to cope with the situation as they've handed it to us." Xers often feel betrayed by the economic strategies of the G.I.s and Silents, who mortgaged cushy retirements for themselves on the backs of younger generations. Ken knows that his labor will be paying for "the good life" of G.I.s and Silents in their twilight years, with very little chance that such generous programs as social security and Medicare will be around when he retires.

THE SPIRITUALITY
OF THE G.I. GENERATION

On the whole, G.I.s are the most overtly religious of all the living generations. Frank, from Overland Park, Kansas, told me, "I feel religion is a very important part of my life," and he is typical of his cohort. G.I.s built the current religious denominations into the powerhouses they were in the 1950s and 60s, and have remained loyal to them, alongside their Silent younger siblings, even as they have been largely abandoned by younger generations.

But for all their overt religiosity, G.I.s are the least articulate generation on matters of faith, the least able to discuss their spirituality in personal terms, and the least likely to reflect critically on their beliefs or religious institutions. For them, faith seems to be a given, and it is largely accepted whole as they have received it. They are not interested in any deconstruction, reframing, or questioning. If they have doubts about any of the beliefs proffered by their institutions, most keep quiet about them.

Yet, ironically, for all their reticence to think critically about faith, their religion is a rational enterprise, not an emotional one. As Howard Rice described the G.I.s he has worked with, "They are quite secular for the most part and they are going to go down and out without asking the fundamental questions. That doesn't mean that they don't go to church, but it doesn't somehow get inside their souls; they don't seem to feel it."[17] In general, they are uncomfortable with pietistic emotionality. Religion is a duty to be performed solemnly and earnestly.

Just as they joined together in the military to preserve freedom, G.I.s join together in churches and synagogues in the service of the greater good, to uphold the values and morals of society as a whole. They feel responsible for preserving the integrity and cohesion of society, and they do this through the public exercise of religion—thinking of it less in terms of personal relationship with God than a social contract between God and a godly nation. Their salvation is collective, their covenant much like that of the ancient Israelites—if they uphold the divine Law, they will earn

God's favor and protection for the nation. Since the primary goal of G.I.s is security, the desire for divine protection is the driving force in their spirituality.

Consequently, they don't question religious authority, they hand on their faiths as they were presented to them, nor do they think about them much in personal terms. If they have deeply intimate relationships with the Divine, they don't talk about them, just as they don't share the intimate details of their romantic relationships. On the whole, they see no distinction between religion and spirituality—spirituality is almost totally experienced in corporate, institutional terms. As Ken, an Episcopalian, said to me, "To be perfectly honest I think it's a matter of the church and the service. And I can't, I don't think any deeper than that." There is little that is warm or fuzzy about their spiritualities, but instead their faiths are lived almost as a continuation of the military discipline they gained in the Second World War. They may have retired from the service, but not from the Lord's army. They are more likely than other generations to use military metaphors when describing their faith. "Fight the good fight," is often on their lips, and indeed, they have not dropped the flag.

The Spiritual Gifts of G.I.s

One of the great gifts that G.I.s have brought to their religious communities has been a fierce and unshakable loyalty. They have donated countless hours, the sweat of their brow and the labor of their hands, all in the service of those religious institutions that serve the greater good of humankind.

As a generation of builders, their religious gift has been edification, building up churches and synagogues, in order to build up future generations—forming them morally and socially to carry on the values that G.I.s fought and died for. (The great sorrow of the G.I. generation is the Boomers' rebellion against these earnest efforts, their rejection of the values that G.I.s believe made America great—values that are required if we are to continue to enjoy God's protection and favor.)

The G.I.s brought a steady hand to the tiller of their institutions, especially through the turbulence of the Cold War and the social upheaval of the 1960s. They honored the wisdom of the past, and sought to preserve it in order to deliver their faith whole to future generations. They sought to be, more than anything else, *faithful*. They took responsibility for their personal morality, expected it of others, and enshrined it where they could in government and culture.

They brought those very virtues that made them great as a generational cohort to bear upon religious life—loyalty, duty, discipline, and personal responsibility. To some extent, the ideal of the separation of church and state eluded them—theirs is a spirituality cut from whole cloth, and in their thinking civic and religious responsibilities are difficult to tease apart. Partly this is because discipline and morality are not seen as private matters, but necessary on a societal level if the terms of the Divine covenant (for protection and favor) are to be fulfilled.

How Divinity Is Imaged

G.I.s value hierarchy and order, and the God of their experience does the same. The Divine is a being who is rational and just, and who expects obedience and responsibility. Thus, Myrtle, in our example above, is upset that her granddaughter is not doing her wedding "right," that is, according to the rules that she believes God has laid down in the Roman Catholic faith. She is genuinely concerned for her granddaughter, and believes that God will not bless her marriage if she is not obedient to the letter of Catholic law.

Overwhelmingly, the G.I. notion of divinity is transcendent, powerful, and demanding. Most G.I.s view God as "out there" somewhere, an exterior presence rather than an interior one. Carol, an Episcopalian, told me, "Certainly [he] is all powerful and someone who looks over the whole world . . . . I felt many many times that there's somebody watching over me." Diane, a Christian from Tucson, Arizona, used similar language when she said, "God is always with you. God is looking down and watching over you."

Most G.I.s speak of the Divine in anthropomorphic terms, typically congruent with the images used by their spiritual communities. They normally think of God as male, as a (mostly) benevolent father figure. Like a father, God has high expectations for "his" children, and holds us to high standards. Their spirituality is one of rules and grace in equal measure. William McDermott told Tom Brokaw, "God is a God of necessity. He sets the morals. If people break them, that's their issue, not God's."[18]

There are consequences to not "measuring up" to their God's expectations. Many G.I.s expressed a significant fear of the Divine that served as a motivating factor in their faith. Cairin, a Roman Catholic originally from Ireland, alluded to this when she said, "It's not a personal relationship. He's divine . . . the Father, God the Son, and God the Holy Spirit. People are to live our faith. We are to help people, to be kind and to be loving towards the poor, handicapped, sick, and [in] jail . . . . Fear of God was taught to us. You did anything like commit a mortal sin, you [should] be afraid of God. It decreased a bit after moving to the United States. I started questioning more of this fear of God when [I] moved to the United States."

Episcopalian Betty emphasized God's power in our discussion, indicating that God is not to be crossed. She said, "My image of God is he's the great I Am . . . he's the almighty, and I have nothing but respect. I don't see him as an old man with a beard. I don't even see him, he's just there. He's great and he's kind and good. That you do justice and [love] kindness and walk humbly with your God. He made us so he must love us, but he must get awful sick of our antics." Earl, an Evangelical Christian, put it succinctly: "I'm nothing, he is supreme and almighty."

While G.I.s may use anthropomorphic language and images, most of them are aware that these are metaphors. Some tried to break out of this way of speaking, but often lapsed back into it. Katherine, who attends the United Church of Christ, displays this tendency—and her response is beautiful as well. "God is a presence, to me. When I focus on it, I know it's always there. I know that it's intent is good. I can trust whatever I get from it. I don't always have the strength to follow through what he wants me to . . . . God is the essence of the world."

Dominant Faith Style

G.I.s tend to be "traditional" believers, valuing doctrine and tradition, and investing wholeheartedly in religious institutions.[19] As I describe in my book *Faith Styles: Ways People Hold Faith*, Traditional Believers live in a universe that is highly structured. Divinity is all-powerful, and in control of all things at all times. The Divine is usually imaged as male, often as a father figure, the head of a metaphorical family that extends to include each individual believer.

The cosmology of this belief system is hierarchical, with a clear delineation of authority in both heaven and earth. Every person in society has a proper place in this system, and life is easiest when roles are respected and embodied willingly. Family systems mirror the celestial hierarchy, with the father in charge, the mother obedient to him, and the children under the authority of both of them. The Divine is supremely beneficent, but also expects every creature to maintain its proper station.

Meaning in this system is found by discerning the Divine will for one's life, and aligning with that will to the greatest degree possible. Spiritual wisdom is found primarily through scripture and tradition.

Spiritual growth for Traditional Believers is likely to be evaluated by the extent to which one has submitted one's own will to the Divine will, and surrendered one's own understanding to the external authority of scripture and tradition. Failure to submit or surrender is seen as rebelliousness, which is inherently sinful.

Obviously, there are many parallels between G.I.s and Traditional Believers, yet they are not identical. Certainly, many G.I.s are Traditional Believers, but many are not. Nevertheless, even those who are not Traditional Believers will resonate with many aspects of the Traditional paradigm. The G.I.s in my own congregation, for instance, are not religious fundamentalists, but are deeply conservative in many areas of their lives, and their approach to faith has many elements in common with those who are Traditional Believers. For instance, while they do not share a sense of great intimacy with the Divine (many Traditional Believers do), they do have great respect for what has gone before and do not presume to know better or to question the tradition.

Spiritual Focus and Spiritual Community

G.I.s are a communal generation. They consider the needs of individuals to be less important than the needs of the family, or the nation. They are a people of personal sacrifice and group effort, and their approach to faith is very much in the same vein.

G.I.s view religion as a corporate activity. It is not a private affair, but a public one. Prayer happens not primarily in the solitude of one's bedroom, but in the midst of one's congregation. Common prayer—congregational prayer—is what G.I.s think of as "proper" prayer. As Betty told me, "You can pray by yourself, but there is something about praying in a community that I feel the strength of it. I would not want to live without Christian belief or a church." When I asked Norma, a Baptist from Springfield, VT if it was important to pray with others, she answered, "Yes, it says so in the Bible. Perhaps because it has a stronger effect."

Their spiritual focus, therefore, is extroverted. Religion is done in the midst of others, it is a group effort. Personal piety is less important to G.I.s than cooperation with one's fellows. G.I.s consider church or synagogue important, in part, because it is good to be *seen* at worship. This is not hypocrisy, but participation. When we asked Norma if it was important to be seen at worship, she said, "I think so. I think it makes an impression on people, to know that you're a church member." She admitted it wasn't absolutely necessary, however. "You can still worship God and not go to church. But I *miss* going to church. I miss seeing the people, and worshiping together."

G.I.s were responsible for building up the religious institutions that are largely in decline today. Despite the separation of church and state, participating in public worship is looked upon by G.I.s as a civic duty. They aren't particular about which spiritual community one is involved in, just as long as one is involved. To eschew "the gathering of yourselves together" (as the Epistle to the Hebrews put it[20]) is frequently seen by G.I.s as a rebellious individualism, which, for them, is indistinguishable from selfishness and immaturity.

Mildred, who grew up Methodist, said to me, "People who go to church have their religion and say 'I belong to this church, and

I'm a Christian and so on,' but to the extent of which they are actually practicing what they ought to be practicing—they don't take it to themselves personally, and they don't show it forth. Almost everybody I know does go to church or has gone to church. I suppose you could do good without being told to, [but] the church gives you an aura of inspiration and authority."

One of the most surprising things about G.I.s is that many of them do not actually consider themselves "believers," but that doesn't stop them from being involved in spiritual community. Lloyd, who was raised Catholic, told me, "I believe the church is a good thing, it teaches good things. I just don't happen to be a believer. I took my children to Sunday School. I *taught* Sunday School."

This is congruent with my experience as pastor of a federated congregation of G.I. Episcopalians and Congregationalists. Several of them were not particularly religious (most have passed away), and if you asked them about their relationship with God, they would instantly become very uncomfortable and change the subject. Yet, they were there in the pews every week. For them, going to church was their rock, a connection with a time that had largely passed away. Katherine told me, "Church gives me stability and a space to be where I feel like I am surrounded by God."

Prayer Style

Since religion is largely seen by G.I.s as a corporate effort, "common prayer," as the Anglican tradition calls it, is their norm. While G.I.s do pray privately, it is not their preferred mode— they pray less often when alone. Often, devout G.I. couples pray together. Gerald, a Baptist from Anchorage, Alaska, said, "We have our devotional every morning—we read from the Bible, we pray together. We have a prayer for every meal. I usually end up reading several chapters of the Bible every night. We read in between times, different things on the Bible." But when one spouse dies, the surviving spouse can find prayer less satisfying. Earl reported, "I try to have some time with the Lord in the morning, first thing when I get up. For thirty years my wife and I read aloud from the Bible every morning, then we'd kneel by the couch and pray. My devotions are less now since she died. Prayer, worship, memorizing a few scriptures in the morning. Then in the evening, pray before bedtime."

What do G.I.s actually mean when they talk of prayer? From my experience pastoring them, and from the interviews we conducted, it is clear that, by and large, prayer means *petitionary* prayer. To pray is to ask God for things—especially healing and protection. Betty, for instance, said that when she prays, "We always thank God for our food, and think of others who are hungry and homeless. Most of the time I pray for people who are ill and are having problems of any kind. As for how I do it, you could do it all day long. You can walk around and do it. I still say 'Now I lay me down to sleep.'" Likewise, Cairin said, "I pray for good health, peace in the whole world, peace for Israel, and [I] pray for a cure for all the diseases including Alzheimer's and cancer."

For G.I.s, prayer is not a particularly intimate affair. God, for them, is judge, general, or at "his" coziest, father. God is not friend, lover, or co-worker, as later generations would image the Divine. As Betty told me, "I don't think he's my buddy." Prayer understood as intimacy with the Divine will usually leave G.I.s cold. That kind of talk sounds suspiciously like the touchy-feely spirituality of their children, which has always made them uncomfortable. The most "intimate" response I heard was from Marian, a Catholic, who said, "I think that for me, since I became a widow early, I talk to God as if he was my husband."

Like so many other things in life, G.I.s see prayer as a responsibility, a duty, a religious obligation. Since G.I.s value constancy and responsibility, they pray. Often these prayers are done according to a traditional form. When I asked Carl, an Episcopalian, about his prayer life, he said succinctly, "Start with accepted prayers; then individual, branching out to 'all sorts and conditions.'" Mildred was much more expansive in her reply: "I do a morning prayer session every morning. I do the Lord's Prayer, the 23rd psalm, St. Francis' prayer, then I have the family prayer. I pray for the church, whoever has to be prayed for that day, and for our own minister, and then I pray for the United Nations, and I pray for our clergy at St. Michael's, and a couple of others in Seattle and

Riverside, and then I pray for all the places where there is fighting. I support half a dozen charities I send twenty dollars to whenever I can, food for the poor and so on. I pray for all of them. I pray for all people who are so angry, depressed, or misguided that they are doing the wrong thing. [Then] I do Compline at night before I go to bed."

While common, such discipline is not the norm among G.I.s. if they do not have others to pray with. While most of them pray frequently, it is most often on an "as needed" basis. As Carol described her practice, "Well I have to say there is one time in the morning we ask for guidance for the day, and for any of our friends who need help. I think all through the day you send up a little message, 'help me,' and that's about what it is. I have not had a practice of going off to a place by myself and doing it regularly."

One theme that emerged from my conversations with G.I.s was that saying "help me," as Carol put it, is sometimes hard for them. It seems to injure G.I. pride to admit that they are not self-sufficient. As Congregationalist Dorothy put it, "My prayer is mental, not verbal, unless I'm in a group. I'm a private person. I pray the Lord's Prayer, but I don't really do a lot of prayer. The Lord helps those who help themselves." United Church of Christ member Charlie is also not likely to ask for Divine help, but instead sees "prayer" as a reflective practice leading to personal responsibility. He said, "I think of what needs to be done in the world, and that motivates me to make some change. Holding down a job and doing the best I could, that was part of my life. You have a lot of time to think about what's going on in the world. My friend, an astrophysicist in Pakistan, called prayer 'deep thinking,' thinking seriously about the problems of the world. Asking God to solve all the problems doesn't do much good, but thinking what you can do can do a lot of good."

One petition that cropped up several times was entreating the Divine to assist G.I.s in simply being better people. G.I.s recognize the sacred duty to mentor younger generations, and although they feel much pride and confidence in themselves, they want to be better, more faithful stewards of their skill and knowledge. Nellie, who describes herself as a deist, told me that when she prays, "I usually say, 'Holy Spirit, help heal any wounds in my family, [and] let me be a better role model." Likewise Ellie, a United Methodist, prays for herself in this way: "When I pray, I pray for improving myself. I don't pray for any material things because I don't believe in that. I pray for courage and patience."

Even though G.I.s see prayer in mostly petitionary terms, they temper their expectations regarding results. This isn't to say that they question the efficacy of their prayer, only that they trust that God's wisdom is greater than theirs, and their desires are subordinate to the Divine Plan. Diane's answer was refreshingly matter-of-fact about this: "The Lord is busy, and he cannot stop what he is doing to help people just because they need help. You will get it when he deems it fit."

Spiritual Guidance Style

Because of their deep appreciation for hierarchy and order, and an innate respect for authority, G.I.s will welcome a more directive approach in spiritual guidance. While they know, cognitively, that their pastors, rabbis, and imams are human, they will still have them on a bit of a pedestal (or will think they ought to, in cases where they don't actually respect their clergy as much as they consider fitting). They have great respect for clergy and professional religious. They expect their guides to be experts, to know more than they do.

In spiritual direction, they will expect to be given "assignments" and to be held accountable for doing them. They will do best in one-on-one guidance relationships. Their experience of being "right" with God is founded less in raw, intimate sharing with the Divine, and even less in mysticism. In fact, the language of Divine intimacy will most likely confuse them and make them uncomfortable. The God of their experience is removed from creation, and, though loving, is like an emotionally distant father figure who desires, more than anything else, well-behaved children.

Thus, their "rightness" with God will be grounded in their conception of faithfulness: doing all that is required, following the rules, being an obedient follower. Spiritual guides who can help them discern God's will and to live it in their daily lives will succeed in the eyes of their clients.

If our opening vignette were to continue, Margaret might serve Myrtle well by reminding her that God's judgment is tempered by mercy, and that Myrtle was once young and foolish as well. God did not abandon Myrtle in her foolishness—it took time for her to grow into a mature person of faith, and she must trust that her granddaughter will do the same. In the meantime, it is Myrtle's responsibility to pray for her granddaughter.

Spiritual Growth Continuum

There was a clear consensus on spiritual growth from G.I.s, but it wasn't exactly what I was asking for. I asked them to describe what a spiritually mature person is like, in contrast to a spiritually immature person. But G.I.s seemed to have trouble separating the demands of their spiritual community from the fruits of those demands. Thus, they described mature people as those who were religiously active, but not one described the kind of character that was formed in such a person. Since G.I.s do not generally distinguish between religion and spirituality, perhaps this was to be expected.

Thus, G.I.s overwhelmingly agreed that spiritually mature people keep the obligations of their religious traditions and communities. As Bert, who attends the Evangelical Free Church, told me, "Spiritual growth is to get into a church, a Protestant church, and to understand all you can of the Bible." Cairin gave me the Catholic version of this. She said that spiritual growth was, "Attending mass, keeping [the] commandments, and making sure you say your prayers."

A couple of people acknowledged that there are people who go to church who *don't* develop spiritually. Mildred said, "You can't tell by whether they go to church or not." But then she acknowledges, "Someone who is spiritually developed *would* go to church of course. Of course they would be a regular in church attendance. They would be involved in at least one church activity."

Similarly, Gerald noted, "Usually one believes in God or they don't. Some people think that they believe in God, but you can't tell by looking at them or talking with them. There are people who go to church who think that they're Christians, probably have been baptized, but still go out and do things. A spiritually mature person *acts* like a Christian."

Interestingly, Nancy, an Episcopalian, acknowledged that going to church isn't strictly speaking necessary, but this "truth" didn't square with her own experience: "You have to read, pray, go to church. I can't manage too well if I don't go to church. Some people say you don't need to go to church, and I know that, but if I don't things run amuck."

A minority theme also emerged from my interviews, in which people *did* distinguish the fruits of spiritual maturity from conformity with the demands of a tradition. This theme identified maturity with the ability to "walk a mile in another's shoes," being genuinely empathetic and caring towards others. As Dorothy put it, "To have spiritual growth, I think you have to have the ability to see things from another person's perspective." Likewise Charlie told me, "Understanding other people's point of view matures a person, and being willing to work for change."

Donald, originally from Louisiana, said that he can identify a spiritually mature person "because he's trying to live a good life. I see one trying to live a good life, and the other one doesn't care. I see one trying to do everything to help his family, the other one don't care about his family, so long as he can get by. I have no use for that man." Similarly, Katherine said, "A spiritually developed person has an awareness of what's going on with other people and cares. A spiritually undeveloped person just goes his own way, and doesn't listen to advice."

In general, the majority of G.I.s see spiritual growth in terms of *obedience*. Sincere conformity with the ideal held up by one's religious tradition constitutes a spiritually mature person, whereas non-conformity and rebellion define spiritual immaturity. A person who is mature in faith is a person who is responsible and obedient, a person who knows the rules and keeps them. In this kind of person, God is well pleased—and it is this kind of person that they aspire to be.[21] In our opening vignette, Myrtle no doubt sees her granddaughter as being spiritually immature, and prays that she will develop a maturity that will surely manifest itself through obedience with the Roman Catholic Church's teachings.

MINISTERING TO G.I.S

The notion of faithfulness is very important for G.I.s. They feel they have worked very hard to be diligent, responsible, even heroic. I hesitate to say that there is a prevalent attitude among them that goes something like, "I've suffered and now God owes me," but it's not too far off the mark, in my experience. When their faithfulness is not rewarded—when tragedy strikes a loved one, when illness threatens to cut life short, or when children go astray—they often feel betrayed by the Divine. Their frustration and sorrow are clear, and they may even voice their outrage. How could God be so ungrateful? Questioning authority—especially Divine authority—is uncharacteristic of them, but when pushed to extremes, they will, like Job, voice their protest.[22]

Of course, there is no adequate answer for questions of this nature. We can't say why there is suffering, and the old chestnuts offered by our traditions to explain it ("it's a mystery," "what doesn't kill you makes you stronger," "free will is necessary") are ultimately unsatisfying. The best we can do for these noble elders is to sit with them in empathetic solidarity, even if we don't exactly agree with the reasons for their mourning. Their lament might be for a rebellious daughter (whom we know has actually done very well for herself) but there's no use trying to talk a G.I. out of his or her opinions.

Medically, there comes a point where the desire for a cure gives way to palliative care. There is a distinct parallel in spiritual guidance. The world has simply changed so much that many G.I.s have not been able to adjust, and often their lamentations seem to younger generations misguided or unnecessary. There is no way to reset the clock, no "do over" that might allow the world to unfold in a way more in line with G.I. values. There is no way to "fix" the issues that trouble them. The best we can do is provide supportive presence as they voice their frustrations and sorrows.

Some G.I.s have been able to "surf" the vicissitudes of the times more easily than others, of course, and I don't mean to suggest that all G.I.s are bitter, angry, disappointed people. Many have marvelous relationships with younger generations, and are facing their twilight years held in loving, supportive environments. These are, however, the minority. Most of the G.I.s I have ministered to in the past ten years are confused and frightened by the tenor of the world, have alienated their children or are experiencing some degree of estrangement, and all have lost, by this time, most of their friends, many of whom suffered greatly as they neared their ends.

This is, you might argue, "the way of all flesh," as Samuel Butler put it, but G.I.s possess a sense of earned generational entitlement that has led them to expect better. The idea that God has let them down is commonly voiced. The answer for us younger generations is to embody the divine presence, to hold their hands, to assure them that they are not alone or abandoned, and above all, to love them despite their occasional outbursts of frustration and blame.

For those doing congregational ministry among G.I.s, you have already discovered a fierce resistance to any change in worship style. It is difficult to find a spiritual community in which G.I.s and younger generations worship together congenially. I remember when my own community was discussing an update to our liturgy. When we were discussing a move to embrace more inclusive language and less harsh theological expressions—among other issues—there was a broad consensus among younger parishioners that the "there is no health in us" line in the confession simply *had to go*.

We called a meeting to discuss the matter, and one of our stalwart G.I.s attended. It reminded me of Martin Luther's historic meeting with Zwingli, where he answered the Swiss reformer's every objection by stabbing with his knife at the words "this is my body" etched in the tabletop. Zwingli left in tears, and we nearly did, too, as our G.I. parishioner answered every objection by pounding his 1928 *Book of Common Prayer.* "I have prayed these words my entire life," he told us, "I'm sure as *hell* not going to stop now."

Younger generations, who might see older styles of worship as antiquated, sexist, or even abusive, need to take a step back and consider the effect of these forms on G.I. worshipers. The very words that cause pain in Boomers bring comfort to G.I.s. The same words that seem to uphold "the system" as far as Xers are concerned, feel like safety to G.I.s. So allow me to be absolutely clear: *to take these things away from them is violence.* This is especially hard for Boomers to hear, because for them worship should always heal, never hurt. Boomers are impelled to create liturgies that are congruent with their highest ideals. Yet, this is a place where Boomers need to step back and consider the lesser of two evils. Is the greatest harm going to be done by continuing to pray the suspect words, or will even more harm result in wresting those beloved words away from older parishioners?

People I interviewed definitely weighed in on this subject. Ken's response echoed my G.I. parishioner when he said, "I go to church, I hear the service that I've always heard, it all seems kind of right to me." Norma's response, however, is more plaintive: "We like the old form of the service—with a regular format, you know. We like the sermon in the same place, we like to sing 'Praise God from Whom All Blessings Flow' at the offertory. One of my friends said, 'When I used to walk into the church and heard the organ play, it gave me a feeling of calmness. I could get my feelings together, I could pray.' Now it's not the same, it's noisy. But as my friend says, 'I guess we've got to go with the flow' with the younger generation. They're still worshiping God, they're just doing it their way."

G.I.s may give in to younger generations in order to keep a community together, but they are rarely happy about it or satisfied with the turn that their worship takes. There is no easy answer to this problem, either. Communities that are large enough to have a "contemporary" service as well as a "traditional" service run the risk of losing a sense of congregational cohesion, but succeed in keeping most people happy. More eclectic approaches—those that try to please everyone with a little of this, a little of that—usually end up pleasing no one, but may be the best that smaller congregations can do.

Sensitivity to the needs of G.I.s to pray in the way that feels most appropriate and is the most effective for them—corporate prayer—is vital for successful ministry to this generation. Likewise, sensitivity to the issues that anger or frustrate them is paramount, without trying to talk them out of it, or minimize their concerns. The world they have loved, fought for, and sacrificed for has passed away. Their grief is appropriate, and must be held with respect and responded to with empathy and love.

When ministering to G.I.s in their homes, remember that they are more comfortable with corporate prayer than private prayer. You will probably find that they will not usually initiate prayer, but will gratefully join you in prayer if you suggest it—especially if you lead it. Don't confuse or embarrass them with prayer that is overly intimate or touchy-feely, overly familiar or experimental. Again, G.I.s value the kind of prayer they heard as children—prayer that is formal, respectful, directed to a powerful, Father-figure kind of deity, and often according to a set script. Praying "with" the grain of their style of faith, rather than "against" their preferred style will yield far more effective results. That thing about "old dogs" and "new tricks" is not, strictly speaking, true. But it is *wise*.

Silents Ministering to G.I.s

In one way or another, Silents have been ministering to G.I.s their entire lives, and not just in the religious sense. They have been serving them in spiritual communities, yes, but also in business, in politics, and in every other arena of human endeavor. Silents took orders from G.I.s in the Second World War, and never really stopped. Silents provided a pliable work force for G.I.s in the post-war years. They were sympathetic to G.I. ambitions, made cooperative employees, and were strong team players. They rarely challenged G.I. motivations or methods directly (although they were indirectly subversive, as we shall see later).

Of all the living generations, Silents understand and sympathize with G.I.s the most. They don't always agree with G.I.s, but they "get" them, and they are experts at the delicate task of G.I. diplomacy. They understand the things that upset and frustrate G.I.s. They share many of the same opinions[23] and can express their sympathy with a sincerity that is difficult for younger generations to muster.

Part of what Silents really have going for them is that, while other generations may understand the greatness of individual G.I.s, Silents understand the greatness of the G.I. project, and the generation as a whole. They approve of them (if not always their methods) and they truly support them. G.I.s, in turn, trust Silents (even if they do not always respect them), and will confide in them and commiserate with them.

Thus, Silents are in a unique place to minister effectively to G.I.s. Silents alone truly understand them and share their confidence. Silents have by this time earned the gravitas that G.I.s expect and require from their clergy and spiritual guides. G.I.s will gladly be led in prayer by Silents, will listen to Silent advice and counsel, and will, on occasion, submit to Silent correction and exhortation. Silents understand the directive role that G.I.s respond to well in a spiritual leader, and can "step up" and embody that authority (and they mostly already inhabit it by this time).

G.I.s prefer Silent pastors, feel most comfortable with Silent chaplains, and can be most vulnerable and teachable under Silent spiritual directors. The natural affinity that has always united these two generations in companionable cooperation definitely works in the G.I.s favor when it comes to ministry.

Silents, remember that G.I.s pray differently than you do. While your primary form of prayer is private, intimate prayer, G.I.s pray best in groups. Encouraging them toward the kind of prayer that is meaningful to you may be effective in individual G.I.s, but will not be effective for most. Encouraging them to join in corporate prayer will prevent them from cocooning themselves where the temptations of despair and self-pity threaten to overcome them. Spiritual community is essential as G.I.s get older, and the more opportunities they have for corporate prayer the better off they will be. Community is always salvific, and for those who are shut-in by illness or depression, it is essential.

In my experience of ministry, G.I.s are nearly universally resistant to entering managed-care facilities because they fear losing their autonomy. Yet, once they actually enter such homes, their quality of life increases substantially.[24] For here they find both the support that they need to continue an active life, but also the community that actually makes life worth living. Such places usually have several opportunities for corporate worship each week. Often, G.I.s will attend every service, regardless of the denomination, so great is their hunger for prayer that speaks to them. Silents who can encourage, support, and offer such prayer will be effective ministers indeed.

Boomers Ministering to G.I.s

Of all the pairings in this book, this is the most difficult. The generation gap between Boomers and G.I.s is the largest among all living generations. Most people know someone who is estranged from his or her G.I. parents—and most G.I./Boomer relationships have had rocky patches, if not rocky roads all the way along. The reasons for this will be explored in depth in the chapter on Boomers, but here we are concerned with how Boomers can minister effectively to G.I.s. The fact is, you may not be able to. Part of being a good minister or spiritual guide is knowing where one's limitations are. If you are a Boomer who has a terrible relationship with your G.I. parents, it may be difficult or even impossible for you to offer responsible ministry to those who remind you of them. Saying, "allow me to refer you to just the right person," may be the most loving thing you can do. You have my permission to do it.

On the other hand, perhaps you have done your work in therapy, or are fortunate to have had good relationships with G.I.s. In that case, it is important to see the ways in which generational distinctiveness can lead to missed connections in ministry.

Even if you get along well with G.I.s in your life, even though you are professional through-and-through, don't expect G.I.s to behave around you. They are elderly, and many elderly people feel at liberty—due precisely to the venerable status their age affords them—to give you the benefit of their unfiltered opinions. Do not let this trigger you. As often as not, a G.I. is trying to get your goat. The rest of the time you are hearing genuine feelings articulated by people who simply have no sensitivity to how their words will impact you. So sometimes it will be personal, sometimes it won't be. *You* must be the professional, regardless.

Boomers, you must realize that you are walking around with a bull's-eye taped to your back, due to your placement in your generational cohort. G.I.s are still angry, and they will take it out on you, even if they have never met you before. So be ready for it, take care of your own inner child, and put a lid on your reactions.

It may be tempting for Boomers to interpret G.I. spirituality as insincere. It is not. It simply does not come from the same heart place in which the Boomers' spirituality resides. For G.I.s, spirituality is indistinguishable from institutional religion. To serve the institution is to serve God, and worship according to the liturgies and forms of the institution is what God requires and what is personally meaningful for them. Boomers must respect these forms and offer them to G.I.s with humility and dutifulness. Boomers must not give in to temptations to "update" the liturgy so that they (Boomers) don't choke on the words. Yes, the language is sexist, hierarchical, monarchical, and militant. Typically, so is the G.I. God. And yet, "he" should *not* be taken away from them.

Replacing "her" for "him" in God language may make Boomers feel better, but will ruin the experience for G.I.s. Boomers, you are not here (in this ministry context) for *you*. You are here for *them*. And you must serve them in the way that is most effective for *them*, regardless of how wrong it feels to *you*.

If you are a congregational minister, serving mostly G.I.s and Silents, you know that you couldn't get away with changing your worship language if you tried. Instead, you must take responsibility for yourself and make sure you meet your own spiritual needs elsewhere.[25]

Xers Ministering to G.I.s

Xers generally get along well with their G.I. grandparents, and this fondness carries over to other G.I.s in their lives. There is

33

no perceivable generation gap between these generations. This is paradoxical, because in many ways, G.I.s are just as powerfully idealistic as Boomers (although in mirror-opposite ways). Strangely, though, G.I. idealism doesn't annoy Xers the way Boomer idealism does.

Educated Xers appreciate the sacrifice and struggle of G.I.s. Xers know that necessity drove G.I.s, and respect the fact that G.I.s leaped in and got dirty, doing what had to be done. Xers meet G.I. jingoism with amusement, and dismiss their economic reactionary positions with a wave. This is both good and bad. Good, because Xers are not triggered by G.I.s in the way Boomers are, and can be fully present to them. They make effective ministers for G.I.s. But Xer attitudes can be problematic if G.I.s sense that they are being patronized or even quietly mocked.[26]

Xers who want to be good ministers to G.I.s must be willing to set aside their generationally required smarminess and irony. G.I.s are deadly serious about their loyalties and values. Xers must pretend, for the duration of their visit, to do the same. I know, I know—I'm advocating inauthenticity for Xers, which is the antithesis of Xer spiritual values. Tough. If being a good spiritual guide for G.I.s means being inauthentic for a short time, then so be it. *Pretend* that you care about the things they care about. Do not mock their ideals and values. G.I.s do not understand your humor, so don't try to be funny. Vent and make jokes about it later to your supervisor. But when you're there, in the room with a G.I., be sure to mirror his or her values.

That means not dismissing institutions, attitudes, and morals upon which the G.I. world is built. I know this is asking a lot of Xers, but in practical terms, this is what it takes to be effective. So suck it up and make it work. If you care for them, you must care about the things that make them who they are. (Or, at the very least, you must *appear* to care about these things.)

Xers must remember that G.I. spirituality is based on the idea of *faithfulness*. This is an idea bound up with other ideals such as duty, responsibility, and obedience. Xers will comfort G.I.s by affirming their fidelity to the goals and demands of their faiths, and the institutions to which they belong. G.I.s are too far along on their path for major, life-disrupting about-faces in ideology or theology. Selling them on the latest deconstructive theologian is pointless. The goal should be to affirm them in the faith that has sustained them thus far, strengthening that faith, reinforcing it, and encouraging it.

"Building up" is counter-intuitive to Xers, whose generational project is primarily deconstructive. But to be a good minister to G.I.s, you must find a place within yourself to do it with a whole heart. You must master the practice of *edification*, the building up of faith—even if it is a form of faith that makes no intuitive sense to you.

This requires acts of imagination and empathy. You must *imagine* what an obedient faith means to the G.I. You must *imagine* what building, belonging to, and serving an institution means to a G.I. This requires creativity and deep caring in order to effectively make such imaginative leaps. These are large leaps, and not easy to do. They go against the grain of every knee-jerk response Xers possess. But if you want to minister effectively to G.I.s, you must be willing to make the effort.

The most important thing Xers can do, however, is to love G.I.s as people. They will sense the authenticity in this, and it will cover a multitude of wise-cracking asides. G.I.s will be deeply grateful for your time, your care, and your friendship. Just see them as people, love them as people, and treat them as you would hope to be treated. Lose the cynical humor (just while you're in the room—twenty minutes won't kill you), and you'll do just fine.

Millennials Ministering to G.I.s

Millennials are a great fit for ministering to G.I.s. Both generations understand the importance of family in a deep and primal way. Both are possessed of a strong "cohort" mentality—group-think and collaboration come naturally to both generations. Both generations are creative and action-oriented. They are both relentlessly positive, kind to strangers, and dedicated to those they care about.

The biggest problem for Millennial ministers and spiritual guides is being taken seriously as religious professionals, simply because of their age. I remember how odd I felt (and how awkward my parishioners were) when, in their 80s they were calling me (in my early 30s) "Father John." We got through the awkwardness, but it was more than just the ironic title. It took a great deal of time—many years of dedicated service—before they started seeing me as their pastor and not just a kid. You may have similar difficulties, especially with G.I.s.

A fine strategy here is actually a ruse: ask their advice on something. If you can position your G.I. parishioner/patient/client as the mentor, and yourself as the "mentee"[27] you will instantly have their cooperation and goodwill. They'll start talking, and all you really need do is listen, nod, and ask questions. The relationship will unfold and deepen and real ministry will happen. As you are well aware, it is the Divine actually doing this work, anyway, not you.

The added benefit to this strategy is that G.I.s actually do have great wisdom to impart. Ask to learn from them, and you will. Yeah, you'll have to glean the good stuff from amidst numerous stories about the Second World War and life on the farm, but you know, there's good stuff to learn there, too. G.I.s grew up in a very different world than you did. It made them different people. To empathize and connect with them in a deep way, you have to understand what makes them tick, what *formed* them into the people they are today. The "life on the farm" stories aren't just boring or irrelevant, they are foundational to G.I. identity and psychology.

G.I.s' reliance on (and devotion to) religious institutions may puzzle you. What *is* it about sitting together in a room singing honky-tonk piano songs from the 1920s about the blood of Jesus that means so much to these folks? It *is* a little puzzling, I'll grant you. Remember that G.I.s aren't tech-savvy. They have to rely on analog means for connection. Music, tradition, and institutions—*these things are how they connect.*

Admittedly, in part this is a mystical, emotional connection, rather than an informational one. (Ironic in some ways, since the G.I.s are not terribly emotive—don't let that fool you. Their emotions are huge, they are just not showy about them.) But the connection is real to them. Tradition (including music) connects them to the past, to the dead, to the Divine, to one another. It's no smart phone, but it does the job.

The institutions they belong to and support are ways of creating and maintaining connections with others beyond their families. They require old fashioned physical proximity, but they don't consider that a liability, but rather an advantage. There's wisdom in this. Don't be afraid to hold their hands. Many of them are starving for affection and human touch. They won't think it's weird, even if you do. Make it a habit. They will be so grateful they'll look right past the fact that you can't yet grow a full beard.

They will, in fact, love you—and if you can love them in return it will be the best ministry you can do for them.

CHAPTER TWO

THE "COMPASSIONATE" GENERATION—THE SILENTS

Joel sat up in his hospital bed, wincing a bit as he did it. "Don't get up for me," Rachel, his rabbi said, placing a kind hand on his shoulder as she approached.

"I think I won't," he said, and shot her a pained smile. "Thanks for coming."

"I'm glad to see you doing so well," she assured him. She sat near him, but continued to keep a hand on his arm. For a while they made small talk, but after a lull, Rachel looked him in the eye. "How are you doing?"

"Well, the doctor said—"

"I know the medical report," she interrupted him. "I want to know how you are doing, emotionally."

"Where I come from, youngsters don't interrupt their elders." He scowled at Rachel, fully thirty years his junior.

"I thought you were Jewish," she shot back. "And don't evade the question. How are you doing?" He looked down and there was silence between them for a while. Finally, she prompted him. "What is your prayer like right now?"

"That's an awfully personal question," he complained.

"There's no one here but us bears," she smiled at him.

"I heard Schwartz made a fuss at the meeting last week," he said.

"Are you going to tell me about your prayer?" she chided.

"He loves to make trouble, but he's a good guy to have in your corner."

"I'm holding out for the prayer talk," Rachel said.

*"Let me tell you how to handle him," he said, and winced a
bit as he adjusted himself in bed. "He's really a good guy, but
he just needs to know he's needed . . . ."*

Introducing the Silents

The G.I. generation was a tough act to follow, so much so that the
generation that came after them didn't even try. Like the introverted little brother of an extroverted star, the so-called "Silent
Generation" seemed resigned (if not content) to follow in the
G.I.s' shadow, continuing pet G.I. projects, and letting big brother
call all the shots. Often seen by others as lacking a generational
spine, Silents became the "gophers" of the G.I. generation, even
after the G.I. Generation had largely retired. Strauss and Howe,
more kindly, labeled them "a consummate helpmate generation."[1]

It's hard to exaggerate the degree to which Silents took a
back seat—though plenty of them were movers and shakers in
the entertainment world (Clint Eastwood, Woody Allen, and Bob
Dylan are all Silents), they made little mark politically. As Strauss
and Howe point out, there were no Silent presidents—we jumped
directly from G.I. George H. Bush, to Boomer Bill Clinton.[2] Thus,
the nickname "Silent" for a generation that was seen but not heard,
who seemed to have skipped over any hint of messy adolescence
and proceeded directly to boring, respectable suburban adulthood.

Birth Years and Place in the Cycle

The Silent Generation was born between 1925 and 1942, a minor
cohort among the living generations, small in duration, number,
and power. Following, as they do, a mighty Civic generation, the
Silents had their work cut out for them. Strauss and Howe identify
generations that follow Civic generations as Adaptive generations.
An Adaptive generation, they say, grows up "overprotected and
suffocated youths during a secular crisis; matures into risk-averse,
conformist rising adults, produces indecisive midlife arbitrator-
leaders during a spiritual awakening; and maintains influence (but
less respect) as sensitive elders."[3]

Adaptive generations by necessity ride the historical coattails of the more dominant Civics that precede them. While Civics are movers and shakers, Adaptives are shake-averse, conflict-averse, and argument-averse. They are a generation of humanitarians, peacemakers, and arbitrators who generally approve of the Civic project, but seek to smooth out its rough edges, to make sure that our collective actions live up to our stated principles.

This dynamic is easy to see when looking at the G.I.s and Silents. The G.I.s created "the Great Society" that we enjoy today, but the Silents made sure that it was honest and that it applied to everyone, not just to a privileged few. The Silents engineered a tricky and important transition in how the world perceived America—from a respect based on military superiority to one based on moral authority.[4]

Formative Events

As children, Silents were born too late to have any knowledge of the prosperity that followed the Great War or the youthful abandon of the Roaring Twenties. Instead, they were forced to grow up quickly and assume adult responsibilities before they were even in their teens as many of them left school to enter the work-place in order to help their families weather the Great Depression.

No sooner had the nation begun to emerge from that great Dark Night of the Depression than it was plunged into another one—the U.S.'s entrance into the Second World War. While this war was an affair entirely led by G.I.s, the first wave of Silents were among the young infantrymen in the trenches under fire. Younger Silents back home were swept up in the patriotic euphoria of wartime boosterism, while at the same time enduring a second "Great Depression" of rationing and economic asceticism.

The ending of the Second World War did not see the end of Silent militarism. As Debra, originally from Tennessee, described it to me, her generation endured, "one war after another." Silents went back to war in Korea, and achieved middle management positions in Vietnam. The longest war in which the Silents engaged, however, was the Cold War, and it was in this struggle—a triumph of diplomacy, double-speak, and arbitration—that their true colors and formidable conciliatory skills were most needed and most successfully employed. They saw the necessity of the bomb, but at the same time they understood the gravity and foolhardiness of its employment.[5]

Silents were as crushed as the rest of America by the assassination of John F. Kennedy. And while the Silents' only great generational achievement, the Civil Rights Movement, boosted their self esteem, it was fiercely buffeted by more assassinations. Their most important leaders—Martin Luther King, Jr. and Robert Kennedy—were lost to radical ideologues opposed to the Silent ideals of liberty, peace, and justice for all.

Silent hopes were raised once again during the space race—the moon landing made many of the lists of "formative events" returned to me by Silents who participated in my survey. But that triumph was short-lived, as, five years later, the Watergate scandal exploded the illusion of political integrity and propriety for subsequent generations. Even though it was a G.I. president in office at the time, the albatross of the event was passed to the Silents and has been dutifully worn by them ever since.

Experience of the World and Disposition

Since first-wave Silents grew up during the Great Depression and last-wave Silents grew up under the rationing system of the Second World War, it is not surprising that their overwhelming experience of the world was one of scarcity and depravation. Stan, from Anchorage, Alaska, wrote that he was "born during the Great Depression. My parents moved to California because they could not find employment in Oklahoma. The depression continued as World War II broke out and rationing of foods, gasoline, and consumer goods was very real. My parents raised rabbits and chickens (in Los Angeles) to have meat and eggs."

Olivia, from Minden, Nevada, reported a similar experience. She said, "My parents were products of the Depression and were very conservative with their money, indeed with all resources." Because of this hardship, Silents are the least likely of all the living generations to be extravagant with their resources. They are reserved, cautious, and fiscally conservative.

Their hardship may have formed their experience as children, but their young adulthood was far more prosperous. As Strauss and Howe report, "Silents have enjoyed a lifetime of steadily rising affluence, have suffered relatively few war casualties, and have shown the twentieth century's lowest rates for almost every social pathology of youth (crime, suicide, illegitimate births, and teen unemployment)."[6]

After the war, the Silents had reason to be hopeful. As Opal, from Denver, Colorado, remembers it, she was "hopeful for economic improvement over my parents' generation," and held to a "belief that better times were to come," having "immense faith that science would solve all problems."

The Silents, by and large, bought the Ozzy and Harriet version of idealized suburban American life hook, line, and sinker. As a generation, Silents were the ultimate co-dependents, mollifying the volatile G.I.s on one hand and affirming the outraged Boomers on the other (while advising restraint, of course). As with all such "peacemakers," managing image became of primary importance—a caricature that is expertly and accurately depicted on the current hit television series *Mad Men*, a show that is entirely about Silents and their preoccupation with image. The image of prosperity equals prosperity, the image of family harmony equals family harmony, and Silents cultivated these images diligently and effortlessly.

But there was certainly a difference between image and reality, and the affluence of the post-war years didn't mean that Silent life was stress-free. As Olivia described this time to me, "Because of the threat of nuclear attack, we were taught to 'duck and cover' in school and had drills frequently. We would jump under our desks or march down to the basement of the school where we would sit. Mother set up an area in our basement with water and canned foods just in case the world exploded. We were taught that we needed to follow directions and that our country was led by competent and good men (always men, of course), but that as good citizens we needed to be prepared for whatever catastrophe might be brought on by evil people in other countries."

Olivia's statement reveals an important feature of the Silent mindset—an intrinsic trust in the integrity of governmental authority, and authority figures in general. Silents were always in awe of the G.I. generation, and generally trusted them. They believed in the G.I. project, and were glad to add their labor to the effort when they were old enough to do so.

Silents contributed greatly to the space race, and they took considerable pride in their country and its spectacular accomplishment of landing a man on the moon. Yet, again, the race was a G.I. project, and Silents were sometimes ambivalent about their involvement. As Rebecca, from Emeryville, California, remembered, "We were living at Cape Canaveral during the boom of the NASA era. I watched launchings and was of mixed mind. How exciting, yet, did it make sense to start 'conquering' space when we clearly had so much work to do here at home?"

Despite the very real pain they witnessed and experienced, the Silent generational disposition is overwhelmingly optimistic. Although their experience of the world was shaped by financial scarcity, they emerged from that rich in patriotic spirit, hope for the future, and faith in their elders, their own efforts, and in the wisdom of science "to lead them into all truth."[7]

In a Word and a Song

When I asked survey respondents about a generational motto or a song that summed up their cohort, no clear consensus emerged. Nevertheless, there were few surprises among the themes that many of the responses contained. Many picked songs that were popular, but held little that was psychologically revealing—such as "New York, New York," "Sentimental Journey," or "Fly Me to the Moon." This is significant in one way, in that it points to the fact that Silents (much like G.I.s before them) come from a time in which music was seen as escapist entertainment, rather than as confessional or political in nature.

Nevertheless, two songs emerged that were selected by more than one respondent, and the juxtaposition of them speaks directly to the ambivalence in the Silent psyche that I frequently encountered. These songs are "America the Beautiful" and "We Shall Overcome."[8] While these songs are not in conflict—most Silents would affirm the essential messages of both—they are nevertheless in tension, speaking power-fully to the Silent love of their country *and* their desire to reform it.

There was great diversity in sugges-tions for a generational motto as well. One of my Boomer students suggested that "Yes, sir," summed up the Silents she knew pretty well—no doubt refer-ring to the Silent tendency to capitulate to almost anything the G.I.s directed them to do. This is only humorous, of course, because there is some truth to it. But it was the responses of Silents them-selves that I was the most interested in. Hank, from Montgomery, AL responded, "a penny saved is a penny earned," which speaks to the deprivation that formed the Silent experience. Kal, from Juneau, Alaska, suggested, "If we can imagine it, we can build it," which speaks to their optimistic, can-do spirit, as does San Franciscan Oliver's "Onward and upward!"

Caitlin, originally from Ireland and now living in Baltimore, Maryland, reflected the Silents' patriotism, listing her generation's priorities: "Defend your country, respect your generation, look up to your President." Caroline, from San Lorenzo, California, had some patri-otic vacation advice, "See America first," which made me laugh, because I have heard my father say those exact words.

Sam, from Oakland, California, reflected the Silents' generational project in his response: "We stand with the underdog!" as well as "Social justice for all," suggested by Diane, from Ashland, Oregon. But it seems to me that Stan's response was the most comprehensive

WE SHALL OVERCOME

We shall overcome, we shall overcome,
We shall overcome someday;
Oh, deep in my heart, I do believe,
We shall overcome someday.

The Lord will see us through, the Lord will see us through,
The Lord will see us through someday;
Oh, deep in my heart, I do believe,
We shall overcome someday.

We'll walk hand in hand, we'll walk hand in hand,
We'll walk hand in hand someday;
Oh, deep in my heart, I do believe,
We'll walk hand in hand someday.

We are not afraid, we are not afraid,
We are not afraid today;
Oh, deep in my heart, I do believe,
We are not afraid today.

The truth shall make us free, the truth shall make us free,
The truth shall make us free someday;
Oh, deep in my heart, I do believe,
The truth shall make us free someday.

We shall live in peace, we shall live in peace,
We shall live in peace someday;
Oh, deep in my heart, I do believe,
We shall live in peace someday.

and reflective of the cohort as a whole: "For God, for country, for family, and for self. Our actions and motives were in that order."

Generational Project

The G.I.s did great things, they wielded great might, they saved the world, they built the infrastructure that America runs on even today—but they did it with all the poise and grace of a bull in a china shop. To say that "toes were stepped on" may qualify as an extreme understatement, to which G.I.s reply with their standard answers, "collateral damage," "necessary losses," or a dismissive "suck it up." The Bull wrecked its constructive havoc across the globe, followed dutifully by the Silents with broom and dustpan in hand, unruffling the feathers the G.I.s seemed oblivious (or uncaring) of having ruffled, smoothing over hurt feelings, cleaning up the detritus, and undoing a mountain of damage.

In teaching this material, I sometimes twist the title of Silent James Dean's famous film, and call them "conformists without a cause"[9]—yet that is hardly fair. As an adaptive generation, they *did* have a cause, and that was to humanize the institutions built by the G.I.s. The G.I. impulse for the common good at the expense of the individual left a lot of pain in its wake, to which the Silents were particularly sensitive. This is a generation of empaths, highly compassionate people who see the value of the G.I. project and the institutions they built, but Silents took it upon themselves to oil and tinker with those institutions to make them both more efficient and more responsive to human pain and need. As Strauss and Howe wrote, "Silent appeals for change have seldom arisen from power or fury, but rather through a self-conscious humanity and tender social conscience."[10]

As much as they trusted the G.I.s' basic motives and valued their institutions, Silents struggled with an ambivalence about G.I. *methods*. Nowhere is this more evident than in the push-and-pull between Senator Joe McCarthy's Communist witch-hunt throughout the 1950s and basic civil rights. Silents were divided—internally, and politically—around the issue, but it was emblematic of a larger ambivalence in play in the generation. As much as the Silents were invested in G.I. projects, they found the G.I.

steam-roller-over-any-opposition approach to be unnecessarily bullying. Inwardly they reacted negatively to the harshness of G.I. methods, and strove to accomplish many of the same goals by more compassionate means.

Sandwiched between two dominant, loud generations, each with more than their share of ideologues, Silents in general were motivated by compassion rather than ideology. As Olivia described her experience, "I remember when all the Vietnam 'fuss' started being very confused. I found it difficult to understand why people were marching or being beaten and arrested. At that time, I thought that if we were at war, the President and all the other leaders must have very good reasons for doing that. A good part of me thought the young people should have calmed down and, if they felt so adamant about their positions, they should protest in more civilized ways. I also felt that the authorities should have reacted in more moderate ways."

Silents are curiously flexible ideologically, valuing peace and harmony over any particular party line. As Strauss and Howe describe them, "Lacking an independent voice, they have adopted the moral relativism of the skilled arbitrator, mediating arguments between others—and reaching out to people of all cultures, races, ages, and handicaps."[11]

In light of this perceived "wishy-washy" nature of Silents, it is tempting to see Woody Allen's brilliant film, *Zelig*, as a work of generational autobiography. Zelig, a chameleonlike figure with no significant identity of his own, is "defined" by the events he happens to be present at and the company he keeps.

What Are They Seeking?

Although rejecting the hard, mutually opposed ideologies of the G.I.s behind them and the Boomers in front of them, the Silents nevertheless discovered a sense of purpose for themselves. Partly this manifested in the humanizing reforms of G.I. institutions already mentioned, but this was part of a larger concern: justice.

The desire for "liberty and justice for all," so foundational to the American dream, became a guiding impulse for Silents in every arena of society. Influenced in part by the horrors of the

Second World War, Silents were outraged by "the cruelty displayed by Germany as they attempted to destroy 'inferior beings,'" as Stan described it. They keenly felt the responsibility and discernment that American military might required of them.

As Strauss and Howe report, "16% of Harvard's Class of '64 joined the Peace Corps, Harvard's top postgraduate destination for that year."[12] Debra told me, "I was very unhappy about the state and condition of the world, and have felt called to help, especially in terms of what God has shown me is the root problem, a lack of equality or not practicing the universal message of the Golden Rule to treat others with equal fairness and respect, that results in inequality."

The Silent generation sought justice for all who suffer around the world, but, especially at first, at home. As Strauss and Howe point out, "The Silent Generation has produced virtually every major figure in the modern civil rights movement—from the Little Rock children to the youths at the Greensboro lunch counter, from Martin Luther King, Jr., to Malcolm X, from Cesar Chavez's farm workers' union to Russell Means' American Indian Movement."[13] As Rebecca wrote, "After growing up protected within the environs of a small town in Ohio, I was stunned at the Civil Rights era. That is, although I knew there was such a thing as prejudice, it had not really dawned on me how outrageously inhumane and far-reaching it was. A challenge loomed big—justice, tolerance, finding a way to mediate differences."

Silents reached out in small ways, as well, excelling in "helping professions" such as teaching, medicine, ministry, and government.[14] Nick, from Berkeley, California, told me, "I know a whole lot of people—my age—who really seem to have made a lot of effort to make the world better. I belong to a Rotary Club! These people are so different: blue collar and management, black and white."

In whatever arena Silents found themselves, they championed human and equal rights generally, engineering efforts for racial equality, women's liberation, gay and lesbian liberation, and by increasing international pressure for human rights abroad.

How Silents Are Perceived

The portrait of the Silent generation that Strauss and Howe paint can be summed up in one word: weak.[15] We may have to trust them on this, because when I asked people to tell me what they thought of *other* generations, there were opinions aplenty about G.I.s, Boomers, Xers, and Millennials—but, perhaps tellingly, not a single person commented on the Silents. Beth, from Martinez, California, was so right when she commented, "The small era I group myself into seems largely unnoticed." Oliver concurs, "I doubt if other generations think about us." Ona, from Novato, California, told me, "I think we're becoming irrelevant to the younger generations."

Yet Silents themselves certainly have plenty of opinions on how others probably see them. Opal offered several other one-word descriptions: "Conventional," "Boring," "Square," "Rigid," "Practical," and "Expedient." Nancy, from Durham, North Carolina, is more articulate in her generational self-assessment: "I feel like I am the generation after what they called the 'greatest generation,' those who went to war, whom the whole nation rallied around. My generation doesn't have that. [That] generation was so much influenced by the Depression, that they were very much seeking financial security and a good, safe life. They kind of shook their heads on those of us who wanted to shake up things—like the Civil Rights movement. They would have regarded us as unwise. I see my children's generation are perhaps seeing us as irrelevant. When the Berlin wall fell I told my children, 'this is the biggest event in world history since WW II,' and [they said,] 'Oh?' It seemed like they did not even see it. They are probably worried we are a burden on them now because they're going to have to take care of us as we age, since most of us are not contributing to the economy any more. I cannot see them turning to us for wisdom, either."

Olivia reiterated the theme of being a burden when she wrote, "Up until the past several years, I thought we were held in good esteem and respect, however that seems to be totally falling apart. Today, I think the younger generations feel that we are sucking up all the limited resources to be had and that we ought to just fade away. I feel angry about having made so many sacrifices and contributed so much money only to see unimaginably rampant greed in leaders of large corporations drive us, as a country, into a state where huge numbers of people live in poverty and we have lost our competitive edge in the world. I think my generation is now considered irrelevant at best."

Stan told me that younger generations "think we are a generation of hypocrites, always talking about the 'old days' and old ways. They think we do not understand the pressures they are subjected to and the situations they have to deal with. The complaints from younger generations has been that my generation was not truthful. Using marijuana and other drugs did not kill them, like they were told . . . and while they do not refute that WWII was for a noble cause, they do question what 'really' happened . . . . My generation was responsible for our nation's involvement in Korea and Vietnam. Younger generations question the motive and wonder why we were really there."

How Silents Perceive Themselves

Although other generations may perceive them as weak or irrelevant, Silents see themselves as compassionate, as indeed, they are. They feel proud of their accomplishments, even if others don't see them. As Olivia wrote, "I think of us as the ones who fought the big war, who created prosperity for this country, who worked hard and contributed to the Social Security and Medicare coffers. I believed that we would be rewarded for our hard work and for not making a big stink about things. I thought that would be enough and that society would take care of us for our devotion, hard work, and sacrifice. I think of my generation with admiration and respect and believed we would be accorded the same. I think we were very successful at doing those things we set out to do . . . . Looking back, I perceive my generation to be proud, resilient, hard working, and naïve."

Regardless of how positively or negatively Silents are perceived—when they are perceived at all—they get along well with other generations. They can play ball just fine with G.I.s, providing them with reliable if unremarkable team players. They also relate well with the idealistic aims of Boomers, even if they don't always share Boomers' over-the-top passion and grandiose means of bringing those dreams about. They share the pragmatic spirit of Xers. And although they love their Millennial grandchildren to tears, they are aware that these children have entered another world into which they cannot follow—a realization that makes them sad and proud at the same time.

Overall, Silents view themselves as caring and compassionate, moderate and fair, practical and cautious. Whatever else they may be, they are not wrong about these things. They may never lay claim to being the greatest generation, but they are certainly the most just.

THE SPIRITUALITY OF THE SILENT GENERATION

The Spiritual Gifts of Silents

Silents will always be defined by what they are not. To borrow Teddy Roosevelt's metaphor, the G.I.s carried big sticks. The Boomers also carried big sticks, and although they pretended they were not for beating, they did plenty of it. The Silents, however, true to their name, spoke softly. If Jesus' words about the Peacemakers carry any weight in eternity, then the Silents are the children of God indeed. And Silents also know better than anyone that the saying "No justice, no peace" is true, and their pursuit of both is integral to their spirituality. Peacemaking is their first calling, and their great spiritual gift.

Joel, in this chapter's opening vignette, might have been eager to avoid talking about his private prayer practice, but he really *did* want to talk about making peace in his synagogue, offering advice to his rabbi about how to work with a troublesome member of the congregation.

Few of the Silents' neighbor generations are generous about

their calling as peacemakers, however. G.I.s often complain that "politics have no place in church," and decry any "peace and justice" language in their spiritual communities. They are likely to lump Silents who raise concerns about peace and justice in their spiritual communities in with Boomer "radicals" who challenge everything the G.I.s stand for and shed their blood to build.

Silents likewise get grief from Boomers, who idealistically champion Truth over Peace, and see the Silents' flexibility when it comes to placating G.I.s to be dishonest capitulation. They, too, see Silents as weak, because Silents refuse to stand up to G.I.s, especially when it comes to issues on which Silents and Boomers agree.

Xers get Silents, however. They see the G.I. rock and the Boomer hard place that Silents are wedged uncomfortably between. They also understand the pragmatism that drives Silents. They don't understand Silents' desire to work within the system to change things, but shrug it off without much judgment.

The Silent generation's greatest spiritual gift is reformation. Unlike Luther's Boomer-like "Here I stand! I can do no other!" stance, however, Silents work quietly for reform within their spiritual communities and secular institutions, appreciating and affirming the contributions of G.I.s, and finding rational, reasonable motivations for slight course corrections that G.I.s can accept (couched diplomatically in their own language and pointed toward ends G.I.s consider desirable). At the same time, out of the other side of their mouths, they work to motivate Boomers to hit the pavement to enact their reforms—which Boomers are eager to do.

Boomers should be careful not to label this disingenuity. Silents are not ideologues, as both G.I.s and Boomers tend to be. They are pragmatists who nevertheless are working towards what they see to be necessary and achievable ideals. Ideals that they have indeed been successful at bringing about, both in society and in their spiritual communities. G.I.s would criticize these as not being "spiritual" concerns. But Silents know better.

How Divinity is Imaged

Silents value traditional faith, but hold it less rigidly than G.I.s. Their reforming spirit is just as evident in their religious lives as in their civil endeavors, and the form of Divinity they experience rejects harsh dogmatism and instead reflects the kind of care and compassion that guide the Silents themselves. Indeed, many of them attribute their reforming fervor to their faith, believing that it is the Divine that calls them to and empowers them for compassionate action in the world.

The Divine, for Silents, is a loving parental figure, transcendent but also intimate. While most of them will use traditional images to speak of Divinity, they are aware that these are metaphors, and do not confuse images with reality. Violet, a Lutheran from Missouri, describes her faith this way: "The Divine to me is God, and it's personal. It helps me to believe that there's something out there that's watching over me. I trust the Divine to keep me safe, to keep my family safe, and to help me when I'm troubled."

While the Divine for G.I.s is concerned more for the community than the individual, for Silents the Divine is deeply concerned for the needs and health of each and every person. Sam, who "hangs out with Episcopalians and Lutherans," told me, "The Divine is a prayer away . . . very near and personal. No man has seen the Divine . . . with the exception of looking to Jesus. God wants us to love our neighbor as God loves us, as mirrored in what Jesus Christ did for us . . . . God is forever reaching out to us in the presence of the Holy Spirit. God is gracious, and seeking relationship with us."

The Divine mirrors the forgiving and compassionate nature of Silents themselves. As Kevin, an Episcopalian from Petaluma describes his faith, "I trust in an extravagantly loving Higher Power who is in control and intimately involved in all aspects of life, who has empowered us as co-creators . . . . I sense that my Higher Power's 'requirement' is simply one of responding to the Divine love, loving God/Goddess and each other. I feel, too, that my Higher Power has a limitless sense of humor and ability to accept us as we are, foibles and all."

Because of their recognition of the "conditional" nature of metaphors, rarely mistaking them for "the Truth," Silents may use masculine language for the Divine because it is traditional and comfortable (and indeed, may be uncomfortable with feminine or gender neutral language), but they recognize that this masculinity is metaphorical and not literal. Hank, a Roman Catholic deacon, put it this way: "I have learned that God is pure Spirit, but to tell the truth I must say that I have no idea what that means. So I picture God as Father/Provider and I also think of God as Mother, very nurturing. Also there are times when I have God as my best friend, by my side, always for me and never against me (especially when times are hard, but that is the human condition and I realize that life is not always fair)."

Because they expect an intimate relationship with the Divine— and hold this as a spiritual ideal—Silents are understandably distressed when they hit occasional rough patches in their spiritual lives. Hank wrote, "There are times in my life when I feel that God is very intimate and at others I may experience a dry spell when I feel that God is distant . . . . God wants us to realize that we are all brothers and sisters in God's family and therefore we love and take care of each other."

For Silents, the Divine demands justice and opportunity for all people, especially those who have few opportunities. Therefore, religion and spirituality, for Silents, contains a strong impulse toward justice. Caitlin, a Roman Catholic, told me, "People are to live our faith. We are to help people, to be kind and to be loving towards the poor, handicapped, the sick, and those in jail."

Theirs is not an "anything goes" kind of deity, however. Silents are painfully aware—no doubt due to their own hard-won experiences—that actions have serious consequences, and that people must take responsibility for themselves while at the same time reaching out to lift up others. Ed, a UCC congregant from Mill Valley, California, wrote, "I have no idea how the Divine *feels* about people, but I do know that actions have consequences, some of which are predictable and some not."

Debra, a Roman Catholic, sums up a lot about her generation's spirituality concisely when she reports that she believes in a "personal God, who personally came to me as God's hand on the wall on the morning of my fifth birthday. God is love, a Spirit, neither male or female but both . . . . God requires us to seek God, and God's Holy Spirit guides us to love one another . . . . God gave us free will and we grow in spirituality or suffer the consequences."

While G.I.s find safety and security in having a sense of who the Divine is, Silents are keenly aware of the mysterious nature of Divinity. Ed wrote, "The Divine is a supreme mystery rather than a personal or anthropomorphic deity . . . not necessarily distant since I see the Divine mystery in all things."

Olivia, an Episcopalian, struggles to articulate what she knows is ineffable: "The closest I can come to an image for the Divine is the power that holds the universe together. I believe that this force is both intimate and distant—immanent and transcendent—that it urges, but does not compel, and that it calls us to our own greatness . . . . My experience is not so much one of being loved and of loving God, it feels even more intimate than that. Ultimately, I fail to have words to describe the closeness I feel which is beyond human emotion and human intellect."

Nancy, a witch, even names the Divine "Mystery." She told me, "My view of the Divine is that it is something . . . immanent in all things and all beings—everything takes part in the Divine. The Divine is mystery, actually. The Divine creates and shapes our lives, but in ways we have no way of understanding . . . Very immanent, at the same time very distant. That is the mystery . . . . Human comprehension just can take in so much, we are animals with self-consciousness. We are not capable of understanding the mystery out there."

Dominant Faith Style

While G.I.s are likely to identify with the strict, top-down, "do what you're told" approach of religious traditionalism, the Silents are much closer to what I label "Liberal Believers" in my *Faith Styles* book. Liberal Believers read the same scriptures as Traditional Believers, they sing the same songs, they pray the same prayers, and, in fact, their worship services may be in every detail identical with Traditional Believer congregations. The difference, however, is how they hold these things.

While Traditional believers typically hold scripture, stories of the faithful, and revered images of the Divine as literal truth, Liberal Believers, while still honoring these things, see them as metaphorical—pointing to something true but essentially incomprehensible to the human mind. At best, these symbols and images are an approximation, at worst, a distortion, of the unknowable Mystery with which we still desire—with all that is in us—to be intimate.

This leads to some very different attitudes—differences clearly evident in many arenas when comparing G.I.s and Silents. For instance, while a Traditional Believer may hold that only his religion is correct, and that anyone who does not believe as he does is damned or lost, a Liberal Believer assumes a much more humble stance. The Liberal Believer sees her faith as partial, not whole, and since her images and stories are symbols and metaphors for the Incomprehensible that nevertheless facilitate relationship and salvation, she is much more likely to see other faiths in precisely the same way: partial truths whose symbols and metaphors also point to the Incomprehensible in life-giving ways.

While Traditional Believers insist on a structure that has been handed down to them, Liberal Believers are more open to experimentation and new ideas, including influence from non-religious arenas of life. And while Traditional Believers are most concerned with correct doctrine (orthodoxy), Liberal Believers (realizing that the "correct" doctrine is partial anyway and therefore cannot be *entirely* correct) are concerned with correct action (orthopraxy). This "correct action" is determined by what the scriptures and revered figures say a "holy person" acts like.

In the case of Christianity, then, Liberal Christians are not so much interested in whether one believes in the Virgin Birth or the divinity of Christ, but whether one does what Christ said to do. As Jesus told the "sheep" in the sermon on the mount, "I was hungry and you gave me food, I was thirsty and you gave me something to drink, I was a stranger and you welcomed me, I was naked and you gave me clothing, I was sick and you took care of me, I was in prison and you visited me" (Matthew 24:35–36). Certainly, Liberal Believers may believe traditional teachings, but unlike Traditional Believers, they do not insist that others in their fellowships do so. The "test of faith" for Liberal Believers is actions, not beliefs.

By the time Silents appeared on the scene, a liberal-fundamentalist split in mainline Protestantism had been brewing for some time in the United States, but it was the Silent generation that really brought Protestant liberalism into the mainstream. While not all Silents are religious liberals, the Liberal Believer ethos captures well the overall religious project of Silents, which is more focused on the compassion of the Divine than its judgment.[16] Even fundamentalist Silents take a more intellectual and reasoned approach to their faith than G.I.s do, valuing rationality over blind obedience, and insisting that even the most conservative religious institutions live up to the humanitarian ideals enshrined in their traditions.

Unlike Boomers, many of whom simply threw off the religion of their G.I. parents altogether, Silents can and do worship comfortably side-by-side with Traditional-Believing G.I.s. Yet, as they did with other G.I.-built and led institutions, they softened and humanized those institutions—the churches and synagogues—shifting the focus from obedience to God toward service of human beings (understood *as* obedience to God). Compassion and mercy supplanted fidelity and loyalty as the most exalted virtues in American religious life—congruent in every way with the divergent priorities of G.I.s and Silents.

Spiritual Focus and Prayer Style

Silents, by and large, have an introverted spiritual focus—in our opening vignette, Rabbi Rachel had a hard time getting Joel to open up to her about his prayer life, and indeed, faith is not something that people of this generation talk about openly or easily. Religion and spirituality are overwhelmingly seen by them as private affairs. It is nobody's business whether or not one goes to church or synagogue or temple.

Prayer, for Silents, is ideally done in one's room, alone with the Divine. When I asked Debra, a Roman Catholic, to describe her spiritual practice, she said that it is mostly "silence, talking personally with God, listening, practicing virtues of patience, faith, charity, humility, perseverance, kindness—and most of all love for one another and all the Saints and Angels." Deeply influenced by Hinduism and Buddhism, Beth's practice is similar to Debra's, even though her theology is very different. She wrote, "I meditate daily. One form is sitting after breathing and *asanas*,[17] silently chanting 'Om,' gently bringing that stray puppy of my mind back

to Om, each time she wanders. The other form is practicing presence, anywhere, everywhere, as often as I think to become 'in the
moment.'"

The subject of the Silents' prayers are also deeply congruent
with their generational project. As Hank reported, "Since I am
now a widower I have more time for prayer. Sometimes I will sit
in my prayer corner and just . . . enjoy the presence of God. The
only things I pray for are peace and justice in the world." Matt,
a Buddhist from San Francisco, echoes this generational theme
in describing his practice: "When I meditate I try to be mindful,
aware of what is happening in my body, in my mind. I attempt to
increase my concentration on what is occurring. The equivalent of
what we pray for . . . well-being, and less suffering in others and
myself."

While the prayer form used may still be primarily petitionary,
its purpose is not so much to lobby the Divine (as it is for G.I.s)
but to establish intimacy, as one would when one shares one's daily
struggles or frustrations with one's mate. As Neal—a Canadian
with a Lutheran upbringing—describes it, he prays "for people
that are ill, for people fighting despair, for people in trouble, for
guidance, wisdom, generosity of spirit. What I find surprising
about this is that I do not really believe that God intervenes."

Olivia, an Episcopalian living in Nevada, also finds this
strange: "I use the *Book of Common Prayer* and follow the daily
office readings . . . . I end with prayer and meditation. During the
day I attempt to practice the presence of God in my daily activities.
. . . I pray every day for healing for my daughters (one has cancer,
and the other is an addict). I have thought about why I would pray
for a particular outcome when I don't believe God works that way
exactly. Although I don't believe God listens and responds (or not)
to each individual prayer, I certainly don't understand how God
works anyway. I do think that putting the vibration of healing into
the world may, in some way, have an effect—and besides, what
else can I do for them? In the same way, when I am working with
someone who requests a prayer, I am happy to comply for the
relief and healing it certainly will bring to that person."

While Silents do indeed engage in common prayer (prayer

together with others in a worship service) it is not what they automatically think of when you say the word "prayer." Say "prayer" to Silents, and they are most likely to resonate with Jesus' words, "whenever you pray, go into your room and shut the door and pray to your Father who is in secret; and your Father who sees in secret will reward you" (Matthew 6:6).

Silents in Community

The heyday of liberal Protestantism was a largely Silent-driven phenomenon. Silents believed in the great religious institutions, and brought to them their reforming instincts when it was their time to lead. As Carol from Los Gatos, California, told me, it's "very important to have a church, a community, a family, and more balanced, supported organized religion," even though Carol herself does not attend. Indeed, when the Silents were young and in their prime, church attendance was very common—yet it is less common now than it used to be, as is true for all Americans. Still, according to Gallop studies among both Catholics and Protestants, church attendance is higher among Silents than any other generation.[18]

Silents feel comfortable in spiritual community, and since they work well with others, they naturally find others of like mind in their churches and synagogues. When in their prime they brought their concern for justice and peace first to the governance of their religious institutions, and then positioned those institutions to advocate for justice in society at large.

Although this trend upset many G.I.s, this was not a devious manipulation of teaching or resources on the part of Silents, but a mobilization toward what they considered to be the clear mandates of their faiths—for Christians and Jews, the scriptures clearly state that God's concern is for the poor, the widow, and the alien. The Silents believed their cause was God's, and they were convinced that cause was just.

Thus, the Silent-led liberal Protestant churches provided much of the backbone for the Civil Rights struggle, with white church leaders standing alongside black leaders, providing moral, numerical, and financial support for the struggle. All through the 1960s and 1970s, Silent-led Protestant churches issued statement after statement in support of economic and social justice, denouncing racism and unjust war, and advocating environmental justice.

Silents provided much of the energy for the ecumenical movement of the 1950s, which attempted to unite Protestant Christianity into one super-church. This grand ideal failed, of course, but the temptation to end centuries of rancor and division and create peace and harmony among Christians of good will with much in common proved irresistible to Silents, and seemed a tailor-made project for their skills and proclivities.

In the United States, the most successful outcome of this impulse was the United Church of Christ, in which churches of English reformed backgrounds (Congregationalists and Christian Churches, united in 1931) and of German reformed backgrounds (Lutheran and Calvinist congregations, united in 1934) merged in 1957. UCC leaders expected Presbyterians, Methodists, Lutherans, and Episcopalians to jump on the bandwagon and swell the membership of the United Church even further, but in this they were disappointed. Silents, undaunted, organized bodies such as the Consultation on Church Union to further this conciliatory end, but to no avail.

Like the G.I.s, Silents are less likely than younger generations to draw a distinction between spirituality and religion. Only about half of them recognized such a difference, and—true to their generational type—many of those were conciliatory in their comparisons. For instance, Hank wrote, "Spirituality is a personal relationship with God. Most people are spiritual. Religion is that facet that helps us to live out our spirituality." Olivia agrees, but expands on this theme: "I define religion as an institution and spirituality as the engagement with the Divine which may, or may not, be encouraged by religion . . . . I believe that for some people being part of a religion provides a great opportunity to encourage spiritual development. A religion also has the power to discourage that development and to subtly, or not so subtly, coerce people into believing a particular type of 'truth.' For me, religion provided an entry point and a direction for the development of my spirituality, as I think it does for many."

Although spiritual community and corporate prayer are

important to Silents, it is important to remember that their primary spiritual practice is solitary prayer. Olivia describes an ambivalence that seems to resonate with many Silents today: "When I spend too much time inside—and in an intimate relationship with—the church, I become anxious and need to step away for a more solitary discovery . . . . When I am very active in a church, I find I cannot do the individual questioning that advances my understanding and then my experience. When I am outside the church, I am freer yet I miss the uplifting of spirit which is gained in community. On the surface, it would seem there is no impediment to having the best of both worlds, yet for me this does not work out that way."

Spiritual Guidance Style

Silents, by and large, have a healthy respect for authority—healthy in the sense of being plentiful, but also healthy in that they are keenly aware of the limits and dangers of authority, as well. They appreciate structures, but are also critical of them. Just so, this "both/and" approach manifests itself in their approach to spiritual guidance as well.

Silents are deeply contemplative in their spirituality—the Divine for them being both friend and lover. Effective spiritual guides allow silence and space for Silent discernment to emerge. Generally, a non-directive approach will work best, as Silents often will need to explore and "feel out" where Spirit is moving for them. They are comfortable leading in this dance. On occasion, however, Silents appreciate a more directive touch—a suggested reading or practice, or even a bit of teaching where it is called for, will be welcomed. To paraphrase Lao Tzu's advice, "Be ready with the directive, but overall keep to the non-directive."[19]

Just as Silents prefer private prayer to corporate prayer, they also usually prefer individual, one-on-one spiritual guidance to being in groups. They can appreciate groups, and enjoy participating in them—such as during group retreats, or community discernment. But for the purpose of exploring and discerning their own relationship with the Divine, privacy is important.

Spiritual Growth Continuum

As we have seen, the Silent imperative toward justice is linked to their spirituality. Faith compels them to confront injustice, to make peace, to bring harmony to difficult situations. This is what a spiritually aware person *does*. A person who is spiritually immature, on the other hand, does not "play well with others," and has no concern for other peoples' feelings or well-being. Thus, Silents tend to see spiritual immaturity in terms of indifference (to suffering, injustice, etc.), while on the other side of the continuum, a spiritually mature person will be motivated by a highly developed sense of compassion. As Matt described it, "Undeveloped would be little awareness or thought of the nature of existence, a focus on sense desires and aversions, indifference towards others. Someone who is well developed would have a more plausible concept of the nature of existence, more compassion towards others, less aversion, more being present in many moments, or each moment."

Ona, a Unitarian Universalist from Novato, California, concurs: "Self-absorption is at the low end of the continuum—that, and the illusion that one knows enough and can control one's destiny (the Greek *hubris*). Growth in spiritual maturity, then, involves being open to life, all life, but especially other people, respecting them as *persons*, being serious about life and its tragedies and joys; shedding illusions, vain hopes of escape, and embracing this life."

Stan, a Southern Baptist, is also very much in line with this. He told me, "The more like God we become, the more understanding and love we exhibit. Someone who is very undeveloped is generally egocentric and selfish. Everything is about them and all decisions and actions are to enhance their image or reward them in some manner. Someone whose spiritual growth is very well developed exhibits love and consideration for others; although I may not agree with them."

Although Silents tend to think of spiritual growth in terms of one's degree of—or capacity for—compassion, another theme emerged from the survey responses that is both related and insightful: openness to new information. Carla, a lapsed Catholic from Kansas, makes the link between the two when she wrote, "Someone underdeveloped or undeveloped is probably not very attuned to a world outside of his or her immediate world—family, school, community; kind of just in a bubble-shell. You don't really need or want to think beyond your own parameters. And I think once that shell begins to break, whether it's through experience or education or anything like that, that's when they start to become more developed spiritually, when they see beyond themselves in a wider kind of view of the world."

Bernard, a Presbyterian from Chesterfield, Missouri, was one of many who touched on this "open-minded" theme, saying, "The more you expose yourself to positions and attitudes, the more your own perspective will change and I consider that to be growth." Caroline, a member of various New Thought communities, summed this perspective up pithily when she wrote, "Spiritual growth is not being afraid to explore ideas. It is expansive, not contracted."

The two ideas are both well-represented, but as Carla suggests, they are also definitely connected. Open-mindedness, for Silents, is not a virtue in a vacuum—it is valuable only so long as it serves a purpose. And that purpose is to generate empathy for other people's perspectives, an achievement which invariably results in changes in attitudes, policies, and behaviors that move us—both personally, and socially—toward more just and equitable relationships.

Thus, in spiritually companioning Silents, it is important to keep in mind the importance of both compassion and the willingness to learn and change. Helping a Silent move from indifference to compassion will seem like success for most Silents, for in doing so a client is moving closer to the heart of the Divine.

MINISTERING
TO SILENTS

G.I.s Ministering to Silents

This is one of the easiest pairings in this book. Silents have been ministered to by G.I.s their entire lives. They respect G.I.s, they understand them, they even like them. They're the older brothers and sisters that have always hovered over the Silents' shoulders, giving advice and supplying leadership.

G.I.s, you should understand that while Silents are cooperative, committed members of their spiritual communities, they have some distinctive characteristics that can trip you up if you are not aware or prepared for them. Yes, Silents are good followers, but they also have a mind of their own, and while they will say "yes" to your face, they will work behind the scenes to make things come out the way they think they should. This is not to say Silents are not trustworthy—you can *always* trust them to do what is just and compassionate.

G.I.s should remember that Silents have a different approach to prayer. They love praying together in community, but their primary prayer practice is individual and private. They also have a deeply contemplative orientation and rich inner lives that do not mesh well with the nuts-and-bolts approach to things that G.I.s employ by default. G.I.s doing ministry with Silents may feel uncomfortable asking questions like, "How do your feelings change when you pray about this? Do you feel closer to God or further away?" but Silents will be deeply grateful for this, because it will demonstrate that G.I. ministers understand and care about the intimacy with the Divine that is so central to their spiritual lives.

G.I. spiritual directors should be prepared to talk much more about their Silent clients' feelings and longings than clients who belong to their own cohort. G.I.s, please avoid rolling your eyes or "pull yourself up by your bootstrap" language when discussing spiritual disciplines or practices. Silents are going to be much more interested in subtle affective nuances than you are, and it may drive you crazy. Do resist the urge to stare at them as if they are crazy, or chasten them into talking about "real things."

When it comes to community life, since Silents are natural peacemakers, why not employ them to do what they do best? G.I.s long ago handed leadership over to the Silents, and by and large this has been a good thing for spiritual communities, as Silents are sympathetic to both G.I.s and Boomers and have been able to provide a bridge between them that has allowed religious institutions to endure, although one cannot say they prosper. G.I. pastors who are still in ministry would do well to leave lay leadership in Silent hands for the sake of the continued well-being of the community. I would venture to say that if lay leadership of a community is still in G.I. hands, it is a shrinking and dying community, with few Boomers and even fewer Xers or Millennials. G.I.s would do well to recognize their limitations—both physical and psychological— and practice being good "team players" with other generations.

The truth, however, sad as it may be, is that by the time of this writing there are few G.I.s in active ministry, although that was not true twelve years ago when I began researching in this area. Certainly there are still a few pastors, many pastor emeriti, and a goodly number of G.I. nuns still practicing spiritual direction— but by and large G.I.s have retired from ministry.

Boomers Ministering to Silents

This is also a very happy match. Silents and Boomers have long been generational partners. They are driven by many of the same issues—although they approach them in different ways. The Silent approach is introverted, while the Boomer approach is extroverted. The same holds true for issues of the Spirit as well.

Silents have a tendency to be more conservative than Boomers, as far as religion is concerned. By this I don't mean a knee-jerk fundamentalism, but a reticence to wander very far afield in their spiritual explorations. The Boomers went to India for enlightenment, the Silents went only as far as Selma, and they're more than content with this.

Boomers who minister to Silents would do well to respect this reticence. Even though you may be great friends and in agreement on most things, your Silent parishioner or spiritual direction client just isn't likely to be as enthusiastic about that Pema Chödrön book as you are. That's okay. (That new Dietrich Bonheoffer biography, however, is probably right in the pocket, although that may not interest *you* as much.) It's not that Silents don't approve or think that there's Truth to be found in other traditions, it's just that it's foreign and they are less likely to see its relevance for their own personal spirituality.

Silents are also introverted when it comes to religious activism. They are naturally followers, and now that the G.I.s are generally too old to lead, they almost automatically fall into line behind Boomers, and are usually content to do so. They are not likely to instigate protests or marches, but they are not hard to mobilize, especially with effective Boomer leadership. Boomers who honor their institutions and want to work within them for change and justice and compassion will find in Silents fast and steady friends, and invaluable partners in ministry.

Boomers should keep in mind the private nature of Silent spirituality. Boomers like to shout their spirituality from the rooftops, but Silents recoil from this kind of display, which they consider unseemly and invasive. They are more than happy to talk privately and intimately about their faith, once they know you and trust you. They feel awkward, however, speaking about spiritual matters in groups or to strangers. Some, like Joel in our opening vignette, may be reticent to speak of it at all.

Boomers who work as hospital chaplains or in other helping professions would do well to be sensitive to this aspect of the Silent personality, and not simply charge in expecting Silents to open up quickly or easily about such intimate matters (as most fellow Boomers do). Silents will need to know and trust that you care about them as people before inviting you into their "temple space." Take time to get to know them first. Make sure they know that you care about them, establish some interests in common, and inquire about their families.

As a beloved Silent colleague in ministry advised me when I was first starting out in ministry, "Don't talk to them about religious nonsense. Just *enjoy* them." It was the wisest advice I have ever received, and tailor-made for ministry with Silents. Enjoy them, and they will enjoy you. Then they will trust you, and they will entrust you with their secrets. And Silent spirituality is indeed a secret and precious thing they guard protectively.

Xers Ministering to Silents

Xers and Silents are not natural allies, but there is no discernable animosity between these generations, and their relationships are generally harmonious and friendly. Still, projections abound. Silents might confuse them with Boomers (and then end up confused when their attitudes and behaviors don't turn out to be what they expect), or see them as an alien species that they can't really relate to.

Silents also may have trouble seeing such "youngsters" (even though Xers are solidly at midlife, now) as figures bearing spiritual authority, and Joel jokingly refers to this in the opening vignette. This can be awkward, but Silents will get through it—mostly because they have little choice. More and more pastors, chaplains, and spiritual directors are Xers, and Silents by necessity are warming up to them.

Xers must battle their own projections, being careful not to confuse Silents with Boomers or G.I.s. Xers should resist seeing Silents as irrelevant fuddy-duddies. And indeed, once Xers and Silents withdraw their projections and actually work together and get to know each other, a great affection usually develops. Xers see that Silents lack precisely those traits that drive them crazy about Boomers, and Silents see that Xers are actually much more like themselves than they thought.

Indeed, Silents and Xers have much in common. Xers ministering to Silents will find that these parishioners and clients have the same reticence in speaking about spiritual issues that Xers do. For both generations, religion and spirituality are deeply private, personal matters. Neither of them speak lightly or easily about them with strangers or in groups (unless it is a group with which they are intimate). Indeed, Xer ministers may have to overcome some formidable internal resistance in order to broach the subject of spiritual needs at all.

Silents will sense that this is difficult for Xers, too, and will be compassionate and cooperative, but both will experience a shared discomfort that, ironically and happily, may provide necessary bonding.

Xers should remember that Silents love their institutions, and are distressed by the dismissive attitude that they hear from Xers regarding them. Institutions are sacred for Silents. They have served them all their lives, they believe in them, they are proud of what they have built. Xers should be very careful not to discount this contribution, for in doing so they dismiss the life work of their Silent parishioners and clients. Xers may need to work to see past the impersonal facelessness of institutions—and when they do they will see the faces of Silents. If Xers have done the work of connecting with and loving Silents, they may begin to see these institutions—certainly not all institutions, but these few with which they are connected—in a different and more sympathetic light.

Xers must learn to affirm Silents in the value of their life's work, especially now that this work is largely done and Silents are in their retirement. This may be hard for some Xers and may require an act of imagination to achieve. Xers, "fake it 'til you make it" isn't just an eye-roll-worthy Boomer cliché, it's a ministry necessity when working with generations that you don't fully understand.

Xers should also remember that for most Silents, the Divine is deeply personal. Silents don't share the mystical orientation that Boomers and Xers take for granted. God is a separate being with whom Silents deeply desire an intimate, personal relationship. Their religious rhetoric is filled with this kind of language, and it is a deeply felt reality for them. Xers must be on guard against "leaking" their own cynicism about the unlikelihood of the Divine being concerned with individuals when they are ministering to Silents.

Xers must remember to surf into the Silent universe to meet them where they are. Xers must be willing to enter into what is, for them, a different universe for the good of those to whom they are ministering—and indeed they *must* if they are to be responsible and effective ministers. Fortunately, Xers are generally pretty good at such feats of imagination, although they may need to decompensate with other Xer ministers in order to feel "okay" about them. These conversations must be confidential or they may be misconstrued as mean or mocking. They are neither. Remember that Xers use humor and irony to describe the things they love—when those things include Silents, the Xer minister will have fully arrived.

Millennials Ministering to Silents

When Millennials have opportunity to minister to Silents, they are being afforded a valuable opportunity to learn. And Silents, more than any other living generation, are easy to learn from, since they are kind and patient teachers. If Millennials can approach ministry situations with Silents as being valuable for themselves (rather than simply for those they serve) they can open themselves to wisdom that can round out the Millennial worldview in precisely the ways that will benefit them most.

Millennials and Silents play similar roles in regard to other generations—both are conciliators. Silents do their work through negotiation, while Millennials tend to employ innovation. Silents and Millennials are both fiercely collaborative generations, less interested in credit than with results.

Both are creative problem solvers who work and play well with others. Both have a deep need for extra-generational approval, and are driven to make things work *better*. Both are extremely social generations, deriving value from their connections with family, friends, and co-workers.

Millennials who minister to Silents, then, will find much common ground. And yet there are significant differences that will require considerable acts of imagination on the part of Millennials in order to be effective. For instance, while both value community, they define community in different ways. Millennials view community as a web of interrelationship, while Silents view community as a thing—usually an institution of some kind—that people build together. Millennials must overcome a hurdle in seeing the value of this kind of objectified communal goal.

Both feel that people are important, but for Silents, human community is defined by the *what* that humans build together. Millennials must understand the importance of that *whatness* if they are going to understand and find common cause with Silents. Millennials must keep in mind that Silents are far less comfortable with virtuality, and should act *as if* the *whatness* is important so that they can work together toward the common goal of genuine interconnectedness. The true value that you Millennials seek will manifest itself along the way if you do.

Although both generations are optimists, they tend to be optimistic about different things. Millennials tend to see equality and justice as *fait accompli*—at least in the United States and other developed nations. Silents, who have, by their own sweat, wrought the advances of justice over the past fifty years are painfully aware of how far short both society and religious institutions fall short of this ideal. Silent optimism is based on the human value of diligence, while millennial optimism is more based in a magical "thinking will make it so" approach that, maddeningly, for Silents, will probably win out eventually.

Millennials must use imagination to understand that change, for Silents, has been hard won, and that society has not always rewarded a "just do it" approach to problem-solving. Millennials must muster patience with the Silent obsession with diligence and due process. Millennials who work in spiritual institutions can learn much about the value of *process* as it relates to empathy. But caution must be observed since Silents tend to see empathy as an end, while Millennials view it as a means.

Millennials will also need to use their imaginations to understand the Silent approach to Divinity, and the supreme importance Silents place on personal relationship with it. Millennials and Silents both view Divinity as transcendent, but while Millennials tend to see it as largely irrelevant to daily human living, Silents see it as being intimately involved in every part of life. Millennials may benefit from imagining that the web of interrelationships that they value is itself the very Divinity to which Silents are pointing, and that objectifying and personifying it—giving it *whatness*, in other words—helps Silents manifest its benefits and experience connection.

Personal prayer is therefore important to Silents as a way of accessing that affective sense of connection. Millennials should keep in mind that Silents lead with their hearts, and *feel* their way into connection. Prayer is the medium of this feeling, and Silents will be grateful for your support and encouragement of it. They frequently feel lost or abandoned when, even after many hours of prayer, they do not feel a connection with Spirit. Millennials fear disconnection more than most, and I encourage them to draw upon this to empathize with Silents experiencing dryness in their spiritual practices.

Both generations see the value of happiness, but while Millennials generally see it as a personal goal—to which each individual is committed, and for which each is responsible (similarities to the previous Civic generation—the G.I.s—are not coincidental)—Silents take it for granted that we are expected to sacrifice our own comfort, health, wealth, and happiness to create happiness for society as a whole. More simply put, personal happiness is the goal for Millennials while global happiness is the goal for Silents. Millennials will benefit from noticing just how much their happiness was bought at the expense of Silent happiness. The Silents are never appreciated enough. See and acknowledge that debt, and you will have Silent friends forever.

CHAPTER THREE

THE "TRANSFORMATIVE" GENERATION —THE BABY BOOMERS

Evelyn began her session with her spiritual coach, Vic, by beating up on herself. Vic just nodded, since this was not unusual. Evelyn had been part of a study group for The Secret, a New Thought-inspired bestseller that asserts that you manifest what you think. She was not manifesting the kind of prosperity she wanted in her life, nor the kind of peace in her family that she wanted to have.

"I know it's my fault," she moaned. "I'm not thinking right, and my whole family is suffering for it."

Vic listened until Evelyn had tired herself out with her verbal self-flagellation. "Evelyn, are you open to hearing about what I am noticing?" She sniffed a bit, and nodded, not looking at him. She clenched and unclenched her hands.

"Here's what I see: you have this image of this perfect life, this perfect family, and when real life doesn't live up to your image, you hate yourself for it, and beat up on yourself—as if you could make it happen exactly the way you want—if you could only get the trick right."

She nodded.

"My dear, listen to me," he said, his voice softening. "There is no perfect life. There are no perfect families. Everything is messy, and it's not your fault . . . ." he trailed off, because she had buried her face in her hands and begun to sob.

He waited patiently while the feelings swept through her.
"This is bigger than that, isn't it?" he asked.
She nodded.
"It isn't just me," she started, as the tears subsided. "We
had such marvelous dreams for the world. None of it has
worked out. None of it. You used the right word, I think.
Everything is messy, and I feel like a failure. I feel like we
all failed."

Introducing the Boomers

Just as the grim resolve of the G.I.s shaped the first half of the twentieth century, the exuberant and vocal idealism of the Baby Boomers shaped the second half. They are, to be sure, the *"other* Greatest Generation" of the twentieth century. They are, in many ways, a reaction to—and the mirror opposite of—the G.I. generation, and their impact on culture, politics, religion, and every other arena of contemporary life is just as great as the G.I.s.

But while the G.I. generation was shaped by necessity, the Boomers were formed by outrage, rebelling against the status quo so cherished by the G.I.s and driven by a vision of a better future for the whole of the earth, a vision that is very much still alive and driving this exceptional generation.

Birth Years and Place in the Cycle

The name "Boomer" comes from the Baby Boom—that period directly after the Second World War when birth rates skyrocketed as G.I.s (and barely out-of-their-teens Silents) returned home from overseas and reached for their slice of American Pie—a dream of blissful domestic life complete with a beautiful wife, a solid job, a tract home in the suburbs, the obligatory white picket fence, 2.5 children, and a dog.

Born between 1943 and 1960, Baby Boomers are the twentieth century's Idealistic generation. An Idealistic generation, according to Strauss and Howe's model of generational cycles, is a dominant, inner-fixated group that inevitably follows an Adaptive generation. An Idealistic generation "grows up as increasingly indulged youths after a secular crisis," whose coming of age sparks "a spiritual awakening," then "fragments into narcissistic rising adults; cultivates principle as moralistic midlifers; and emerges as visionary elders guiding the next secular crisis."[1]

The antipathy between G.I.s and the Boomers is both legendary and real, and constitutes the greatest generational divide of our time. The clash between grizzled, patriotic pragmatism and runaway idealism created a profound and wide-reaching conflict that raged in the media during the Boomers' youth, moved into the mainstream as they grew into their majority, and continues to ripple out in our red-state/blue-state controversies.

Formative Events

The Boomers came of age during the Cold War, during the 1950s and early 1960s. As Quincy put it, he had a "placid, peaceful middle class 'Ozzie and Harriet' 50s boyhood." Yet as serene as that sounds, the world beyond the suburban oasis was anything but peaceful. When asked about the events that stand out for them, most of my respondents mentioned the Cold War, the Cuban Missile Crisis, and the assassinations of John F. Kennedy, Robert Kennedy, and Martin Luther King, Jr. As Linda of Taos, New Mexico, wrote, "During the late 60s and early 70s my generation was encouraged to be 'free thinkers.' Thinking outside the box got these three men killed. Apparently thinking outside the typical boundaries was a fine idea . . . acting on it was not."

Boomers remember living under the constant threat of nuclear annihilation, "ducking and covering" at school, and the ominous image of Khrushchev pounding his shoe on the lectern, swearing that he would "bury" the U.S. Many mentioned the Civil Rights and the Women's Liberation movements, and the protests against the Vietnam War, all struggles for peace and justice, as well as the burgeoning awareness of environmental peril.

There were triumphs, too, of course. Many remembered the Beatles on the Ed Sullivan show as a breakthrough, but nothing could compare to the moon landing. Kelly, from Phoenix, Oregon, told me, "I can remember waiting tables . . . when Armstrong touched down. Eggs went cold, coffee wasn't served, and the whole place erupted in cheers and applause. I hugged some old guy (he was probably thirty) and I didn't have the sense he was copping a feel. I was so happy."

This had a profound effect on the Boomers' self-esteem. As Linda wrote, "Putting a man on the moon—this event spurred my generation to believe anything was possible . . . we only needed to have a good imagination, dedication, and persistence. It also created the dichotomy of 'if we can do this, why can't we do that?' All the excuses for not solving problems here on earth seemed pretty lame after we visited the moon."

Indeed, it seemed that anything was possible, all dreams were achievable—all it took was ingenuity and a willingness to change.

Experience of the World

The dichotomy between the "appearance" of the happy, perfect, suburban home life and the reality of many homes in which domestic violence, patriarchal dominance, and unbridled prejudice held sway created the impression in Boomers that their elders were hypocrites, a situation they saw writ large in the political arena.

As Linda recalls, "It was a given in my household that the U.S. was 'the most powerful nation on earth.' Considering this power, I found it confusing that we could not win this war, nor could we as a nation even agree on the necessity of this war [Vietnam]. I was also deeply disturbed by the fact that every year at Christmas time we could enter into a long period of cease fire for 'peace during the holidays.' It never made sense to me why we couldn't just permanently extend the cease fire."

Indeed, as their political awareness bloomed, young Boomers were horrified and outraged by what they saw. As Kelly remembers it, "I was unsettled about all the changes that swirled around me. I was appalled by man's inhumane treatment of one another. I chose to believe that the alarming news broadcasts coming out of the South were not real. I couldn't really wrap my mind about John Kennedy, Martin Luther King, or Bobby Kennedy's assassinations, although I remember getting teary eyed when the record, 'Abraham, Martin, and John' played on the radio."

Thus, the Boomers' primary experience of the world was of the injustice and hypocrisy of 1950s America, and this led them to rebel against everything their G.I. parents stood for. Theirs was a generation kicking against the goads of everything they saw as corrupt, moribund, or unjust: white privilege, male privilege, first-world narcissism, and exploitation of the earth—all of this fueled the rage that drove Boomers to speak out, protest, get arrested, make art, music, and no little bit of love.

This sense of the world has not left the Boomers, either. Their formative view of the world is still very much in evidence, even as they enter their seniority. As Becca, in Alberta, Canada, told me, "I feel the world is at a tipping point. Politically and economically, the world is in chaos; environmentally, it is under great stress and threat; polarization and fragmentation increase; intolerance and division are on the rise; we are perhaps one of the first generations to behold the possibility of the demise of human civilization." Karl, from Fox Island, Washington, is equally bitter: "I am disgusted with the corruption that has taken over democracy . . . disgust with wars, politics, insensitivity, ignorance, and this ruthless and hypocritical corporacy that has replaced democracy, etc. Still a Boomer!"

Yet Boomers are overwhelmingly optimistic, even to the point of being self-congratulatory at times. They take pride in the fact that they stood up to power, and believe they made important and substantive changes. Donna, from Delaware, Ohio, writes, "I think we are getting better at standing up about injustice. Specifically, abuse against children and other powerless groups of people, rights for handicapped, mentally challenged, nursing home residents, and minorities of all types." Katie from Canmore, Alberta, adds, "Hearing the news is cause for despair, but I resist falling into that state, and believe we are all called to be co-creators of a better world."

In a Word and a Song

The first generation to grow up with television and nightly news, the Boomers mastered the art of the sound bite early, displaying a talent for heartfelt catchphrases unrivaled by the calculated propagandizers of the G.I.s. Those Boomers who responded to my surveys didn't really reach a consensus on a single catchphrase that summed up their peers, but definite trends emerged. "Make love, not war," made an appearance, as did "Power to the people." John Lennon's "Give Peace a Chance" got the highest number of votes; other possibilities included, "If it feels good, do it!," "We shall overcome," all of which reflect the attitudes and ideals of the 1960s. Only one suggestion came from a later period: "Follow your bliss"[2] became a catchphrase for Boomers in the 1980s as they entered their middle years and were the driving force behind the New Age movement.

While all of these were compelling and certainly rang true, none struck me as forcefully as the words of writer and lyricist Jacob Brackman: "You build it up, mother, we gonna tear it down,"[3] referring in part to the G.I. institutions which they saw as hopelessly marred by corruption. Or, as Linda put it, speaking to her G.I. parents, "We can clean up your mistakes—we can do better than you did."

Perhaps more than any other generation in history, Boomers expressed themselves through music. With the rise of the singer/songwriter (actually a pretty new concept in the music business), Boomers came to embrace less-than-perfect performers on the strength of their songwriting, and indeed, their prophetic power. Bob Dylan's voice, for instance, is definitely an acquired taste, and in an earlier generation, would never have been given a hearing. But there is no denying the force of his lyrics or delivery. Boomers were united as a generation by their music, and popular music did more than any other medium to advance the utopian visions of the emerging Boomers.

By far, the song that most people point to as iconic is Bob Dylan's "The Times They Are A-Changin'." The song rang a bell, loud and clear, sending a message to all who had ears that the old (G.I.) order was passing away, and you could either pitch in, get out of the way, or get trampled. Dylan's song conveys well both the giddy idealism of the Boomers, and the blustering resistance of the G.I.s.

Other songs that people pointed to as iconic were "War! What Is It Good For?" by Edwin Starr, "All You Need is Love," by the Beatles, and "Imagine," by John Lennon. A very interesting suggestion cropped up more than once—that melancholy ode to disillusionment, "American Pie," by Don McLean, suggesting that the song was prophetic of how the idealism of the Boomers was to be, in superficial ways, at least, fleeting and misguided.

What Are They Seeking?

The late 1960s and early 1970s was the heyday of their awakening sense of power, and the next three decades were marked by the very public continuing saga of a generation's quest to find itself. To replace what they perceive as the hopelessly corrupt G.I. institutions, Boomers used their imaginations to propose fanciful schemes of Utopian proportions, enshrining egalitarian ideals and experimental strategies. As David from Penn Valley, California, put it, they sought to "Change the thinking of the nation, its consciousness" and thereby to transform society itself.

> AN EXCERPT FROM
> THE TIMES THEY ARE A-CHANGIN'"
> by Bob Dylan
>
> Come senators, congressmen
> Please heed the call
> Don't stand in the doorway
> Don't block up the hall
> For he that gets hurt
> Will be he who has stalled
> There's a battle outside and it is ragin'
> It'll soon shake your windows and
>   rattle your walls
> For the times they are a-changin'
>
> Come mothers and fathers
> Throughout the land
> And don't criticize
> What you can't understand
> Your sons and your daughters
> Are beyond your command
> Your old road is rapidly agin'
> Please get out of the new one if you
>   can't lend your hand
> For the times they are a-changin'
>
> Copyright © 1963, 1964 by Warner Bros. Inc.; renewed
> 1991, 1992 by Special Rider Music. Used by permission.

Too often, however, when they actually had the opportunity to put their ideas into practice, they tore down the old institutions only to discover that the very human pathologies that plagued their parents' efforts undermined their own grand schemes as well, as greed, ignorance, prejudice, and simple ineptitude crippled their own efforts. As Kelly described it, they "wanted the power to make fundamental changes but . . . didn't want the responsibilities that accompanies leadership."

The youthful idealism of the 1970s was severely challenged by the "get down to business" 1980s, during which time the Boomers' idealism hit a brick wall as sexually transmitted diseases, years of riotous living, and the financial demands of their preferred standard of living all took their tolls. This resulted in a softening of their political and economic idealism (when they traded fighting The Man for actually becoming The Man).

The 1990s, in fact, saw the Boomers taking up the reigns of previously reviled American institutions (a frightening proposition to G.I.s and Boomers alike), exemplified by Bill Clinton taking his seat in the White House. Nora (who shares her time between Whitefish, Montana, and San Francisco, California) wrote, "We were a generation who wanted to cross boundaries, but once we did, we found roadblocks and barriers on the other side as well . . . . We found that institutionalized thought goes very deep, and we were not able to make meaningful changes in many systems that we felt were corrupt."

Quincy described this progression, "At first, we sought change: some of it for what we saw as social good, much because we wanted our own way. Later, we sought *stuff*, and possessions beyond the dreams of our parents. Now, we're seeking security (which is perhaps what we were seeking all along), agonizing over underwater stock options and mortgages, wounded 401(k)'s, and a vision of a cozy, and hopefully early, retirement that suddenly seems out of reach and frighteningly unrealistic."

The idealism of the Boomers wasn't dead, though, it merely changed focus, from societal change to spiritual transformation, leading to the flowering of the New Age movement, where the "transformation of consciousness" was the primary goal. Through Eastern philosophies and channeled entities they sought guidance for how to transcend the messed-up material world to discover a reality of pure spirit, where everything is perfect just as it is. Dualism was identified as the enemy of happiness, and a multi-billion dollar industry erupted as Boomers chased after their lost innocence into the non-material realm where they must surely still be whole and undefiled. Books, CDs, VHS tapes, conferences, and charlatans abounded, money changed hands, and millions of Boomers spent a lot of time on their butts doing nothing, convincing themselves that they were changing the world by changing themselves.

Even Boomer Evangelicals sought to change the fuddy-duddy rules-bound churches into transformed seeker-friendly mega-churches where the power of the Holy Spirit reigned, both within the believer, and within the body of believers, changing hearts and lives, and yes, institutions.

As a generation, the Baby Boomers are seeking *transformation*:

from injustice to justice, from bondage to freedom, from material to spiritual. They have sought this transformation in every arena of life: societal, educational, institutional, personal, and religious. For all of the disappointment they have seen in their lives, they retain much of their youthful idealism and seem undaunted even now, striding into their senior years with their optimism and their fighting spirit intact. As Katie told me, "I believe the spark that was lit during the sixties is still burning."

Generational Project

Boomers saw keenly what was wrong with the Ozzie and Harriet culture they grew up in, how out of touch with real life and hypocritical it was, and how it institutionalized inequality in a variety of arenas. Almost as one, this generation stood up and courageously spoke out against injustice, inequality, and privilege. But more than simply seeing what was wrong with society, they imagined what society *could* be. They saw, in fact, what it *should be*, driven by values of peace, justice, and inclusion.

Thus, their generational project was *visionary*. They spoke possibilities, and worked to make them come about. Unfortunately, the path from their visions to a reality that pragmatically reflected their values has not always been clear, and they have been better at *seeing* a better world than figuring out how to *make one*. As Bette, a Christian Scientist from Mendocino put it (speaking of her peers in the third person), "they wanted to change the world; in some areas they did—technology and some gains in human rights—but in others they weren't very successful, [in terms of] peace and harmony among people."

But you cannot say that they haven't tried. Indeed, Boomers, more than any other living generation, have devoted their lives, resources, and time to making their dreams of a better world come true. They were not only marching for peace in 1968, they are marching now, continuing to see a better world, a world that *could be*, and contributing selflessly to make it come about. They continue to "see visions and dream dreams,"[4] and to contribute to a world that is increasingly diverse, egalitarian, and just, largely due to their efforts.

How Boomers Are Perceived

There is a true love/hate relationship between Boomers and other generations. No other living generation is so polarizing, or arouses so much resentment and hostility from those around them. The biggest conflict is with G.I.s, many of whom were parents to the Boomers. It is the G.I. "project" to which Boomers reacted so strongly, it was the harshness and hypocrisy they perceived in the G.I.s that sparked their "rebellion." Remember that, for G.I.s, rebellion is synonymous with spiritual immaturity. As Kelly told me, "My parents' generation would describe us as naïve and self-indulgent."

Linda wrote, "My dad's generation of men seems to view our generation as threatening. They see the shift of power moving away from them (the conservative white guys) and say 'what is this world coming to?'" (Linda doesn't mention how she thinks women of the G.I. generation feel.)

While G.I.s are likely to see Boomers as having betrayed everything that they held dear, Silents have more sympathy for the younger cohort. The Silents cooperated with the G.I. agenda— indeed, they would not have the strength to oppose it if they had wanted to. So the Silents hold some admiration for the Boomers for standing up to the G.I.s with a ferocity that they would never have dreamed of. They also approve of what the Boomers were trying to do, as it was, in a way, a logical continuation—and intensification—of their own compassionate and humanizing project. Most, however, while silently applauding the motivation, would criticize the means by which they went about it as impolitic, ill-advised, and incautious.

Xers feel a lot of resentment towards Boomers—nothing near the magnitude of antipathy felt by G.I.s, but certainly more than other generations. Maya, an Xer from Columbus, Ohio, put it pithily: "Baby Boomers messed a lot of crap up." Xers often perceive Boomers as self-indulgent and self-centered, but one Xer, Kevin, a Canadian from Salt Spring Island, British Colombia, was unusually sympathetic about this: "When I look at the Boomers, I think, well, I'd probably have done the same. 'Really? The concept of limit has no meaning and I can do whatever I want heedless of consequence?' And *everybody* is telling me this all the time? Hell yeah, I'd have fallen for it, too."

Xers roll their eyes at the grandiose schemes for a better world that drive the Boomers' efforts, are dismissive of Boomers' spiritual aspirations due to the hypocrisy they've witnessed in their Boomer parents and older siblings, and are resentful that the Boomer stampede sucked up every available job in the market and have yet to relinquish them.

Cathy, a Boomer from Fremont, California, noted this when she mentioned, "Some . . . might be envious of the opportunities that we had that they didn't." Some Boomers have made real efforts to understand the pain that Xers experience. Karl told me, "We were the iconoclasts that shook things up too much, traumatizing our children, leaving a trail of disruptions and insecurity . . . . I know that many of the younger folks resent and distrust us. My daughter has an MBA from UCLA and consults with companies on generational issues (e.g., work attitudes, loyalty, turnover) so I have heard how much her generation, and the one after, still feels a bit shattered by all we shook up." The most poignant and insightful response I got from a Boomer on this question was from Ian, from Minden, Nevada, who said, "I'd guess there is a good deal of resentment—our kids for the most part are not doing as well as we did, the world is as scary a place as ever, and it seems we took more than we gave."

Millennials love their Boomer parents and grandparents, appreciating their *joi de vive* and even their visionary approach to life. They also enjoy their hit-and-miss attempts at technological proficiency and sometimes embarrassing bids to remain relevant. Millennials and Boomers generally have wonderful relationships, and Millennials may, in fact, have trouble understanding what all the fuss is about between Boomers and Xers. This can be particularly troubling in a family with Boomer grandparents, Xer parents, and Millennial children where the Boomer/Xer generation gap is very much in play.

Interestingly, I found a great deal of myopia among Boomers as they described how they think others see them. Several respondents believe that other generations would judge them according to issues that matter most to Boomers! For instance, Becca wrote, "I would think there's a lot of resentment and bitterness about what we have allowed to happen to the environment, both earthwise but also politically and economically. The rich have become super rich, the poor have been dealt a terrible blow, and the middle class is thinning out toward either extreme. The opportunity to own one's own home, determine one's own destiny to some extent, is much curtailed. From my own point of view, I would say, I think we blew it." While the self-critical lens is helpful, I'm not sure that these are the issues to which Xers or Millennials would point as the qualities wanting in the Boomer generation.

How Boomers Perceive Themselves

Given that Boomers were the driving force behind the self-esteem push in education, perhaps it is only appropriate that they should have imbibed a bit of their own medicine—indeed, the Boomers have an overwhelmingly positive self-image. Teri, from San Diego, California, sums up her generation this way: "Transformed, powerful, and courageous. My generation has been the voice of change and transformation." Donna agrees, "We are like the boy in 'The Emperor's New Clothes.' Everybody else was going along with the trend in order to fit in. In his innocence, the boy maintained that the emperor was not wearing fine clothes, in spite of what everybody else said." With a bit of pride, she adds, "Yes, we have been and continue to be whistle-blowers of this type." Nick, from Oakland, California, was downright effusive when he wrote that the Boomers are "absolutely successful as a generation, even with failures and disillusionments."

Although none of my respondents used the word, their answers overwhelmingly speak to the fact that Boomers see themselves as *righteous*—which was even a catchphrase in their youth. Admittedly, this was more blatant in their youth, and the generation has gained some modesty as they have aged, but Boomers are still likely to see the ideals that drove them as being very righteous indeed. Other generations may snidely add the prefix "self-" to this description, but for Boomers, their generational mission was nothing short of a divine mandate, which they executed imperfectly but faithfully.

Although they are united in the belief that their cause was righteous, many of them are certainly forthcoming about the imperfect way they manifested it. As Linda put it, "We have succeeded in being diverse and adventurous, we have failed at being completely present to the moment we live in, always looking for the next task." Kelly described her cohort as, "idealistic, raging against the abuses of our parents. Then we *became* our parents, with a little bit of weed thrown in. I do feel that we probably are not as responsible, but we are kinder." Katie adds, "I think we have also been guilty of sinking into complacency, as we achieved a high level of material success. Living lives of comfort, we have at times turned our backs on the values and passion that fired us up as young adults."

Others are more self-critical. Louis (originally from the United Kingdom, but now living in Oregon) wrote, "Our generation, like every one before it, thought we could change the world for the better—and for the common good. Instead, we got sucked into the corporate machine and created no real wealth for the world, just for a few individuals." Quincy's response was among the most insightful and moving I received: "We fancied ourselves the counter-culture, and then *became* the culture. We rejected many of our parents' rules, and then found ourselves in a society stripped of its guardrails. We nurtured and coddled our children, and then saw—too late—what happened when we failed to set limits and realistic expectations. If I had to characterize my own generation now, I'd say we're shell-shocked: What happened? We were proud of cutting free from old roots and ties, trying our wings. Now, our wings are tired, and so many of us seem essentially rootless, in a world we helped strip of its certainties. We were successful for a long time—at doing our own thing—and to the degree many of us cared about civil liberties and civil rights as idealistic youth, we were successful, but an unintended consequence of decades of social sensitivity seems to be that which has morphed into the hypersensitive demon of political correctness stalking our public discourse."

THE SPIRITUALITY
OF THE BABY BOOMERS

More than any other living generation, Baby Boomers made a break from the traditional faiths of their childhoods. The pull of the East has been great for this generation, and the myth that Hinduism or Buddhism is less patriarchal or abusive than Christianity or Judaism has been strong (those native to Eastern faiths can, but rarely do, correct this misperception). Nevertheless, Eastern concepts of karma, reincarnation, and "the Divine within" are popular amongst Boomers, and even Evangelical Boomers have been known to court yoga and meditation.

Many Boomers see themselves as "spiritual but not religious," and have cultivated a kind of spiritual eclecticism, constructing an idiosyncratic spirituality consisting of a patchwork of ideas, images, and practices drawn from many faith traditions and psychological schools.[5] As Donna, who declined to state her religion, described her spirituality, "People can be spiritual and feel that the sun, the moon, the tides, whatever, control their lives. They can feel close to creation by admiring a raindrop on a rose petal. They can write and enjoy lovely images in poetry and in poetic prose. But that is not religion, I feel. Religion is believing that one humanoid is in charge of everything."

Indeed, many Boomers are fiercely allergic to "organized religion," which is inseparable in their minds from the G.I. institutions they denounced in their youth. Even though Evelyn, in our opening example, subscribes to the New Thought-originated ideas in *The Secret*,[6] she does not identify with the New Thought movement, and does not attend Unity or the Church of Religious Science—the ideas drawn from them are just more pieces in the eclectic jigsaw puzzle of her personal spirituality, which also includes Christianity, yoga, and some Wicca practices.

As Boomers began to enter midlife in the 1980s and 1990s, asking the Big Questions, they turned not to traditional religious institutions, as previous generations had done, but instead created a movement as eclectic as they were, the New Age movement.

The New Age isn't really new, of course—it is a hodge-podge of Hinduism, Buddhism, native traditions, transpersonal psychology, Spiritualism (séances, or as it is called nowadays, "channeling"), and other occult practices.

The goal, as always for Boomers, is *transformation*. But in the realm of spirituality, it isn't the transformation of society that is desired, but the transformation of consciousness—or the "raising of consciousness," as Boomers like to put it—a kind of spiritual re-education, Gnostic in character (by which I mean an experiential and non-rational kind of knowing), which will ripple out and effect societal and global change.

Drugs may have been the avenue to enlightenment in the 1960s, sex in the 1970s, but in the 1980s meditation became the favored path. Channeled entities provided the scriptures, women's and men's spirituality circles provided the community, and gradually all that was required for a full-fledged religious movement was in place, albeit in a uniquely "anything goes," "do-it-yourself" fashion.

Which is not to say that Boomer spirituality didn't have its dark side. Charlatan channellers and gurus preyed upon Boomer gullibility that elevated every new channeled entity to the status of a spiritual authority, and—with no system of accountability in place—child, sexual, emotional, and spiritual abuse in Boomer spiritual communities was widespread.[7]

Even Boomers that stayed within the bounds of a formal religious tradition did it in their own unique, anti-authoritarian fashion. Boomer Evangelical Christians abandoned the denominations they grew up in, forming "non-denominational" churches (even forming affiliations of non-denominational congregations—effectively, non-denominational denominations). They tossed out their parents' hymnals and brought in rock bands, to the point where, by the mid-1990s, soft-rock "praise choruses" had effectively replaced (or at least existed uncomfortably side-by-side with) traditional hymnody in a majority of Evangelical churches. Out went the ties and dresses, in came the blue jeans and t-shirts.

Boomers pioneered the seeker-friendly megachurch, where Evangelical theology was dispensed gradually, with sermon messages designed to be non-threatening and "in tune" with modern life. An individual could feel free to be as anonymous as he or she chose in such congregations—the membership frequently numbering in the thousands—or could belong to an intimate "core group," meeting regularly outside of the gigantic worship experiences for Bible study, prayer, and fellowship.

Boomers mostly stayed away from mainline Protestant denominations, a point painfully obvious to all in such churches as their enrollment continues to decline as their G.I. and Silent stalwarts pass on. But a few Boomers have stayed, and where they have, they have once again reinvented these institutions—reorienting their foci from sin and salvation to such reliable Boomer concerns as peace and social justice. Notable figures such as Rabbi Michael Lerner and Roman Catholic (later Episcopal) priest Matthew Fox have re-visioned Judaism and Christianity, respectively, putting specifically Boomer spins on them, making them more individualistic, eclectic, and oriented towards social justice and the transformation of both consciousness and society.

The Spiritual Gifts of Baby Boomers

The Baby Boomers possess powerful spiritual gifts that have impacted and shaped contemporary culture more than any living generation. It is impossible to list the many ways in which the Boomers have impacted the spiritual landscape, but there are a few gifts that seem to emerge across the wide and varied spectrum of this amazing generation:

Vitality

The Boomers invented the phrase, "fifty is the new thirty" and now as the first wave of them are entering their 70s, they are no less active or energized. Boomers live large, out loud, and make no apologies for their love of life, of pleasure, of the goodness of the world around them and their joy in it. While they may be anxious about the political and environmental future of the country and the world, they are almost uniformly upbeat about their lives, their families, and their communities. Boomers are not taking old age lying down, but are transforming our ideas about what midlife is supposed to be like. The rocking chairs can wait—there are trips to be taken, causes to be promoted, wrongs to be righted, parties to attend, and art (and love) to be made. The Boomers are nothing if not exuberant, and time has not diminished this quality—indeed, it seems only to have enhanced it.

Spiritually, they are just as active. Boomers are now the leaders of most spiritual institutions, and although those that are historic and traditional may be smaller, they have a renewed sense of focus, vitality, and purpose, thanks to Boomer leadership. New Boomer-implemented institutions are flourishing, especially seeker-friendly churches and alternative spiritual centers. Time has not tempered their idealism, but it has taught them a thing or two about pragmatism and diplomacy, which they have learned can only help them to succeed (a spiritual lesson many Boomers call "skillful means," after the Buddhist Eightfold Noble Path).

Reformation

In charge of these many institutions, Boomers have, over the past twenty years, thought long and hard about how to reform them to make them relevant (at least to themselves). Old mission statements have been reframed, old systems overhauled, and old attitudes replaced. Boomers are generally suspicious of institutions, but this suspicion lessened as they began to take them over—turns out it was the leadership that was suspect, not the institution itself. Boomers have fearlessly taken stock and discerned carefully (and often at considerable length) the call and vocation of their institutions, guiding them to live into the best of their espoused values.

Prophetic

As a generation, the Boomers are keenly sensitive to injustice and hypocrisy, especially where such are institutionalized and embedded in culture. Both within institutions and in society at large, Boomers have courageously (and often at great personal cost) called those in leadership to accountability. Ever the idealists, Boomers hold aloft the shining dream of how society or an institution ought to be, critique its failings, and draft action plans to bring the dream and the reality into alignment. They aren't always (or, actually, often) successful at this—or not entirely successful—but that doesn't stop them, which is a positive trait right there.

Artistic and Creative

Early in their generational career, Boomers clued into the power of art and music as tools for transmitting vision and catalysts of transformation. In their drive for reformation, Boomers were quick to adopt artistic methods, and have championed "whole person" approaches to education and spirituality, emphasizing a balance of left-brained (linear) and right-brained (artistic) methods. Boomer pastors are known to sing or dance their sermons. Boomer activists employ puppet shows, mystery plays, and performance art to broadcast their prophetic message. Boomers use contemporary music (sounding these days remarkably similar to the folk-rock of the 1960s) to drive their worship.

More than any other living generation, Boomers have embraced creativity and art as tools for transformation, both societal, personal, and spiritual. Boomer spirituality is strong on art, as the runaway popularity of such books as *The Artists Way* by Julia Cameron and the storytelling of Clarissa Pinkola Estes, Robert Bly, Paulo Coelho, and many others attest. The boom in popularity of Coleman Barks' translations of Rumi, translations of Hafiz, Rabia, Julian of Norwich and other spiritual poets and mystics of a variety of traditions also speak to the Boomers' embrace of art as a medium for spiritual change.

Tolerant and Eclectic

More than any generation before them, Boomers are open to wisdom from spiritual and religious traditions other than their own. Even those who practice a single tradition do not evidence the kind of brand loyalty of their elders, nor do they insist that their way holds the exclusive patent on truth. Boomers are *much* more likely to be eclectic in their faith than those who went before them. Liberal Jews or Christians often see no conflict with practicing yoga, or reading a Sufi or Hindu text for inspiration. Even more conservative Evangelical Boomers are much more open to Lutheran or Catholic writers then their parents would have been. Boomers are suspicious of the idea that one institution or group has gotten everything right, and are open to truth pretty much wherever they find it.

How Divinity Is Imaged

Many Boomers have rejected the traditional view of the Divine espoused by their parents. As Karl, who describes himself as "an interfaith mystic," put it, "It is . . . definitely not some distant white male on a throne, our Judeo-Christian heritage." Instead, Boomers tend to view the Divine not as a being who is "out there" but as a spiritual force that is imminent and omnipresent. Karl goes on to describe the being he *does* believe in: "The Divine is what is when you erase your beliefs—it is consciousness and being, including what you are. It is omnipresent, intimate, loving . . . . When you experience Presence (pure consciousness), you are changed and become more like the Presence itself—kind, still, peaceful, loving, happy, content, compassionate, slow."

As Becca, a Christian, described it, "The Divine has evolved for me from a transcendent being to an intimate presence, to something I can scarcely describe except to say that when my spiritual director now speaks of God, as in 'How do you think God looks at that?' I almost shudder. Because I sense no separation anymore and I have no sense of a God-out-there anymore. To even name God 'God' seems so far off, I don't know what to do with it anymore . . . . There is something behind everything I still adhere to: whether that is Energy, Dynamic, Intelligence, Wisdom, I don't know how I would name it."

Part of the "imminence" of divinity is the fact that it is present not just in the physical world, but in all people as well. Unitarian Universalist Cathy wrote, "I believe the Divine requires me to recognize the Divine in others, that I recognize the Divine that we create between us, and that I treat each person as the vessel of the Divine that he or she is," and Quincy answered with a quote from Gandhi, "He who does not see God in the next person he meets, need look no further."

Paradoxically, Boomers seem to see the Divine in both personal and impersonal terms—as person and as energy. This is a tension that seems nearly universal, yet which they seem to hold with little difficulty. Kelly wrote, "Even though it lies within, as well as without, I do not think it is personal, which is very odd since I pray to it pretty regularly."

Therese, who attends a United Church of Christ congregation in Oklahoma City, OK told me, "Right now my Divine is much less personal than it was growing up Southern Baptist. I think I most relate to fire as my Divine Image. As it burns it gives light and warmth. It must be given fuel and it must be tended or the fire is put out. At the same time I feel the presence of the Divine inside me when I am quiet." As Louis, a "progressive" Christian, put it, "The Divine is like an infinitely faceted diamond—able to engage each person with a different yet appropriate facet for where they are at any moment in their life . . . . The Divine is very immanent in my personal life, but needs to be worshiped in a more omnipotent way when we gather as church. I do not see these two as being in conflict. And omnipotent is not the same as distant."

Even Boomers involved in more traditional religious traditions question the anthropomorphic depictions. Edie, a committed Christian from Los Angeles, California, wrote, "I used to think the Divine was the 'figure' of Jesus (a white man) that is displayed in most Christian churches. As I've gotten older, I don't think of the Divine as a person. It's more of a spiritual being. I think of it as a light shining down on the world, illuminating good and evil." Even those Boomers who still think of the Divine in personal terms are open to a wider range of images than previous generations, even insisting on gender variety (or at least neutrality) in religious language and imagery.

Dot, an Episcopalian from Tennessee, told me, "I believe all images that are beautiful, calming, or joyful are of him. I believe he can send anyone to impact our life for his glory; that he speaks on the wind, in the rain, and through a butterfly, dancing on a lily."

What does the Divine require of us humans? According to many Boomers, the Divine is focused less on personal sins (such as pre-marital sex or lust) and more on social sins (such as greed, racial prejudice, and economic injustice) that require a prophetic response. As Teri (who described her religion as "oneness") told me, "The Divine requests of people to be responsible, not coming from guilt, shame, fault, or blame—being an outflow of love, vulnerability, intimacy, and giving. The Divine does not judge, the Divine is source and as source only the light of love is experienced and expressed." This is, of course, not universal. Effy, an "interfaith" person from Hayward, California, wrote, "I believe that the Divine requires nothing. The sun, earth, and water require nothing of me. It will be there in spite of my bumbling. Ideal parents do not really require anything of the child in order for it to be loved."

Spiritual Focus

The Boomers live their spirituality out loud, in an extremely extroverted fashion. They are eager to talk about their spirituality, sometimes even with total strangers, and are adventurous when it comes to exploring new ideas and practices. They do not "hide their light under a bushel,"[8] but continue their prophetic calling in both their personal and public lives.

Ironically, even though Boomers are very open and vocal about their spirituality, their practice of it is largely a private affair. Most Boomers are allergic to proselytizing, preferring to take an "I'm okay, you're okay," or "live and let live" approach to spirituality and religion. Compounding the irony is the fact that "consciousness raising" is very important to Boomers, whether this is perceived as a public ministry (educating the general public) or in terms of personal growth (recognizing one's unity with the Divine, or enlightenment).

What is the difference between "raising someone's consciousness" and proselytizing? This is tricky. Boomers often devote their lives to "raising consciousness" around environmental, political, humanitarian, social justice, and spiritual issues—certainly they intend to persuade others to share their views. They are as convinced of the legitimacy of their causes as previous generations were of theirs, and their efforts at persuasion just as sincere. Boomers are not interested (generally) in converting someone to a specific religion or spiritual practice (this is a private affair) but they can be strident about environmental issues (this is a public affair since it effects the survival of the planet) or even some spiritual issues (such as the interconnectedness of all things, since this has bearing on public issues).

Dominant Faith Style

Among the Faith Style types, Boomers are most likely to be Spiritual Eclectics. Eclectics are open to a wide range of images and ideas about Divinity, and assemble their spiritualities and religious practices in an idiosyncratic and piecemeal fashion. This approach has been disparagingly referred to as being "cafeteria-style"—taking a little bit of this from here, a little bit of that from there. A typical Spiritual Eclectic might go to church on Christmas and Easter, practice yoga once a week, go on a Buddhist meditation retreat every couple of months or so, and find spiritual wisdom in the *Tao Te Ching* and quotations from Groucho Marx. They don't believe that any one religion has a lock on truth, and so they feel free to pick and choose from various sources, according to what makes sense in the present moment.

Linda's response is like many I have received, "I practice Catholicism, indigenous rituals, and eastern energy awareness exercises . . . an odd combination of different religions. I have adapted each of them to my personal needs in a way that they now feel very compatible and complimentary."

If Spiritual Eclectics are pressed to describe the Divine, they are likely to describe it as "a spiritual force animating all of nature."[9] They are likely to see their own relationship with the Divine in terms that are pantheistic, meaning that there is no absolute distinction between the Divine and creation, rather that creation is a part of the Divine and an expression of the Divine. Spiritual Eclectics create meaning in their lives by protecting the planet and its creatures, and promoting consciousness of the interconnectedness of all things.

Spiritual Eclectics honor a wide range of sources of spiritual wisdom, including the scriptures of various religions, poetry, art, science, and especially their own experience, including the wisdom of their own bodies. Eclectics tend to view spiritual growth in terms of their success in "seeing through" the illusion of separateness, debunking the claims of the ego so that they can realize their unity with all being. Their spiritual practices include prayer, meditation, ritual, sacred reading, art, exercise, being in nature, and activism of various kinds.

The advantages of a spiritually eclectic spirituality include its openness to wisdom from various sources, its diversity, and its spiritual generosity. The disadvantages include a gullibility that holds new and untried sources of wisdom (such as fly-by-night gurus) in equal esteem with tried-and-true traditions; difficulty in finding spiritual community; and a lack of groundedness resulting from what is often a spiritual dilettantism, in which seekers simply move on to the next spiritual fad when their spiritual practice gets difficult or brings up painful issues. The greatest danger in a Spiritually Eclectic spirituality is a superficiality that never confronts authentically difficult aspects of human nature.

Naturally, not all Boomers are Spiritually Eclectic, but for readers familiar with my previous book, *Faith Styles,* understanding the Spiritually Eclectic faith style will be a good primer on understanding the Boomer spiritual ethos. Even those Boomers who are not Spiritual Eclectics will have eclectic impulses in the practice of their chosen tradition. Boomer Jews will be far more open to Buddhist prayer practices than their parents were. Boomer Evangelical Christians will be more open to the insights of transpersonal psychology or spiritually driven activism (such as Roman Catholics have been practicing for some time) than previous generations.

Prayer Style

Since Boomers tend to see the Divine in terms that are paradoxically both personal and impersonal, it is not perhaps surprising that their prayer practices are split between prayer and meditation—most of them practicing both.

Karl's response to me was typical of those whose practice tends more towards meditation: "I don't pray for things. I pray/meditate to experience Divinity. The form I use is simple: stop thinking, heighten awareness, experience the world as clearly as you can, and come into the Presence. Then, dwelling in this awakened consciousness without thought brings me clarity, joy, wonder, and action when necessary." Is the "Presence" he mentions personal or impersonal? I'm guessing both. Ian, a secular Jew who considers himself a "spiritual person," finds his connection to the Divine tied to the out-of-doors: "The Divine manifests itself to me with intimacy and deep feeling in the natural world. I spend a lot of time hiking in the backcountry of the Sierras, often alone. It is within the quiet and solitude of this space that I simply stop questioning and realize that there is a surrounding presence that is both unknowable and comforting to me."

Although none of those who responded to my survey said they only prayed but did not meditate, I certainly know of Boomers—especially those who practice particular religious traditions—who fit into this category. Although I suspect that, if pressed, most of these would admit to some kind of receptive prayer practice where they "listened" for the voice of the Divine, similar to how Effy described her experience: "I meditate through silencing my mind . . . . In this way I can hear that gentle quiet voice within that gives me answers that I prayed for. I do not ask for this voice to come. I practice meditation so that I will be able to hear the voice when it does speak. And, inspiring ideas often follow a sensation that my body has become more energized." Of course, not all Boomers would call what they are doing "meditation," since this might have uncomfortable (read "Eastern") associations for them.

Nevertheless, most of those who spoke to me practiced a mixture of meditation and prayer. A Roman Catholic, Quincy's description is typical of many I received: "I do a lot of formalized prayer, psalms, and also a lot of wordless, meditative prayer. I pray for the safety of my children and my wife, for the happiness of my deceased family, for help for the victims of starvation and disasters, and for the forgiveness of my own sins."

Becca, a Christian, describes her practice in similar terms: "Nightly I say the Jewish 'Sh'ma' and offer up the names of those who are in trouble and those I am bound to through love. Otherwise my prayer takes the form of sitting in silence, or doing yoga, walking in nature, exercise, listening to or making music, making love, sitting with directees,[10] writing poetry, cooking when I'm doing it because I want to . . . ."

Boomers have an ambivalent relationship with petitionary prayer. Many of them feel deeply conflicted "asking" the Divine for anything, and this hesitation was well represented in the responses I received. Teri wrote, "My meditation is without words but a seeking to contact the Divine within. When I pray I mention people or situations without asking for particular things. I bring the person into the light . . . . When I ask for things it is usually for peace within [myself] and peace within the world. I ask that others know acceptance and love. I do like the stating of things in the positive. I have learned to phrase greetings as blessings and I find blessings become part of my prayers."

It is clear that Nick—a true Spiritual Eclectic—wrestles with this when he wrote, "I would usually not 'ask' anything of my meditation. But really, how can someone *not* ask or desire an outcome? Even when not stated as an appeal or question . . . I think I ask for presence, stillness, state of 'being,' relaxation, health, awareness, awakeness from my illusions . . . . I do currently wonder how being directive for an outcome meditation would or could be. Prayer is useful and powerful. However, I am in process of redefining what prayer is. Raised Christian, prayer was addressed to a powerful human-like but omnipotent invisible God who judged and decided. That on one hand seems absurd now. *But* I see the power of prayer and expressing intentions while looking both inward/outward. I also see prayer as a way of talking to my deep self (is that God?)."

Feeling deeply conflicted about petitionary prayer doesn't actually stop most Boomers from engaging in it, however. Indeed, though many of those who answered my questions expressed ambivalence regarding the practice, almost all of them still practiced it. Cathy said, "I meditate every day, with most of the time taken in silence, emptying the mind. At the end of meditation, I say prayers like the Metta Sutta, and the Twenty-third Psalm. I also say prayers for others who are undergoing a difficult time, to give them strength to make it through, and to let them know they are held in love."

Dot, too, regularly expresses thanks and prays for others: "I thank and praise God for all he has given me for the day, and often shed a few tears, or many. . . then I pray for peace, for healing for those in pain and sickness, and that people would be led to caring for each other and for peace."

Several Boomers articulated their ambivalence in terms of "not wanting to tell God what to do," recognizing the limitations of their own understanding and the supremacy of the Divine judgment in the matter. As David, an independent Catholic, mentioned, "Realizing my own ignorance of the divine will, I always end a prayer with 'if it is in accord with your will.' I pray for financial survival, health of friends suffering cancer, peace in the world."

Donna voices a similar concern: "I pray in thanksgiving. I meditate on how I fit into this world. I meditate on what I should be doing to make my life and others' lives better. I do not pray intercessory prayer. By that I mean that I don't pray for people or events. God will do what he knows is best."

Some, like Elaine, resolve this by keeping their petitions non-specific: "I send out energy into the universe. For myself, I pray for what is best for me. For others, I pray for what is best for them and their families."

As we have already seen, thanksgiving plays a large part in Boomers' prayer practices as well. Katie's response to me is almost stereotypically Boomer in both its range of practice and its eclecticism: "I have a regular ritual of prayer and meditation. I light a candle, inviting the Holy to be present, and spend some time in prayer, first of all giving thanks for blessings, then saying prayers of intercession for family and friends who may be ill or struggling, or particular crises in the world. I often follow this with several minutes of an embodied practice (yoga, qi kung) to ground myself and affirm that I am a soul living out this life in physical form. This also serves as self care. *Lectio divina* follows, perhaps a psalm or other sacred text, with a twenty-minute silent meditation to finish."

More than any other generation, Boomers have achieved a near-perfect balance between speaking (prayer) and listening (meditation) to the Divine. This has resulted in a rich prayer life in which they have experienced a deep communion with the Divine that has been both rewarding and spiritually profitable for them.

Boomers in Community

Distrustful of religious institutions, Boomers invented the "spiritual-but-not-religious," identity. Quincy's description of this echoes what I have heard from many Boomers: "'Religion,' I think, describes a more-or-less fixed set of creeds, rituals, disciplines, and teachings; 'spirituality' describes an interior life that strives to be in touch with 'the Other,' what I think of as the 'Breath of God.'"

Boomers often associate religions and established religious institutions with their parents' beliefs and choices, seeing them as irrelevant, oppressive, or hypocritical. They equate the beliefs of these religions and institutions with "dogma," which is almost universally seen as an evil. Nevertheless, some Boomers try to be "fair and balanced." Effy told me, "There is power in numbers and therefore I believe religion is a necessary 'evil' that has to be tolerated because the good that comes from it outweighs the bad."

There is a prevalent notion among Boomers that Western religions are "bad" while Eastern religions are "good." They are often incredulous when it is pointed out to them that Hinduism or Buddhism can be just as patriarchal, dogmatic, and oppressive as Western religions, for those who grow up in cultures where those religions are dominant.[11] It is precisely the distance we have from these traditions, and their novelty, that makes them look so attractive. Close up, they suffer from the same feet of clay that burdens any human endeavor. The grass is, indeed, always greener on the other side of the fence.

Because of their allergy to organized religion, Boomers have largely abandoned the mainline churches and synagogues (as attendance statistics have alarmingly demonstrated over the past twenty years[12]), opting, as they are wont to do, to build their own spiritual communities from scratch, trading the tired and "corrupt" models of their parents for new versions shaped by their own ideals.

Evangelical megachurches, which are overwhelmingly non-denominational and therefore not tied to the mainline "system" are a largely Boomer phenomenon, doing church "their way," swapping hymns for soft-rock praise choruses, and dogmatic sermons for seeker-friendly "talks" utilizing pop-psychology, Power Point slides, and coaching terminology. The Jewish Renewal

99

movement is a progressive version of the same Boomer re-invention phenomenon.

Again, the very things Boomers were running from jumped right into their laps. The same dogma, drama, and hypocrisy that typified (in their way of thinking) traditional religious communities popped up to bite them in their alternative communities as well.

Some Boomers chose to stay within traditional communities, but for the past thirty years have been working to remake them in their own image, representative of their own values—sometimes resulting in congregations that would have been unrecognizable to the people worshiping in the very same building only twenty years ago. Mainline denominations, under Boomer influence, largely traded the language of salvation and devotion for the language of liberation and social justice.

A great number of Boomers, however, are not involved in spiritual communities as such, doing their spirituality solo, and finding other venues for community. Non-traditional spiritual communities such as Evelyn's book study group, yoga centers, and twelve-step meetings, however, flourish amongst Boomers, since they offer both spirituality and community without requiring the participant to embrace any particular doctrine. Eastern faiths still have quite a following amongst Boomers, and Buddhist sanghas and Hindu ashrams have growing ministries, especially in urban areas, although oftentimes even these are "reinventions" of the more traditional faiths, offering teachings that have been "Boomerized"—"lite" versions of traditional faiths that often leave those born in those religions scratching their heads.

Boomers need spiritual community, and many of them are desperate for it. Many of them are deeply lonely, having poured themselves into "making it" financially in the 1980s and '90s. Old friends have drifted away and lost touch. Sometimes the only friends Boomers have are their spouses, and though they wish they could find some, they don't really know where to look. Spiritual communities that want to attract Boomers will do best with a soft-sell approach to doctrine, emphasizing music and opportunities for service that resonate with Boomer values. Boomers care deeply for peace and justice, and will support communities that care about these things as well.

Boomers may *find* salvation in your midst, but they will come *looking* for transformation. The more a community can present those as the same thing, the more attractive the community will be to Boomers.

Spiritual Growth Continuum

The Boomers who replied to my surveys were far from unanimous in their understanding of spiritual growth. The journey from spiritual immaturity to maturity varied widely in their responses—nevertheless some generalizations can be made.

I believe that, for Boomers, spiritual maturity is a continuum moving from apathy towards commitment to transformation and concern for the welfare of others. The spiritually immature apathete is entirely self-concerned, doesn't care about other people, the state of the world, impending environmental disaster, or the injustice inherent in our political systems, and doesn't lift a finger to change things. As Therese put it: "I think an undeveloped spiritual person is one who is self-centered and unaware of the needs and concerns of others." Nora (raised Catholic, but investigating Sufism and Buddhism) explores this theme further: "Someone who is very undeveloped spiritually is a person who is adrift—not satisfied with herself or the world, seeing no real purpose in life, and not yet motivated, or afraid to dig in to find out why or to discover worlds beyond herself."

The spiritually mature person, however, gives of him- or herself to others. Such a person becomes a seeker and an activist who is involved in personal and global transformation, making a difference in the world. Teri explicates this theme, describing spiritual growth as "a connection with one's self, core beliefs; being responsible, and how that reflects in and around the universe; a connection with others, understanding we are all one with God, spirit, etc.—being responsible for what we have created in our life and not a victim."

Quincy's description is both succinct and well-stated: "I would describe Spiritual Growth as the process of moving from a purely interior focus to an external one: from focusing on self ('just you and me, God') to focusing on others, and ultimately to the Infinite Other as manifested in the call to serve and call to love others. One can be externally religious and still be a 'spiritual dwarf' when one's perspective is stunted into that kind of 'tunnel relationship' with God that excludes all the messy people, awkward circumstances, and uncomfortable needs of all those around whom we live."

Some Boomers saw spiritual growth as an openness to continued questioning. As Linda, a Catholic, wrote, "In my mind, people who are not spiritually developed have a set of beliefs handed to them at a very young age, and never challenge those beliefs for viability in their own personal experience of life. These people are especially unwilling to hold the possibility that what is true for them may not be universally 'correct.' People on the undeveloped side of the continuum would feel personally threatened by questioning of their beliefs. On the other hand, people who are spiritually growing challenge their beliefs as they go through life. They may stick with the concept of their original beliefs, but they will no doubt have a deeper understanding of their 'God' and themselves for having explored the nuances of their beliefs. These people can entertain the idea that there are infinite ways that the Divine works in this world. Spiritual maturity is also reflected in one's ability to hold the tension of opposite possibilities without needing to choose to relieve the discomfort of the tension."

Kelly (who would like to be a Buddhist, but says it's "too hard") echoes this in her description when she says, "I believe individuals who are farther down the spiritual path keep asking questions and, more importantly, listen for answers. Their need to understand their place in the universe is central to who they are. They are more open—to compassion, love, empathy, and understanding. They see other people for who they are. They despise ignorance, but not the ignorant. They are disciplined in their practice. They have a practice. They can separate the important from the mundane. They are not exclusive, they don't use their enlightenment to further their own needs. They live by example." However, Kelly is not hopeful as to the attainability of such maturity, adding, "I haven't met anyone who I have felt is spiritually enlightened."

Another broad theme was spiritual sensitivity and discernment. Effy describes maturity in terms of an "'awareness' level of spirit residing within. The greater awareness one has of Spirit residing within and a perception of the reason for this divine Spirit, the greater a person uses each and every event as an opportunity to understand oneself better. On the other end of the continuum, there is the person who is not aware of the existence of Spirit. This person could even be very benevolent by nature. However, when something goes wrong, the person may see himself/herself as a being the victim. Events or others are blamed for one's circumstances."

A final theme that emerged was the immaturity of materialism. Bette, a Christian Scientist, told me she thinks an undeveloped spirituality "is totally involved with materialism (material existence) and doesn't credit God for good," while a well-developed spirituality "is in constant communion with God, love." David is in complete agreement when he writes, "Undeveloped to me means materially or sense-identified. Well-developed is someone not attached to earthly things though they may possess them."

Connecting these themes is a concern for others as the litmus test for maturity—apathy, selfishness, and self-interest are seen as immature states to be transcended through spiritual attention and practice.

MINISTERING TO BABY BOOMERS

Those doing spiritual guidance with Boomers should be cautious of their aversion to authority, and should hew to a strictly non-directive stance (although, as in our opening example, a good intervention is appropriate now and then). A contemplative orientation will be most effective, allowing the client to lead, and holding an awareness of the immediate presence of the Divine. Boomers enjoy small groups, as the popularity of spiritual book circles and twelve-step groups attest. Loosely structured discernment groups such as Wisdom Circles were invented by Boomers, and these are particularly popular in gender-separated groups such as women's spirituality circles and men's drumming and storytelling circles.[13]

Although idealism is at once the Boomers' greatest asset, it is also their most troublesome liability. Just as with Evelyn, Boomers will often be so fixated on an idealized notion of how life, or their job, or their relationships, or politics *should* be, that they cannot relax into and appreciate the gift of what *is*. The Buddha is reported to have said, "We suffer only so long as we resist what *is*," and this resistance due to rampant idealism has caused Boomers a great deal of suffering indeed.

Ministers and spiritual guides can be of great assistance to Boomers by reminding them that imperfection is normal, and warn them away from self-destructive hyper-scrupulosity. I cannot count the number of times I have counseled suffering Boomers who were beating up on themselves for not being "perfect"—as if anyone ever was. Boomers, more than any other generation, need to be gently invited to embrace the "good enough" spiritual life.

G.I.s Ministering to Boomers

As I have already pointed out, the generation gap is widest between G.I.s and Boomers, as these two have fundamentally different perspectives on spiritual maturity and the place and importance of institutions. G.I.s who find themselves ministering to this generation must realize that Boomer critiques of the society G.I.s built are systemic, not personal, and must be willing to set aside decades of rancor. They must be willing to meet Boomers on their own terms—not an easy feat, and indeed, some G.I.s would be doing the responsible thing in discerning that they simply cannot work with Boomers. This is especially true if the G.I. minister has Boomer children from whom he or she is estranged. It is almost impossible for G.I.s not to project the rage and disappointment they feel towards their Boomer children onto the Boomer generation in general, and this is one reason that Boomers involved in more traditional forms of religious practice have had to break away from established communities to form their own, free of G.I. leadership and judgment.

G.I.s would do well to be mindful of the values that they and Boomers hold in common: freedom and self-determination. Boomers seek these things in different arenas than G.I.s, but it may be helpful for G.I.s to make empathic and creative connections with the Boomer worldview.

G.I.s will do better with Boomers if they can hold their own views with some humility. If a G.I. can admit that, yes, perhaps they were a little harsh, and that yes, institutions often go astray from their founding visions (and often have on the G.I.s' watch), this will go a long way to defusing the ideological stalemate that may impair the ministerial relationship between G.I.s and Boomers.

G.I.s will also make friends among Boomers if they can affirm the things they can see as good in Boomers' visions. Boomers' desire for justice is something that G.I.s can support (even if the means by which Boomers seek to bring it about sometimes seem suspect).

In order to work effectively with Boomers, G.I.s must be comfortable with a wider range of images, metaphors, and symbols for the Divine than they themselves use—including feminine images. They must be able to honor and use these metaphors without ridiculing or disrespecting them in any way.

Furthermore, G.I.s may need to stretch to see public protests, activism, and social justice work as spiritual practice, or indeed, as having anything to do with religion or spirituality at all. They must be able to hear a Boomer's critique of the status quo, of religion, or of social institutions without taking it as a personal attack.

G.I.s must keep in mind that Boomers have a very different attitude towards the public practice of faith. Since G.I.s see prayer as primarily a public enterprise, and being seen at prayer a mark of respectable social standing—the Boomer antipathy towards public displays of piety and their proclivity towards private spiritual practice may be easily misunderstood by G.I.s attempting to minister.

Boomers are likely to consider a concern for public practice to be a form of hypocrisy, and G.I.s simply cannot expect it of them as it violates a major Boomer principle. That doesn't mean that they don't engage in public practice—they do—only that the fact that it is public is not important to the Boomer in any way, and public practice will always be secondary to one's private prayer and meditation.

Speaking of meditation, some G.I.s may have trouble affirming this as a valid spiritual practice. G.I.s should educate themselves about the long history of meditation in their own traditions, and experiment with it themselves in order to gain understanding and empathy for the practice. G.I.s, read my lips: "Different" does not mean "wrong" or "bad."

Silents Ministering to Boomers

Silents are more likely to still be in active ministry than G.I.s at this time, and Boomers, if they think back, will probably remember with relief when the shift from G.I. leadership to Silent leadership occurred. Things have been *much* easier in religious institutions since then.

Even though the Silents got along well with G.I.s,[14] Silents have always been secretly fond of Boomers, seeing them as bold and brave younger versions of themselves. The Boomers had the courage to say all the things that Silents were thinking, but couldn't risk angering G.I.s by actually speaking up. While Silents never would have even dreamed of stepping as far out of line as Boomers did, they are sympathetic to Boomer concerns.

The Boomer "project" was something that the Silents, by and large, understood and—secretly—approved of. The Silents used their influence to "course correct" G.I. institutions to make them more just and humane, but they never voiced the sweeping critiques as Boomers did, and in fact, most Silents probably thought that the Boomers would be more effective if they were more like the Silents themselves. If they would just reign it in a bit, the G.I.s might be able to hear what they were saying. If they would just *play* the game, they could *change* the game.

The Boomers, of course, could do nothing of the kind, and so the Silents watched with helpless anxiety the culture war brew before their eyes, distraught by their divided loyalties, seeing the good points on both sides, and also seeing clearly the myopia of both G.I.s and Boomers. It was a painful place to be, and neither generation on either side of them could hear their voice of reason.

Despite all the turbulent water under the bridge, Silents and Boomers generally have good relationships, and it is largely due to Silent leadership that Boomers have felt "welcomed back," to the religious institutions that had seemed so hostile and inhospitable under G.I. leadership. Boomers might secretly whisper about Silents being the lackeys and "whipping boys" of the G.I.s, but in the end, they gave the Silents something that the G.I.s never did: respect. Silents are in a good position to offer spiritual care and guidance for Boomers—who are now old enough and wise enough to realize that someone with more life experience might actually have a thing or two to teach them.

Silents understand the Boomer antipathy toward public displays of piety, as they share with Boomers a preference for private spiritual practice. Silents may have to stretch a bit to understand the Eastern spiritual influence that Boomers have incorporated into their spiritualities, and this is true even of those practicing in more "traditional" Christian and Jewish denominations.

Silents are in a good position to hold Boomers accountable to their own ideals—something that Xer spiritual guides cannot really accomplish due to the fact that Boomers have a hard time respecting Xers.[15] Silents can reflect back to Boomers the kind of unconditional love and acceptance that they have never experienced from G.I.s. Silents can be a healing presence for Boomers that no other living generation can even come close to.

Silents should be aware that the Boomers' spiritual Achilles heel is the very idealism that drives them. When they do not measure up to their ideals, when they fail to accomplish the grand world-changing visions they launch, Silents can remind them that imperfection is no shame, that limitation is the human condition, and that our best intentions often go awry through no fault of our own. Silents can chasten Boomers' overscrupulosity (a trait G.I.s cannot even see, due to the large gap between what constitutes virtue and vice for the two generations) and teach them to be kind and compassionate towards themselves—a role at which Silents excel.

Xers Ministering to Boomers

The distance between Xers and Boomers is the second widest gap of the generations living today. Boomers are already suspicious of Xers, seeing them as apathetic and lazy versions of themselves who, maddeningly, will not "get with the program." Xers will point out that "the program" is stupid and impractical . . . and they're off and running.

Xers who want to minister effectively to Boomers must do some inner healing work and learn to forgive. So long as you (Xers) are resentful of Boomers, there is no way that you can love them or serve them sincerely. Yes, Boomers are maddeningly myopic. Yes, they are often completely blind to the situations in which they placed you. Yes, they are unwilling to take any responsibility for their actions.

And you know what? They may never clue in—and yet, they *still* need pastoral care. Here's a newsflash for you Xers: you are not in this business for yourself. So grow up, take responsibility for yourself where you are right now, get over it, and get to work.

Xers are in a unique position to assist Boomers with their Achilles Heel—runaway idealism and overscrupulosity. Xers excel at seeing through grand visions to what is actually practical and possible. The trick is to bring Boomers down to ground level and help them root their efforts in what is pragmatic and achievable without bursting their bubbles. Boomers' experience of Xers is that they are perpetual Eeyores, raining on Boomer parades, telling them why things *can't* be done, and ending up doing nothing.

Of course, that is a distorted view, but it is easy to see how Boomers might feel like Xers are such killjoys. Instead, Xers will be most effective when they can affirm the Boomer impulse to transform the wrongs they see around them, and then assist them in discerning achievable goals towards that end. Being as how there is not a single pie in the Xers' skies, they are very good at pointing out the impracticalities of Boomers' visions—what Xers are not so good at is having the patience and diplomacy necessary to steer Boomers toward workable solutions.

Likewise, Xers are very good at seeing exactly how Boomers' idealism is tripping them up. Again, the challenge for Xers is mustering the tact to confront Boomers with their unhealthy idealization in ways that can be heard and not resented and rejected. Since Xers are the kings when it comes to sarcasm and cynicism, this may require some heavy lifting. Thus, any hint of unhealed rancor towards Boomers is going to severely limit an Xers' ability to minister with grace. It is a rare Xer who does not have work to do in this area. Xers cannot look to Boomers to help them with it, either—Boomers, by and large, cannot even see it.

Fortunately, Silents can, and Xers would do well to seek out Silent mentors to help them with their "Boomer issues." Silents can both affirm the goals that Xers are striving for and can give them practical, workable advice on how to approach Boomers and work with them.

"Cusper" Xers—those born in the early 1960s—can also be a great resource for Xers in ministry. I myself was born in 1962, and I often say that I am an Xer who speaks fluent Boomerese. People like myself (a sub-group that some sociologists call Generation Jones) can help translate for later Xers what drives Boomers, and likewise can give guidance to Boomers on "just what is the Xers' problem, anyway?"

Late middle age is not going to be easy for Boomers. Their self-image is of perpetual youth, and equally perpetual coolness. They are not going to surrender these despite the ravages of time, skin cancers, wrinkles, or the fact that they still think music made forty-five years ago is cutting edge. There is no need to disabuse them of these notions—it's part of what makes them endearing, if you can get over your resentments enough to see it.

Far from perfect, Boomers need love and care as much as anyone else. Their generation is as much shaped by woundedness as Xers are. The fact that Boomers *did* the wounding to Xers is something that Xers must forgive and strive to heal if they are to be of any use to them. Xers who can see the woundedness behind the Boomer project will have an advantage in being able to have compassion and empathy for them. Genuinely loving them is just a small step beyond that.

In matters of worship, Xers should keep in mind that Boomers see themselves as experimental and progressive. Xers tend to lean toward an "ancient-future" approach that embraces new worship forms, while bringing with them treasures from the past, including music and ritual from the medieval and reformation eras. Boomers may be reactive to what they perceive as their parents' music or liturgical forms. Xers can help Boomers by honoring their desire for contemporary music and liturgy, and when Boomers are open to it, reframe older media in ways that are fresh and non-triggering.

Xers and Boomers actually make excellent partners in ministry—with Boomers leading the charge with vision, and Xers serving as the detail people, working out the nuts-and-bolts of how to actually implement ministry plans. When both Boomers and Xers are aware of the differences between them—and appreciative of the spiritual gifts each bring to the table—they can create formidable ministries.

Millennials Ministering to Boomers

Boomers and Millennials are a match made in heaven. They already love each other, right from the start. Late Boomers are the cool parents that Millennials "hang out with," and their familial relationships are often deep friendships. Boomers led the way in correcting the errors made with the Xers, instilling in Millennials a positive self-image. They are impressed with the achievements of Millennials—and, in fact, may feel like Millennials can do no wrong.

This idealization of Millennials may leave Xers rolling their eyes, but it's good news for Millennials, who are in an excellent position to provide effective spiritual care to Boomers. Boomers trust Millennials, they cut them a *lot* of slack, their good relationships with them (as both children and grandchildren) cover a multitude of sins. The love and trust are mutual, and Millennials, although they may consider Boomers quaint in some ways, have a deep affection for them, and return their respect.

Millennials, despite their young age, can meet Boomers at the point of their need in a way that Xers could never dream of. Indeed, of all of the living generations, only Silents come close to being able to minister to Boomers as effectively as Millennials.

Millennials should be comforted by this reservoir of good will capital—they may need to draw on it, but should be careful not to abuse it. (Boomers have limits to their patience, too.) But this should rarely be a problem: Millennials are a Civic generation, and thus they are socially sensitive, responsible, and hard working (qualities that Boomers appreciate, even if they couldn't applaud them in their own parents).

Millennials share with Boomers many ideals—especially the importance of interpersonal skills, of relationship, and of community. Boomers feel safe with Millennials, they open up to them easily, and can usually be vulnerable with them. Millennials can be on the lookout for empathy burnout in Boomers, they may need to infuse back to Boomers some of the hope and optimism Boomers worked so hard to impart to them. Boomers will accept this as a great gift, and will feel encouraged and strengthened by the fact that the "younger generation" is on board with some of their ideas.

Indeed, Millennials approve and affirm the ideals that drive Boomers so relentlessly, and while they share the earthy pragmatism of Xers, they feel none of the impatience or resentment Xers harbor toward the older generation. Thus, since Millennials feel no rancor towards Boomers, their care for them is sincere and without reservation.

They work well together, with Millennials often surprising Boomers by generating creative ways to implement Boomer ideas. Boomers are generally open to technology, but often they are just as happy if someone else is handling the details. They appreciate that Millennials seem to move in the technological world so effortlessly (and with none of the grouchiness or prickliness of Xers), and are grateful for Millennial innovation and assistance.

Boomers are delighted by Millennials' initiative, drive, and creativity—especially when these things are in service of things Boomers consider important. Since Millennials live to please, their cooperative ministry efforts are often both fun and fruitful.

CHAPTER FOUR

THE "AUTHENTIC" GENERATION —GENERATION X

Donna felt herself deflate when she realized that Danny was her next client. In her career as a Licensed Clinical Social Worker she had run across few people as intractably depressed as he was. At forty years old, he was unemployed, unshaven, and living on the generosity of friends. He slumped into her office, clad in the same black T-shirt and blue jeans that he always wore. She steeled herself for a pointless hour of sarcastic resistance to her every attempt to help.

"I'd like to pick up where we left off last time, Danny," she began when it became clear that he was not going to lead with anything.

"What's the point?" he moaned, looking at the ceiling. She bit her lip, since she agreed with him.

"I want to talk about where you find meaning."

He scowled at her. "Where I find what?"

"Meaning. How do you find meaning in your life?"

"Dude, are you speaking English?" he looked back at the ceiling. "I see your lips moving, but I don't understand anything you say."

She fought her own frustration with his "so what, nothing matters anyway" demeanor. "I'm going to write you a prescription," she said. That got his attention.

"For what?"

"For hard labor."

"You can't write a prescription, you're not a psychiatrist," he complained.

She ignored him and scratched the address of the local Catholic Worker house on the notepad. She handed it to him.

"What's this?" he took it, looking at her suspiciously.

"It's an address. Go to it. I want you to put in four hours a week."

"Doing what?"

"Doing whatever they tell you to. If you don't get in four hours before our next appointment, don't bother coming."

"Are you serious?"

"As a heart attack," she said.

BLACK CLOTHES, APATHY, moody music and a cynical disposition towards the world—what's up with Generation X? Not previously considered prime candidates for spiritual pursuits, due to their allergy to idealism and institutions, Xers are starting to show up in spiritual communities, and, increasingly, are coming for spiritual direction. Why the change of heart? Because Xers are entering midlife, and as their hair begins to thin and their belts begin to tighten, the myth of their immortality is unraveling and they are beginning to ask the difficult questions that humans have been asking for centuries. So who are these curious, cynical creatures, and what makes them tick?

Birth Years and Place in the Cycle

Xers are placed by most sociologists between the years of 1961 and 1980. Although some may quibble with the exact years, here, beginning the X Generation in 1962 or even as late as 1964, in my own experience, people born as early as 1960 share in the majority of Xers traits (even though they may also have some typically Boomer tendencies).[1]

In Strauss and Howe's model of Generational Cycles, Xers are the inevitable Reactive Generation that follows after Idealistic generations (in our case, the Boomers). The generation gap between Xers and Boomers is the second widest gap of all the living generations. Naturally, this means conflict. Xers get along well—very well, in fact—with every generation *except* for Boomers, with whom their rivalry has achieved epic, almost legendary status. The reason for this will become clear as we explore this enigmatic generation further.

Formative Events

Through no fault of their own, Xers are the most demonized generation alive today. They were the first generation to be born after the introduction of "the pill," and partly because of this, they were the first to be thought of as a burden rather than a blessing. In the free-wheeling 1960s, kids were seen as being "kind of like headaches, things you take pills not to have."[2] Following publication of biologist Paul Ehrlich's bestseller *The Population Bomb* in 1968, children were not only seen as inconvenient, but as an intolerable burden on the ecosystem.[3] This era also saw the rise of a new horror genre that depicted children as demonic, from *Rosemary's Baby* to *The Omen* to *Children of the Corn*. Rarely before were children depicted as so burdensome and dangerous.

Xers could not help but internalize these values and images. Their insecurity regarding their own worth was augmented by the unstable family life experienced by so many. While only 11% of Boomers came from broken homes, nearly half of all Xers are the children of divorce. The stable home life taken for granted by previous generations is alien to most Xers. Even those who did not suffer broken homes were surrounded by the threat as they saw their friends' parents divorcing, and watched television shows that presented a united front of divorced or widowed single-parent families (even the *Brady Bunch* concerned the union of two widowed parents). Maybe one's own parents hadn't split—yet—but the threat hung over every Xer like the sword of Damocles.

This lack of value was reinforced by the "latch-key kid" phenomenon of the 1970s. With liberated women everywhere taking their rightful place beside men in the workplace, this left junior at home to fend for him- or herself. This led many Xers to grow up quicker than they might have, to act out more than was good for them, and to feel unimportant. Because of this, Xers are convinced that no one is going to help them if they do not help themselves, and a fierce, uncomplaining determination is common among Xers.

Ironically, this extreme self-determination exists quietly side-by-side with those who simply couldn't cut it on their own, who just gave up and decided to live in their parents' basements as perpetual teenagers. As Marie, from Saltville, Virginia, described her own experience, "I see many of us still dependent on our parents (economically, emotionally, etc.) in ways that our parents were not dependent on their parents. I can think of several people in my age range who still live with their parents or who have moved back in with their parents—sometimes bringing several children and pets with them. I personally have pawned my two dogs off on my parents!"

Self-doubt does not exhaust the woundedness of Xers. Optimism and faith in others does not come easily for this cynical generation. Before Xers were out of diapers, they were faced with fears and uncertainties unknown to any previous generation. Xers learned to "duck and cover" during bomb drills as early as pre-school and kindergarten, and despaired over the fate of the earth while they were in elementary school, watching the statistics on environmental catastrophe grow grimmer as they grew up.

As Buddhist Xer Lhasa Ray told one journalist, "We share a common sense of powerlessness or despair that has been with us since the very beginning. As early as I can remember, my parents would tell me about nuclear war and how it was this looming threat. I spent a lot of time in fear of these huge powers out there that I had no control over and which were going to determine my fate somehow. So I didn't have a sense of a bright future on a global level."[4] Uma had a similar experience. She writes, "The threat of nuclear war had a big effect on me. I remember being so frightened that an accident like Chernobyl would happen in America. I remember looking at maps of America and figuring out where all the nuclear plants were and figuring out what range I was in. When I saw the photos from Hiroshima, I decided I would rather be right next to a plant and be disintegrated rather than have my skin slip off my body."

It is difficult to overstate the damage that the Watergate and

Iran-Contra episodes did to Xers' trust in public figures. Because of these and other episodes, it is not surprising that Xers are intolerant of authority figures. As Ken told me, "From dictators in far-off places to politicians right here in our own backyard, our leaders have squandered our resources, our money, and our future to fund their own drives for power and prestige." Maya, from Columbus, Ohio, adds her own note of cynicism when she wrote, "My experience tells me that no politicians are trustworthy. They are wealthy and care for the interests of the wealthy. My vote counts very little, although I continue to vote."

While many Boomers can relate to their distrust of authority, they are often impatient with Xers' pervasive cynicism. It is important for Boomers to realize that while they were themselves suspicious of authority, they also believed they could do better than their elders, holding a collective vision for a utopian society that they would bring about. Xers watched the idealistic dreams of their Boomer elders crash and burn in the "Me-Decade" 1980s, and have no comparable idealistic visions.

This distrust of authority extends to the realm of ideas. "If 'grownups' aren't to be trusted, then how can we trust anything they say?" young Xers asked (although all Xers are adults by this point, few feel like it). Thus religious teachings and political ideologies all hold about as much water as the notions of Santa Clause or the Easter Bunny.

The suspicion of anything beyond what they can actually see and feel runs deep. Xers are the first generation to fully internalize a post-modern worldview. No longer are there monolithic answers to the universe. While previous generations had faith that religion, and later, science could determine universal truth, Xers are dubious. All things are relative, and subject to interpretation according to one's gender, ethnicity, and other factors. As homiletics professor Ronald S. Allen wrote, for Xers "the assurance that the human family could arrive at universal truth has given way to the recognition that all statements of truth contain significant interpretive elements that arise from the interpreter's education, class, race, ethnicity, gender, and nationality. [Generation X] is coming to maturity in a culture that is pluralistic and relativistic in its attitudes toward certainty. Different (and sometimes contradictory) versions of truth exist side by side in the mall of human possibilities; people are free to choose which (if any) to follow."[5]

This, of course, creates a difficulty for religious institutions which have, for most of their history, been seen as the repositories of unassailable truth. For Xers, the alleged "truth" offered by religions can no longer be taken for granted. Xers are suspicious of institutions, and even more suspicious of anyone claiming to have the answers. As liturgist (and Boomer) Kevin Yell told me of his ministry to Xers, "If one says in one's attitude or actions 'Congrats, you've found the right way' you've lost them."

Xers have certainly been born into an unenviable era. Following on the heels of the ultra-successful Boomers, they have found themselves marginalized and then blamed for their own marginalization. They are insecure about their place in the universe, as all ideas have been relativized. As a result they feel powerless and suspicious of all authority, possessing a precarious existentialism.[6]

Experience of the World

The nightly horror of Vietnam on the evening news just added to the apocalyptic shadow over Xers' childhoods. It was very clear that this was no "Ozzie and Harriet" world they were born into. Instead, Xers experienced the world as fierce, dangerous, and doomed.

Because they were children, they felt powerless in the face of all this gloom, and so turned it inward. Because they saw the adults around them betraying their own ideals, Xers grew up embracing few, if any—at least none that are not laced with a good dose of irony. Because their parents' generation rejected them (through divorce, a negative attitude toward children, and abandoning them to being perpetually "Home Alone") they feel betrayed, a feeling that is reinforced when they read about how the governmental budget is being balanced by mortgaging *their* future.

As C.K., a digital artist from San Francisco puts it, "We are defined by disenfranchisement." His response to my survey is worth quoting further: "As a whole, my generation seems to be lost and left behind. We are too old to cling to naïveté, but too young to have much power. We are too cynical to buy into pre-vious generations' jingoistic nationalism or materialism, but we don't have much to replace it with. We know that we will only inherit debt and turmoil from the Boomers, don't have enough ambition to build something of our own, and have little hope that civilization will survive in the hands of the kids following us."

Due to this negative confluence of factors, Xers do not feel like they belong—not to this culture, not to this country, some-times not to the world. Their primary experience of the world is one of alienation, a theme that recurs frequently in Xer art and culture.

In a Word and a Song

Generation X has generated a lot of catchphrases, from Bart Simpson's "Don't have a cow," to the ubiquitous and sublimely multivalent and monosyllabic "Dude." But the one that best describes their generational attitude is "Whatever works," which is often shortened to the more dismissive, "Whatever."

This speaks to the practicality of Generation X. Because they are not swayed by grand ideals, nor lured by visions of the world as it "should be" (as Boomers often are), Xers are possessed by an almost mercenary pragmatism that evidences itself in every area of Xer life. Jobs are not a means to personal fulfillment so much as a way to pay the rent, government is nothing but a necessary evil, and relationships are pursued less out of starry-eyed romanticism (an affliction often scoffed at by Xers, or, more likely, kitchily cel-ebrated with an ironic wink) than by an often consciously negoti-ated arrangement for meeting mutual personal needs. They have already given up on the idea of "the nuclear family" as a dysfunc-tional joke, and early on formed enduring "tribes" (the current Boomer parlance for which is the cheesily politically correct "fam-ilies of choice"). Such tribes sport fluid, permeable boundaries, and have an unspoken agreement regarding mutual respect as their center of gravity.

If you want a good laugh, try convincing Xers that they should do something because it is the right, honorable, or noble thing to do. (Oh, by the way, you will not be laughing, they will—at you.)

GOODNESS GRACIOUS
by Kevin Gilbert

Goodness gracious, is there nothing left to say?
When the ones that get to keep looking are the
ones that look away
It's pabulum for the sleepers in the cult
of brighter days

Goodness gracious, at the mercy of the crooks
We're broke and stroking vegetables and there's
way too many cooks
In every pot a pink slip, in every mouth a hook

Goodness gracious, I'm not listening anymore
'Cause the spooks are in the white house and
they've justified a war
So wake me when they notify we're gonna fight
some more

Goodness gracious, not many people care
Concern is getting scarcer, true compassion
really rare
I can see it on our faces, I can feel it in the air
Goodness gracious me

Goodness gracious, my generation's lost
They burned down all our bridges before we
had a chance to cross
Is it the winter of our discontent or just an early
frost?

Goodness gracious, of apathy I sing
The Baby Boomers had it all and wasted
everything
Now recess is almost over and they won't get
off the swing

Goodness gracious, we came in at the end
No sex that isn't dangerous, no money left to
spend
We're the cleanup crew for parties we were too
young to attend
Goodness gracious me

Goodness gracious my grandma used to say
The world's a scary place now, things were
different in her day
What horrors will be commonplace when my
hair starts to grey?

Gilbert, Kevin. "Goodness Gracious," from the CD **Thud** (PRA Records,
1995). Lyrics reprinted by permission of Gilbert Properties Partnership.

If you want one song that best sums up the experience of Xers, there is overwhelming consensus on which it is. No other single lyric defines Generation X like Nirvana's "Smells Like Teen Spirit." Elliot, from Grapevine, Texas, lauds the song's "peculiar sense of self-indulgence, mixed up with outrage, self-disgust and (it's there) ironic humor." Everything pertinent to the Xer view of the world is there: the internalized negative messages, the tribal nature of Xer relationships, contempt for authority, and the overarching conviction that nothing and no one ultimately matters. Of all songs produced by Xers, it is nearly universally hailed as the generational anthem, and among music written by Xers, is probably the most frequently covered song by other artists. Unfortunately, at press time we were unable to procure permission to reprint the lyrics from "Smells Like Teen Spirit."[7]

Less well known than Nirvana's standard, but equally descriptive of a multitude of Gen X themes is Kevin Gilbert's song, "Goodness Gracious." See the sidebar for the complete lyrics to this excellent and evocative song.

What Are they Seeking?

In answer to this question, Ed, from Columbia, South Carolina, responded succinctly: "Survival."

Born of their early latchkey days of foraging for themselves, and the constant threat of nuclear annihilation, Xers have little hope of flourishing, and seek nothing more than to simply survive. One would think that those early situations would be temporary, and the "survivor" mentality a state of mind that Xers would eventually grow out of, but the hits just kept on coming. As Xers attempted to enter the workplace, they found it glutted with Boomers, forcing them, once again, into survival mode. (They did survive, by the way, by inventing an entire industry that didn't exist before—resulting in the dot-com boom of the 1990s.)

Sexually, too, Xers view themselves as "survivors." Left stranded in the wreckage of the Boomers' free love era, Xers seethed at the selfish, hedonistic abandon that stranded them as children, and restricted them as young adults as herpes, genital warts, and most especially AIDS left sexuality not a playground but a minefield to be trepidatiously navigated (a situation Kevin Gilbert alludes to in his song, "Goodness Gracious").

Several of the people who responded to my survey used the word "security" to describe what Xers long for the most—which also underscores the "survival" theme. But it's important to note that this security is different from the security sought by G.I.s — the G.I.'s achieved their security, and were vigilant in maintaining it. Xers have never gained it, and have little hope of it.

Disposition

Whereas every generation that has gone before them has been upbeat about the world, their prospects, and the future, Generation X alone are pessimists. This is partly due to the fact that while every other generation has been driven by a proprietary idealism that has inspired hope and optimism (whether warranted or not), Xers suffer from an almost debilitating idealistic anemia, leaving them without much hope for themselves, the nation, or indeed, the world. Danny, in our opening vignette, wears his generational depression on his sleeve, as indeed, a lot of Xers do.

A bleak cynicism runs through almost all Xer culture and art, although not in a way that is whining or complaining. Instead, it is simply stated as a matter of fact. When the band Fallout Boy sings,

"I will never believe in anything again," they do it to a jaunty, cheerful tune that suggests that all is as it should be. It is little wonder, then, that irony is the form of humor most often employed by this generation. The nearly systematic betrayal of ideals, and the hypocrisy inherent in every facet of American life provide a ripe, almost infinite field for the Generation X humorists' harvest.

Generational Project

Because of their early betrayals, Xers have a nearly universal allergy towards idealism, and a finely tuned cynicism toward stated agendas (there's always a hidden one). Generation X was born with a built-in Bullshit Detector, and it is turned up to eleven. Nothing delights Xers more than tipping other generations' sacred cows, and they especially enjoy sticking pins in Boomer balloons due to the rampant animosity towards their neighboring generation. Their generational project, then, is *deconstructive*, which is not a job that Xers have chosen, but one that they simply can't help doing.

In Xer society, no assumption should go unpacked, no belief unchallenged, and no agenda unquestioned. If anything does slip through, it goes on the To Do list for later dismantling. Answers that placated earlier generations, such as "Because I said so," "Because that is how it has always been done," or "Because that's what God wants" hold no water for Xers. Unlike Boomers, who are likewise suspicious of authority, Xers will not respond to demands (tyrannical or otherwise) with anger, but with an even more damning pity.

This impulse towards deconstruction has left the generation without any one single constructive project around which they can gather, unlike all the other generations. As Kelly, from Waynesville, North Carolina, wrote, "I don't think my generation really had any idea about what they should try to accomplish as a whole." As Kirk, from Gilbert, Arizona, put it, "I don't think my generation has had a direction . . . . We have no great leader or motivator of our time. We are a generation in Limbo." Marie echoed this theme when she wrote, "Many of us seem to still be seeking an identity or a purpose. I know many people my age who are still floundering around, in a sense, trying to establish a career, complete an education, or just establish a basic life or identity."

Meaning and purpose and means must be constructed (otherwise, how or why does one live?) but Xers will not accept these things as constructed by others. Xers must construct their own meaning, indeed their own view of the world, from scratch, and it will be an idiosyncratic and unique construction lacking any semblance of generational cohesion. Xer meaning is a startlingly postmodern experiment in relativistic projection in which competing worldviews are—by mutual consent—permitted to exist in tension with little or no conflict or disagreement. There is no "right" way to see the world. I have mine, and you have yours, and in an environment of mutual respect we can discuss our "meanings"—or not. Whatever.

This impulse toward deconstruction and idiosyncratic reconstruction has been an infuriating aspect of the Xer personality for older generations, but in fact it is a real strength. Xers are always questioning the "why" of things, pinpointing unstated but real agendas, and figuring out more practical and efficient ways of doing things. Their ability to deconstruct and reconstruct reality "on the fly" gives them a valuable kind of street smarts that has enabled them to survive and is a benefit for anyone employing them (so long as they can tolerate the caustic humor in which their critiques and evaluations are inevitably couched).

How Gen X Is Perceived

When I asked C.K. how other generations perceive Xers, he said, "I would guess they are puzzled by us, unable to figure out what we want. We must seem lazy and depressed." Indeed, other generations are not inclined to be sympathetic to Generation X. Violet, from the Silent generation, sums this up well: "I think younger generations are totally crazy. It's hard to understand why everybody's so unhappy."

Seemingly blind to the difficulties faced by Xers in their formative years, other generations fault them for being apathetic and melancholy. As Sofia, from Cleveland, Ohio, wrote, "The older generations don't get us, they don't understand how much harder things are for us. They look down on us paternalistically, using terms like 'boomerang generation,' and pin the blame for these social problems on our individual choices instead of on the shifts in societal policy and realities that happened between when they came of age and when we did."

But because older generations often consider Xers' negative traits and attitudes to be a result of failed Boomer parenting, they are forgiving of Xers. Even some Boomers, such as Nora, feel this way: "I think my generation went too far in trying to give their own kids all the 'freedoms' that we worked hard to achieve, and in doing so, failed to provide a good structure for younger folks to find their own path to independence. As a result, I think we left the generation below us adrift."

Boomers consider Xers to be younger versions of themselves, and they don't understand why Xers don't care about the things that they consider to be of utmost importance. Yet, as Richard Linklater wrote in his screenplay for the Xer manifesto film *Slacker*, "Withdrawal in disgust is not the same as apathy." Xers are not inclined to get excited about projects they deem flawed, unnecessary, or failed from the start.

Older generations are impatient with Xers' lack of allegiance to what they consider to be fundamental values such as patriotism and reverence, and Boomers can't understand why Xers won't get on board with their transformative agenda. But the fact is that Boomer visions for building a better world—universal peace and brotherhood, eradicating global hunger, of the world holding hands in a giant, orgasmic Pepsi moment—make Xers yawn, and that makes Boomer blood boil.

It's not that Xers don't think those things are important—they do, very much so (well, not the Pepsi bit). They just don't think the Boomer agenda, enacted according to the Boomer game plan, is practical or achievable. Instead of grand visions of a shining, peace-filled world, Xers are concerned with helping individual people in their neighborhoods. Xers are active volunteers—more so than any other living generations. Nearly 50% of Xers engage in some kind of volunteer work.[8] Xers are committed to making a difference in small, immediately recognizable ways. They are impatient with Boomer visions of world peace, but they will be the first to line up to feed the homeless, where they can see the fruits of their actions with their own eyes.

How Gen Xers Perceive Themselves

Xers tend to see themselves as *betrayed*. I have already mentioned many of the reasons they feel this way: from their broken homes to their latchkey abandonment as children, from the constant threat of nuclear annihilation to the wanton destruction of the environment, from the Boomers shutting them out of the job market, to the STD minefield they were forced to navigate just as they were coming of age, Xers felt betrayed at every turn. While G.I.s and Silents were passing safety net legislation to make sure their retirements would be comfy and secure, and while Boomers morphed from peaceniks into investment bankers, who was looking out for Gen X? No one.

C.K. told me, "We utterly distrust anyone who desires power over others, and automatically assume that all politicians (and other authority figures) are corrupt and self serving. We value personal experiences over owning property. We can't determine if we are successful as a generation until we figure out what we want. Most of us are going to be unprepared for getting old."

Xers realize that no one is going to look out for them but themselves. Uma said that one of the messages she received growing up was, "Take care of yourself, because no one else will. We were raised with a very 'pull yourself up by your bootstraps and make it' kind of mentality. As a woman, I was not raised to find a man to take care of me. It was very much a feeling of 'you are on your own kid, good luck.'" Some Xers, however, seeing the odds weighted against them, just gave up, not wanting to expend needless effort on a hopeless cause—in this case, tragically, that lost cause was *them*.

Uma goes on, "Honestly, I never had any hopes for our generation. We were and are always in the shadow of our parents. They lived the '60s. They changed the world. What could we possibly do? And this is supported by our parents. Everything we do or say or create in the world can never compare to what *they* did. That being said, I do see my generation as being wonderfully creative and experimental. I see a lot of creative collaboration in folks of my age."

THE SPIRITUALITY OF GENERATION X

The unique psychological makeup of Generation X makes the discernment of anything recognizable as a "conventional" spirituality (as understood by previous generations) difficult. Since they are allergic to idealism, faith and the embracing of dogma are tough sells. They are suspicious whenever religious claims are being made, and they are always keen to spot the ulterior motives of spiritual and religious leaders.

Since they distrust institutions, churches (at least in the traditional sense) hold little appeal for them. While they are likely to agree that spirituality is important, they don't see how institutional religion fits, and typically think of established churches, synagogues, and mosques as self-serving dinosaurs unworthy of their time or attention. "Let them rot," is not an uncommon attitude among Xers, who have a great deal of contempt for institutional religion and the pain, suffering, and intolerance such institutions have foisted upon the world in the name of God.

Instead of the received authority of scripture and tradition, Xers are more likely to trust their own experience, and to value their friends, their own bodies, and even popular culture as equally reliable sources of wisdom. As Interfaith minister Uma described it, "I think that spirituality is the soul and religion is the vessel. There can be many different kinds of vessels for spirituality, such as art-making, gardening, or 12-step programs, and religion is just one of them. Religion is organized and spirituality is a naturally occurring phenomenon."

Ministering to Generation X—especially if you are not from that generation—can be incredibly frustrating. They are not likely to accept time-honored ideas, they find faith in anything they cannot see with their own eyes difficult, and, most irritating of all, they feel free to render caustically cynical judgments about everything others hold dear.

The Spiritual Gifts of Generation X

Before you write them off as hopeless, however, pause to consider the spiritual gifts that Xers bring—for they are many. Xers are excellent at questioning the "why" of tradition—they bring a healthy impulse toward reformation that is helpful for any community, in almost any context. Their built-in facility for deconstruction and reconstruction can help communities reevaluate their mission, their purpose, and root out calcified practices and ideas that no longer yield fruit. Xers can then reframe a community's mission in practical, achievable terms that empower the community as-it-is, rather than in the idealized way it has perceived itself in the past.

Comfortable with ambiguity, Xers are extremely tolerant of coexisting worldviews, and do not need the members of their communities to all think alike, or even believe the same things. Beliefs are held lightly in Xer society, and take a back seat to empirical values such as kindness and respect. Instead of fighting about beliefs (which historically has bogged down spiritual communities, often causing them to split), Xers are experts at finding common ground and orienting efforts toward perceivable goals that everybody can get on board with.

None of this is to say that it is necessarily comfortable being in community or working in ministry with Xers. They love to kill sacred cows, and often annoy with their constant questioning. They also, inexplicably, see irreverence as a form of reverence, leading to religious observances that are confusing to those of other generations, since it appears that Xers are making fun of their own faith, sometimes caustically, even mercilessly. But be careful dismissing this as blasphemy—it is, instead, a form of affection, even intimacy. Xers make fun of things they love, and their joking, however maddeningly blasphemous it might seem to outsiders, is a sincere form of praise.

How Divinity Is Imaged

Xers are not opposed to the notion of God, but theirs is a very different deity than the one worshiped by their grandparents. Xers are quick to reject the "old man in the sky" notion of divinity, or, God forbid, the idea of a literal "Heavenly Father," and this is largely true even of evangelical or fundamentalist Xers, who are far more likely than previous generations to view such language as metaphor. Even so, it is not a metaphor that resonates with Xers, given their abandonment by their human parents. Kal, a clergyperson in the Independent Sacramental Movement[9] living in Nashville, confessed, "I realize that God is more than this particular tradition and its words and images, but it is the language I speak and I tend to stay increasingly firmly within it. I do think I have a stronger sense of the indwelling nature of God (God upholding us and every last bit of creation in existence at every moment) than is sometimes typical."

Indeed, like the Boomers before them, for most Xers God is a much more mystical and imminent sort of being. Rather than locating divinity "out there," as separate from creation, ruling it, as it were, from "above," Xers tend to see divinity as permeating all of creation. Sofia, a Unitarian Universalist from Cleveland, wrote, "To me, 'the Divine' is everything, every atom of the universe is divine, it is both as intimate as the tip of my nose and as distant as stars in other galaxies at the same time."

But unlike Boomers, for whom the Divine is an imminent presence who cares deeply for creation and for them, the Xer deity tends toward the impersonal. As Kate, who described herself as "independent" (not affiliated with any faith), told me, "The Divine is as intimate or distant as I bring my consciousness to it. And when I turn my consciousness to it, I don't know that it is personal or impersonal. There is not a human element to it, so I could say that the Divine is both personal and impersonal . . . and neither."

When I asked Uma (a self-identified Spiritual Eclectic) about her image of divinity, she said, "When I think about God or the

Divine, I think about a greater energetic essence. Something that is bigger than me but is also me. God has no gender, but I often refer to her as a She because it feels good to me—the Great Mother. It also helps me heal the mother and father issues I have by thinking about God as my mother and father. I feel held and guided by the Divine. I think my intuition comes from a divine place. God is both me and not me." Lara, a Christian from Arizona described divinity in similar terms: "All encompassing, mysterious, omnipresent, within, one."

Xers might concede that God cares about what happens to the world as a whole, but does God care about what happens to them, as individuals? Not so much. Xers have largely rejected the idea that the Divine is concerned for them personally, regarding this as spiritual narcissism, nor do they accept the idea that the Divine favors any one particular nation over another. They might *wish* it were otherwise, but they don't, in general, actually *believe* it. As Mia, a non-religious person living in Boulder Creek, California, described it, "I imagine an intelligence that cares but is very distant and removed from people's lives. I don't have a clear picture of what God looks like. I just know that I believe in something. I don't think all this started by accident. On the other hand, I don't feel that someone is checking in on me daily."

Similarly, Xers are hesitant to assert that the Divine favors one religion over another, and are likely to view all religions as helpful but equally flawed pathways to divine communion. Consequently, notions such as "the elect" or divine favor in any form will be hard sells for Xers. Even Xer fundamentalists are more hesitant than their forebears to render judgment on those not of their faith— such judgment, they would say, rightly belongs to God (note the success of Xer minister Rob Bell's book *Love Wins*, which makes this exact point).[10] As Presbyterian Elliot wrote, "I am not part of the crowd that says heaven is for Christians or whatever. . . . I don't set rules or even really think about heaven/hell—it's all bullshit conjecture and makes no sense to me, really. I'm interested in the intersection of the eternal and time in life as lived, not in some perfect afterlife."

Individual salvation is not a doctrine that is an easy fit for the

Xer. Since divinity is not interested in them as individuals, Xers are more open to notions of general salvation, and will be sympathetic to those working for justice or hunger relief (in small, empirically verifiable ways, of course). As C.K. (a non-religious person) described it, "Spiritually evolved people are able to see 'the big picture,' it's not about 'me' so much as it is about 'us,' and even beyond the human race to the well-being of the planet, and the universe as a whole."

Thus, Xers have a hard time accepting a deity's concern for their individual souls (a specious genus to start with), but will concede that the deity might be concerned for the survival of the biosphere and the human race in general. Towards this end, Xers are more than willing to roll up their sleeves and get to work, seeing themselves as co-workers with God in the interest of this general salvation. But unlike Boomers, who will spin grand visions of "saving the world" from hunger, poverty, and injustice, Xers will eschew such pie-in-the-sky grandiosity in favor of modest street-level efforts.

Spiritual Focus

The generations tend to alternate in their spiritual foci. The G.I.s were spiritual extroverts, while their Silent successors were spiritually introverted. Boomers lived their spirituality out loud (way loud), while Xers are once again quieter and more personally circumspect about their spirituality.

This introversion evidences itself first in Xers' lack of spiritual certainty. They are hesitant to make bold spiritual or religious claims because of an innate spiritual humility that rejects the notion that their own spirituality is "the" correct one, or implying that all the others are wrong.

If Xers follow a religious tradition, then, it is not because they are convinced that it is "correct" or "more correct" than any other, simply that it is a good fit for them, individually. Most Xers, even religious Xers, have no problems being friends (even close friends) with those of differing religious traditions, especially if they share similar values. Liberal Christians, liberal Jews, and liberal Buddhists may all be members of a single Xer tribe, and although there may be prodigious teasing about the differences, there will be real respect, too.

Consequently, Xers are loath to "push" their faith or their spirituality on others. They feel free to share what it means for *them*, but feel inauthentic insisting that it might be right for someone else, or, God forbid, for everybody. As neo-pagan Karen put it, "I believe that we each have choices to make regarding our spirituality and we cannot force anyone to chose ours. They know within themselves where they are to be and go and what to believe."

Faith, for Xers, is a profoundly personal matter. It is even considered rude in Xer circles to inquire about someone's religious or spiritual beliefs, unless the topic has emerged organically in conversation, and the information volunteered. Ironically, inquiring about the details of a person's sex life is considered *less* taboo in Xer circles than asking about the details of his or her faith life.

For those wanting to engage Xers in spiritual discussions, related topics such as meaning (and the construction thereof) and values are safe, and will often lead to an Xer volunteering information about his or her beliefs. But be aware that the very notion of "beliefs" for Xers is tricky, since reality is seen as malleable and it is acceptable to discard beliefs when other ideas that make more sense are encountered. Xers are notoriously disloyal to schools of metaphysical thought, and even among the certifiably religious, brand loyalty is rare. As Elliot put it, "I'm a bit of a freelancer when it comes to church, as are most of the people I went to high school or college with."

Dominant Faith Style

Unlike other generations that fit squarely into specific Faith Style categories, Xers generally fall into one of two types, depending upon whether they practice a religious tradition or not. Most Xers do not follow a faith tradition, and those fall into the Ethical Humanist category. Ethical Humanists reject religious truth claims, yet are possessed of a poignant and powerful mysticism nevertheless—an awareness of being a small part of all that is, and an orientation of wonder toward the cosmos. Xers are cognizant of the fact that scientific claims must be reevaluated constantly, and so are not invested in them dogmatically, yet they are a valued source of spiritual wisdom, creating a sense of awe and kinship with the natural world. As C.K. described it, "My conception of God is an entity so vast that it is beyond comprehension at the human scale. I believe the universe was created in the 'big bang,' and by design, unfolds as it must. I consider science to be that portion of the language of God that we have learned to speak ourselves."

Religiously oriented Xers, however, are more likely to fall into the Religious Agnostic category. Religious Agnostics do not know whether or not there is a divine being, but find value in the community, collective wisdom, and historical rootedness of religious traditions. Religious Agnostics practice those traditions, and thereby appropriate their benefits, but they hold them lightly, and reject exclusive truth claims made by "true believers." They choose to live "as if" the tradition were true, "as if" there were a God, without asserting that any of the dogma actually *is* true. This path, difficult as it might be due to the nay-saying of true believers to one side and atheists to the other, affords Xers their integrity, while still also allowing them their historical, family, and ethnic heritage, and the very real benefits that follow from practice of a spiritual tradition. Elliot, reflecting on the difference between "religion" and "spirituality," told me, "Religion is spirituality worrying. But religion is also spirituality with anchors, with orientation—it can make the world quit spinning."

Of course, there are Xers who actually *are* true believers, as the size and clout of the evangelical subculture clearly indicates. This is not surprising, since the burden of living in a relativistic universe is great, and many find it very stressful to have to think through every issue for themselves. Many Xers have, when faced with the gaping maw of a postmodern, deconstructed universe, simply turned tail and run for cover into more traditional paradigms.

But even these do not march in lockstep with their elders, and are likely to deconstruct and reconstruct the issues in ways that square with both their generational biases and the demands of their faith. For instance, evangelical leaders of the eighties and nineties pressed two issues *ad nauseam:* abortion and "the gay agenda." While Xer evangelicals may agree with their elders that both of these are wrong, their horizon is not eclipsed by them, and they take a back seat to issues such as poverty, the death penalty, and environmental stewardship. Evangelical Xers are also more likely to hold their faith with less arrogance and certainty than previous generations, exhibiting a great deal of respect for those of other faith traditions, and none.

Prayer Style

Xers, as spiritual introverts, usually recoil from corporate prayer. They may tolerate it in contexts where such prayer is traditional (such as church or synagogue services), but they will not be *comfortable* with it in any context, and Xers on their own will rarely pray aloud when in groups. Xer religious professionals must work hard to overcome their generational reticence in order to function properly, and this they usually can do, although they may have a good deal of inner work (deconstruction and reconstruction) in order to justify it.

Xer religious professionals can, with effort, supply all the kinds of prayer their jobs demand, but what about Xers who are not religious professionals? How do they pray? How do Xer religious professionals pray when they take off the collar?

Prayer, for Xers, is an exceedingly private affair, and Xers are loathe to speak about it. They share with their Boomer neighbors a mystical orientation, although it is of a vastly different quality. While Boomers are often drawn to a kind of "cosmic consciousness" that pervades the universe and that drove the New Age movement in its heyday in the 1980s, Xers' mysticism is of a much more impersonal variety. While Boomers seek to tap into some mysterious "spiritual energy current" that Platonically nourishes all things, Xers are more naturally Aristotelian, positing no spiritual uber-reality behind or above the phenomenal universe, but affirming the sacredness or awe-fullness of creation as it is in itself. Ken, a Unitarian Universalist, wrote, "The Divine is an ever-present presence—in everything and everyone; in totality—completely unknowable, but knowable in the people around us, the animals, the water, the wind, the rocks, the clouds, in tears and in smiles. . . ."

Their prayer is not likely to be directed towards an anthropomorphized image of divinity, nor is it likely to take the form of meditation designed to mystically connect one with the spiritual energy generating and upholding reality. Instead, Xers are more likely to sit on the beach or stare at the canopy of stars, and to feel their relatedness with the rest of matter. Science and the "New Cosmology" of such writers as Brian Swimme speak well to this orientation of awe towards creation, and a mystical sense of connectedness between the meanest creature and the farthest star. As Nick, a Christian from Texas, wrote, "I do not necessarily pray 'for' anything nor do I pray 'to' anything, but rather I hold peace and stillness and in that space I connect with *love* in its many manifestations. I still hold an expectation that love works through me to create greater good in the world, but I am open to whatever rises in my prayerful meditation. In more contemplative prayer, I follow more of a script that has me focusing on a bit of scripture or core message—and this is more about mental discipline and managing of thought than it is about connection."

In response to my questions regarding prayer, C.K. responded, "I don't pray much, as I don't believe that God really takes much of an active role in our day-to-day affairs, if any. When I want something really bad, I might silently plea to the Creator to help, but it's really more of an expression of my hopes that events transpire as I hope they do than any real expectation of divine intervention."

Sofia told me that her prayer, "takes the form of movement. I cannot meditate/pray sitting still doing nothing, it feels too uncomfortably selfish especially at this point in my life (growing family, early phase of career, etc). I connect with the divine impulses within myself and around me through art projects or dancing or driving, that kind of thing." Unitarian Universalist Ed's response is similar: "I was never much for petitionary prayer, least of all for myself, but I love thanksgiving—yoga as active meditation has been a great boon to me in trying times."

Xer prayer is often very active, and is likely to take the form of work—often on behalf of those in need. LCSW Donna in our opening vignette knows that it is just this sort of "prayer" that might help Danny find meaning in his life. While there may seem to be little in common between a Silent priest on his knees in a cathedral and an Xer spooning soup into a bowl for homeless people, both are, for their respective generations, authentic and vital forms of prayer. As neo-pagan Karen told me, "Religion is all outward trappings. It is based more on what men have said than on what the Spirit leads you to do." Xers may be openly hostile to religious dogma, trappings, and prayer forms, but put them in a situation where they can roll up their sleeves and make a difference in people's daily lives and they will respond with energy and enthusiasm. For Xers, *that's* true prayer.

Xers In Community

As we have already seen, Xers have a natural aversion to religious institutions, and have a hard time reconciling their suspicion of authority, hidden agendas, and dogma with the daily life of churches, temples, societies, or any other form of "organized religion." C.K. goes so far as to say that he rejects "all organized religions outright, and has nothing but contempt for them. They cause more harm than good and are keeping humankind from evolving spiritually." This is a common opinion among Xers.

Even for those not so hostile, it simply does not make sense to Xers to expend energy supporting institutions when, invariably, the institutions' first priority is self-preservation rather than the ideals they espouse. Sofia wrote, "My relationship with religion over the years has changed mostly because of bureaucratic crap that has been going on in my particular congregation. I come to church to connect with people, to feel a part of something bigger and more meaningful than my little day-to-day life struggles, not to play high school-style politics." Xers, therefore, are not keen to be part of traditional faith institutions, leading in part to the continued decline among mainline Christian denominations in the United States, and the lack of religious concern generally in Europe.

Yet, as Sofia's response suggests, Xers are exceedingly social animals, and "connection" is a true value for them. Furthermore, their "tribes," "packs," or "families of choice," usually gather around other common values and concerns. Just being in community, being part of a "tribe" is a spiritual practice, as social demands invariably present Xers with moral dilemmas and provide opportunities to become better people. Donna is hoping that Danny will find just such challenging community at the Catholic Worker house in our opening vignette.

It has been suggested that the coffee shop is the Xer church,[11] and indeed, such places provide a welcoming place for Xers to meet, to share their struggles and concerns, to support one another, to compare notes on literature and pop culture, and to discuss and debate ethical and theological issues. It is not far off the mark to say that, for Xers, more real spiritual inquiry and edification takes place in coffee shops than in churches or other traditional spiritual institutions.

In addition, Xers' concern for social welfare, on the ground level, is infectious, and it is not uncommon for "tribes" to pull in their friends and to gather around such activities. New "tribes" often even form amongst those who are socially engaged around their ministry sites. Xers' impulse towards "action over words" is nowhere as clearly visible as in Xer communities.

Xers who do participate in traditional religious structures will invariably come to them with a critical eye, and will have an agenda (not conscious or chosen, but generationally instilled) toward reform that demands greater transparency, greater institutional and ideological humility, and a ruthless evaluation of the most effective expenditure of effort. Elders would do well not to fight or reject Xers' questioning or ideas out of hand, but to recognize the valuable power for course-correction that they offer, the energy for reinvention that they bring, and harness that energy for the benefit of the institution.

Spiritual Growth Continuum

Although Xers are as likely as anyone else to move through James Fowler's stages of faith development,[12] how they themselves view spiritual progress is unique. Hyper-sensitized as they are to hidden agendas and hypocrisy, for Xers *authenticity = spirituality*. Xers recognize authenticity as being the premiere spiritual virtue, and religious Xers will recognize and appreciate it even in atheistic Xers. Conversely, the greatest human vice is hypocrisy, for which Xers have a very low tolerance. Marie, a Christian, describes her generation as, "less 'fakey' and more honest, natural, and authentic in our interactions with others than our parents were. We are more cultured, creative, inventive, and ingenious. We are less likely to conform just for conformity's sake, and I generally think we are more open-minded and accepting of diversity than previous generations. My generation is less formal and perhaps less pretentious than previous generations. I think we are more open and honest with ourselves and with others."

Spiritual growth, for Xers, consists of moving along a continuum that posits hypocrisy at one end (undeveloped spirituality) and authenticity at the other end (the highest development of spiritual attainment). Authenticity, in Xer estimation, includes such corollary virtues as transparency, sincerity, and personal congruity (harmonious and non-conflicting personas in all arenas of one's life). This is something Uma has been able to achieve for herself. She writes, "I think there is a search for . . . wholeness and authenticity in my generation . . . . I have truly followed an authentic life."

Because of the importance of authenticity, meaningful spiritual leadership for Xers will include "calling people on their shit," and a willingness to be honest about one's own shit (we all have it, after all). Being up front about all one's agendas will be very helpful, and exhortation towards transparency will be welcomed so long as one is transparent oneself.

Although this seems like a novel twist, what Xers are really talking about is honesty. Since, according to the Anglican Book of Common Prayer, the Divine is one before whom "all hearts are open, all desires known," and from whom "no secrets are hid"[13] this impulse to be naked and honest before God is a time-honored one indeed. Until we can be honest with ourselves, with each other, and with the Divine, how can any real spiritual progress be made? The Xers are speaking language that is culturally meaningful for their particular place in history, but the wisdom they present is timeless.

Many of those who responded balked at the notion that spiritual growth might be linear. As Ken noted, "Spiritual growth is like a spiral; I think that people can learn new things through reading, studying, talking with others and allowing themselves to be influenced by experiences. But, once new things are learned, it's important to cycle around to revisit past questions about who we are, what we are doing here, how we can make ourselves and our world better, what we believe, etc." Marie added, "I see spiritual growth as a continual process. We never actually 'get there' (at least not in this earthly life) because wherever we get, there is always somewhere higher to go."

Xers I interviewed offered some alternative continua that are also insightful. A couple of people suggested that spiritual maturity manifested as a concrete concern for others—a recurring theme for Xers. Kirk, a Lutheran, wrote, "People who have an undeveloped spirituality are very inwardly focused. They have a 'me, me, me' attitude, and they just don't have much regard for the well-being of others. Spiritually developed people are outwardly focused on the well-being of others. They lend a helping hand without thought of what's in it for them." Lara (who identifies as non-religious) is in complete agreement when she writes, "I think a person grows spiritually by one's level of acceptance or compassion for others and him or herself. An undeveloped person blames God for circumstances he or she doesn't understand. A developed person takes more responsibility for his or her actions."

One final continuum involved a movement from ignorance to knowledge. Xers are very sympathetic to the idea that knowledge is a form of salvation[14] and indeed, education has been one of the only factors going for them. C.K.'s spin on this is a journey from unconsciousness to wakefulness: "Spiritual growth is an awakening to the universe around us, gathering enough perspective to understand that others are in their skins as we are in ours. The more awake we are, the more we are able to control the infantile animal urges screaming from the more primitive mind, and truly understand what is going on around us, and operate in the ebb and flow of the world around us."

MINISTERING TO GENERATION X

Since Xers are extremely reactive to authority, those privileged to offer spiritual guidance to them would do well to maintain a non-directive style. Allowing them to set the agenda and discover for themselves how ideas and beliefs ought to be deconstructed and reconstructed will yield the most fruit. And be prepared, there will be much deconstruction and reconstruction, as this is the primary form of spiritual inquiry practiced among Xers. It may seem tiresome, tedious, and even depressingly cynical for other generations to listen as Xers pursue their relentless dismantling of reality (and tenuous reconstructions) but this is what Xers must do, and what will have the most meaning for them.

They are, after all, *making meaning*, from scratch, which is the only way Xers can appropriate meaning. Any meaning that is simply handed to them from elders, from tradition, or from any other source will be viewed with suspicion. Xers, brought up in a commercial-saturated culture where everyone is selling something will always be asking "What's the hidden agenda? What's in it for the one telling me this? What is this *really* about?" Spiritual guides who can hang in there and encourage their critical questioning will be most valuable for them.

Xers work well in one-on-one spiritual guidance, but do even better in groups. While few Xers hang out at the sorts of spiritual institutions that offer traditional spiritual direction groups (and would most likely be repelled by the hierarchical and directive method employed by many such groups), many Xers are taking their spirituality into their own hands, forming Wisdom Circles or other communities of discernment or inquiry.[15] This may take any number of forms: a Wicca ritual circle, a salon gathered around Dante's *Divine Comedy*, or a regular gathering of like-minded friends at the pub—all are regular groups that meet for mutual discernment, albeit at differing levels of commitment.

Xer discernment groups are most often self-directed, run by consensus, and operate with an open-door policy. Members come and go as they feel the need, and little peer pressure is brought to bear one way or the other—another manifestation of Xer respect for the integrity of the spiritual processes of others.

G.I.s Ministering to Xers

G.I.s may find in Xers similar traits to the Lost Generation (born between 1883 and 1900) that immediately preceded them, especially in their tendency towards bleakness, despondency, and despair. G.I.s should be careful not to lump Xers in with Boomers— yes, they may both sport outrageous fashions (note how different they are from one another, though), and they may both flaunt the established ideals and institutions you hold dear (note that they do it for different reasons). There is actually a lot of common ground between G.I. and Xers' disdain of Boomer idealism. Try having a bitch session sometime—you'll be surprised how well you get on (do make sure the room is clear of Boomers first).

G.I.s will do well to remember that Xers' critiques of pre- vious generations are not unwarranted. True, they don't respect the ideals and institutions you hold dear, but this is largely because those ideals have been betrayed by those generations that have come before them. Remember that Xers value authenticity above all things. They do not respect things or people because of some received wisdom that states that they *should*, but will only do so if the things or people are truly worthy, in their estimation.

If you want to be effective with Xers, huffy, righteous indigna- tion must be put aside. You must be willing to eat a bit of humble pie, to get in the dirt with them, to be willing to admit your foibles as well as your strengths. Xers will love and respect you even if you are the most sordid sort of rascal—so long as you are up front about it. More than any other generation since . . . well, since your- selves, Xers know the value of a sincere penitent.

Do not take Xers' critiques personally—they are directed at whole generations, not at you individually. If you can bear the burden of their collective anger toward your generation without becoming angry, and especially if you can see their points and take responsibility for what you can, you will go far in making Xer friends. In other words, just let them vent without trying to defend yourself (or your generation). They may be wrong about some things, but they are probably right about others. So fess up to all you can, and you can create a bedrock of mutuality and trust to work from.

Xers share with G.I.s a can-do willingness to roll up their sleeves and work, and working together toward mutually affirmed goals can create community in a powerful way. Xers will appreciate your no-nonsense approach to spirituality, and you will find a lot of common ground in how you live that out. Be aware, however, that your strategies for doing so are diametrically opposed to one another. While Xers and G.I.s will have much agreement in what needs to be done, the G.I. impulse is to create institutions to carry the work forward. Xers, however, are hostile to institutions in general and will seek to avoid involvement with them, preferring to get their own hands dirty and to work on projects where they can see immediate results.

You may think this uncooperative and inefficient, but remember that Xers' distrust of institutions is not unjustified. Neither of you are wrong in your approaches, you are just coming from different generational cultures. If you must, think of it this way: Xers have been wounded by institutions, and so they do not trust them. That's just the reality, and you must deal with it. You will get nowhere trying to talk them out of it.

So while G.I. ministry is largely institutionally focused, Xer spirituality is lived out largely outside of institutions. In those cases where Xers are involved in your institution, do not casually dismiss their critiques or you will blow off the next generation of leaders. Instead, assume that they have valid points and ideas, and seek to accommodate them. After all, if Jesus is to be believed, the institutions are there to serve *people*, the people are not there to serve the institutions.[16]

G.I.s who want to be effective with Xers will seek to understand their institutional allergy and work *with* this idiosyncrasy, rather than against it. Xers will often volunteer for an institution's work project—providing much needed muscle—so long as they do not have to join the institution. And creating good will between Xers and an institution is no mean feat.

G.I. spiritual directors must keep in mind that Xer spirituality is rarely lived out within the bounds of religious institutions, and should not seek to force this issue. Understand that Xers find spiritual community in other places, and this is very much to be encouraged. Xers' view of divinity will be very different from your own, and you must be willing to accommodate that. The Xer God will not usually take a human form, and may not be self-aware. Xers may see themselves as part of a "sacred web of being" that may not be conscious of individuals, or if aware, may not care that much about them. There is some common ground between the G.I. concern for the whole over the individual, here, and the Xer God, although cosmetically they may seem quite different.

The biggest difficulty may be assumptions about spiritual growth. While G.I.s tend to see spiritual development as a movement from rebellion to obedience, Xers will see rebellion against hypocrisy as virtuous. Loyalty to people, ideas, and institutions that are a given for G.I.s will simply not be so for Xers, for whom everything and everyone must initially be viewed with suspicion.

On the other hand, authenticity is a virtue that G.I.s can affirm and relate to under another name: honesty. Honesty is a great virtue for G.I.s and if you can orient yourself towards that in ministry to Xers, you can establish a ground of commonality, trust, and community.

Silents Ministering to Xers

Much of what I have said above regarding G.I. ministry to Xers will pertain to Silents as well, specifically regarding institutions and honesty. A point of pain between Xers and Silents is that the generational project of Silents—the humanization of institutions—will seem meaningless to Xers, for whom institutions should simply be left to rot as lost causes. It is true that Xers do not understand how hard you have worked to address the very issues that have caused them to reject institutions, and if enough trust can be built, they may even be able to acknowledge that.

Silents will find that Xers are sympathetic to their concern for others, and their commitment to compassion. Silent rhetoric typically goes over well with Xers, who can generally support Silent

ideals, if not their means. Preaching for Xers is easy for Silents—
Xers get what they are trying to say, and often agree. Getting Xers
to roll up their sleeves for hands-on ministry is also easy, so long
as the work is directly with the needy and not indirect aid medi-
ated by an institutional hierarchy.

The Xer God is far less interested in individuals than the Silent
God is. Individuals in general matter less, in the Xer schema—a
humble corrective to the hubris of preceding generations. Silents
must be careful when ministering to Xers not to appeal to an
anthropomorphic deity that will sound absurd to Xers. If divinity
is concerned with human life, it is on a grand scale. This is an
interesting dichotomy in Xer thought—Xers are only interested
in helping one-on-one, but do not generally see the deity as being
concerned with individuals. Xers may see themselves as partners
with God, taking up the slack in the grand scheme of things. Not
bad for slackers.

Xers will also be sympathetic to the Silent notion that spirituality is a private matter. Repelled by the must-be-seen-by-the-neigh-
bors, religion-as-public-display approach of the G.I.s and offended
by the obtrusive, in-your-face spirituality of the Boomers, both
Silents and Xers appreciate the personal, quiet, ain't-nobody's-
business-if-I-do approach to spirituality and religious practice.
Silents can trust their instincts in this regard when ministering to
Xers, who are likely to be uncomfortable praying aloud, or even
appealing to a personal deity at all.

Silents are uniquely situated to minister effectively to Xers.
They are too old to automatically trigger them the way Boomers
do, and their simple, quiet, supportive presence may remind them
of their grandparents—not a bad place to start for ministry. Xers
trust Silents more than any other living generation, and are more
likely to open up to them. If Silents can withdraw their own projections, being careful not to confuse Xers with Boomers (a common
and deadly mistake), and have some sympathy for the difficulties
Xers have had to face, a strong and meaningful rapport can be
formed that may facilitate effective ministry and healing.

Silents make excellent therapists and spiritual directors for
Xers, as their naturally compassionate natures bring out the best

in Xers, who are often grateful for the kindness, the attention, and the welcome lack of judgment.

Boomers Ministering to Xers

This is one of the toughest combinations in this book, although Boomers have a hard time seeing it. As already stated, Boomers tend to see Xers as younger versions of themselves, and are often blind to the generational distinctions that separate them. Xers share none of the Boomers' idealism, and, in fact, are forcefully allergic to it. This is not Generation X being adolescent or difficult, this is a different world-view, and Boomers will get nowhere so long as they treat Xers as recalcitrant Boomers.

Boomers and Xers are diametrically opposed in most areas that matter, ministerially. Boomers want to change the world, Xers want to help out in their neighborhood. Boomers want to discover the Truth, Xers want to discover lunch. Boomers live their spirituality out loud and proud, while Xers are quiet and circumspect about such matters. Boomers have a hunger for transcendence, while Xers are so firmly planted on planet earth that they suffer limited mobility.

In order to minister effectively to Generation X, Boomers must be willing to set aside their judgments about them, and meet them as real people with ideas, feelings, and concerns that matter. If you can meet Xers at the point of their need, have compassion for Xers' immediate pain, or help with the problem that is in front of them, you will gain their trust and their appreciation.

Xers will not be the slightest bit interested in grand schemes or ideologies, however, so it is best to leave these on a hook outside the door. Boomers are possessed of an almost irrepressible optimism that is quickly tiresome for Xers. Boomers would do well not to try to talk Xers out of their existential funks, but to simply enter into such dark places with them, in compassion and solidarity. If there is any hint that you are impatient with—or disapprove of—their pessimism or *ennui*, you will lose them.

Boomer therapists and spiritual directors will do well to focus on practical ministry as an expression of Xer spirituality. "Touchy-feely" approaches to faith or personal development are usually repellent to Xers, who will prefer to ground their spirituality in community service, art, or intellectual inquiry rather than in prayer or meditation.

In spite of the formidable generation gap, there is much that Boomers and Xers have in common. Xers and Boomers both distrust hierarchy and authority. The difference is that Boomers think they can do it better, while Xers consider the notion of leadership itself as flawed. Both Xers and Boomers are concerned with reform, both of society and religion, although Xers are less convinced progress can be made in any organized fashion. Both Boomers and Xers are concerned for peace, justice, and human rights—but Boomers must be cautious not to appeal to utopian futures or grand schemes for bringing them about, as such talk will cause Xers to sigh and walk the other way.

Boomers and Xers both enjoy contemporary music in worship, but Xers are far more willing to value tradition (so long as it is held in an experimental and non-dogmatic way). If you ask Xers which they would prefer for worship music, a rock band or Gregorian chant, most Boomers will take the rock band, but fully half of the Xers will choose the chants.

There is a great deal of healing that needs to be done between Boomers and Xers, and any relationship between these two generations will be rocky until it is done. Xers feel powerfully betrayed by Boomers, and so long as Boomers are convinced of their own righteousness and refuse to admit their mistakes or make amends, this is not likely to change. The fact is that the runaway idealism of Boomers caused them to behave in irresponsible ways that directly and negatively impacted Generation X. Boomers, as a whole, refuse to acknowledge this, and until they do, the chasm between these two vital generations will remain a wide one.

This problem is compounded by generational tendencies, theologically. The majority of Boomers felt oppressed by G.I. and Silent institutional religion, and threw out as cruel and misguided such notions as sin and redemption, substituting more user-friendly (and often Eastern-inflected) concepts such as illusion and mindfulness. At worst, Boomers might admit to "mistakes," but in general Boomers are allergic to theological notions that smack of judgment or absolutism. Xers, however, believe in sin—on both the personal and societal levels—and they want Boomers to confess. The stalemate—and the estrangement—is most likely going to be a long one.

Millennials Ministering to Xers

Millennials have much in common with Xers—both are wired, both are connected, both have a tendency to form "tribes" and have a grounded, realistic view of the world. But there are major differences, too, that impact Millennials' ability to minister effectively to Xers.

For one thing, Xers are not likely to view happiness as a virtue, and if Millennials try to talk Xers out of their misery they will turn them off quickly. Sure, it's an intuitive approach that works well for other Millennials, but "happiness" is not a coin with much worth in the Xer universe. Xers take it for granted that happiness is an ephemeral emotion that comes and goes, not a permanent residence to be pursued and dwelt within. I know this is maddening, Millennials, and doesn't make much sense, but trust me on this one. Xers have nothing against *being* happy, they just don't see it as a realistic goal for themselves. They value *survival* over happiness, and if they can survive, they will be happy (or the functional equivalent thereof). So, no happy-talk, please.

Xers are too wounded by their childhoods to be as hopeful as you are. Millennials who are impatient with them will lose them. Compassion is a better strategy, even if it is hard to see where they are coming from. Remember that even though Xers may seem a dreary and depressed lot to you, they are hard-working, resilient, and able to bear a lot of punishment. They actually kind of thrive on it. Go figure.

Xers will appreciate your no-nonsense approach to problem solving and your creativity, so when you encounter Xers in a tough place, brainstorming strategies with them will be helpful. This is especially true when cooperating with them in ministry or working with them in the field.

When working with them as therapists or spiritual directors, however, be careful not to veer into "fixing" or "problem solving" too quickly or too often. The temptation can be great, since Xers often seem "stuck" in negative thinking or behaviors, and ways ahead seem so clear (to you). Our opening vignette shows a therapist responding out of this very kind of frustration. Who knows, it *might* help Danny, but it's best to let him find his own way to daylight.

In worship, remember that Xers are likely to be very identified with their own pain, and will bring that into their worship experience. They will want to focus on difficult questions such as "Why is there suffering if God has the power to stop it?" and "How can I make meaning in a world that has none?" This may seem overdramatic to you, and you might be right. Nevertheless, such issues are important to Xers, and to the extent that you can indulge them a certain amount of darkness and negativity in their worship, they will be. . . well, not happy, but fulfilled. You may feel yourself becoming impatient with yet another song in a minor key, but at least Xers know how to keep the toes tapping.

Go ahead and roll your eyes at Xers' bleak assessment of the landscape, too. They know it's over the top and mock it themselves, so they won't be offended if you do it, too. Plus, humor is, for them, a means of making meaning, of promoting intimacy and bonding. You grew up on Xer humor so you know how that works. A well-placed barb can serve as a useful corrective for Xers, who are more likely to take the hint than to take offense.

Millennials and Xers share a roll-up-your-sleeves approach to spirituality, and work well together. Millennials have more capacity for vision than Xers do, though, so while the Millennials would do better (and will go farther) tending to the big picture, they can utilize Xer muscle well by putting them to work in the trenches. Xers don't mind, that's where they feel like they are doing the most good. Unlike Boomers, however, Millennials can see the big picture without a distorted sense of proportion and can make plans that are both idealistic *and* achievable—a combination that is going to serve Millennials well. Consequently Xers are more likely to trust Millennial visioning because it seems grounded in reality and in touch with basic human needs, and can be convinced to commit to their projects.

Now, Millennials, I know you don't need Xers' help, but take pity on them and let them do the grunt work. They like it, and it will leave you freer to actually save the world.

CHAPTER FIVE

THE "CONNECTED" GENERATION —MILLENNIALS

Eighteen-year-old Justin received an invitation to join a Facebook group called Sexuality and Spirit. Since he considers himself keenly interested in both of these subjects, he joined to see what other people had to say about it.

For the first few days, most of the postings were banal, making smutty jokes, but then he read a posting that stopped him in his tracks. A girl named Elvira asserted that sexuality and spirituality were the same thing, that sexuality is the desire to connect, and spirituality was the awareness of connection.

That insight made his head swim, and he began to look at his family, his friends, and even the guy he had a crush on in a new light. He reposted Elvira's remarks to his Facebook wall and articulated how this insight had affected him. He followed up on the Sexuality and Spirit page with an extended post on his change in perspective.

Some of his friends pooh-poohed this insight. His mother (also a Facebook friend) asked him what he had been smoking, and could she have some of that, too? But the best response came from the Sexuality and Spirit page, when he received a friend request from Elvira.

THE FIRST WAVE of Millennials are now in early adulthood. They are the largest generation the United States has ever known—nearly eighty million strong,[1] they are 21% larger than the Baby Boomer generation.[2] They will soon be exerting an irresistible influence in our culture, and their tastes and sensibilities are already strongly reflected in popular media.

It is hard to generalize about a group as wildly diverse as the Millennials—especially since diversity is something that they embrace and cherish. Most Millennials have close friends who are nothing like themselves, not because it is "politically correct" to do so, but simply because they *are* this way—"everybody's different" is one of their favorite phrases, and difference is simply not an issue.[3] Nevertheless, based on my own interviews and extensive research by several sociologists,[4] many generalizations are possible: the Millennials are relentlessly hopeful, relationship-driven, well educated, and committed to making peace wherever they happen to be. Of course, they have their problems, too, as we shall see.

Birth Years and Place in the Cycle

Millennials were born between 1981 and 2001. At first, generational theorists called this generation "Generation Y," seeing them as a kind of Gen X "lite." Yet in many ways, Millennials seem like mirror opposites of their Gen X neighbors. They are hopeful, optimistic, and largely happy (a very significant factor in Millennial spirituality). Millennial children have known more care, companionship, and privilege than any previous generation in history—which, as we shall see, has turned out to be a mixed blessing.

Following the reactive Xers, the wheel would appear to have come full circle: according to Strauss and Howe's theory of generational cycles, Millennials are expected to be the next Civic generation in the cycle. And yet, the Millennials are shaping up to be a stunningly un-civic generation—the watchwords of the G.I. Civics simply ring false to Millennials. Concepts like "personal responsibility" or "civic duty" are likely to be met with incomprehension.

I will proceed with the assumption that Millennials are indeed a new Civic generation—they are young, and this theme may simply be slow in emerging, as indeed it was for the first-wave G.I.s. But there is also the possibility that we have skipped a Civic generation, and the Millennials are actually a new Adaptive generation.[5] As we shall see below, the Millennials are strongly conciliatory, and they exhibit many more traits in common with Silents than they do with G.I.s, at least on the surface of things.

If the Millennials are indeed Civic, they are clearly *not* your grandfather's Civic generation. This is not a generation who believes in "shoulds"—which for Millennials smacks of division, coercion, and judgment (an unholy trinity in the Millennial universe).[6] They live instead in a world in which moral and cultural relativism reigns supreme.

Formative Events

By the time the first Millennials were born, the disastrous results of the poor parenting practices that resulted in the "latchkey" kids of Generation X had become screamingly obvious. First wave Xer parents and last wave Boomer parents were united in vowing that it would be different for their children—and so it was.

It was a cultural about-face that went almost completely unrecognized in the media, and yet was nearly universal. No longer did most homes have two working parents—latchkey kids were a thing of the past. Overwhelmingly, parents of Millennials committed to one parent being home at all times. Furthermore, Millennial children were doted upon to a degree unknown by previous generations. No hurt went unassuaged, no owie went unkissed. Rarely did Millennials have an unscheduled hour—their calendars were as full as their parents'. Soccer, music lessons, folk dancing, tutors, you name it—Millennial children were given more attention than they could possibly absorb.

The parents of Millennials were dubbed "helicopter parents" because of the close attention they gave to every aspect of their children's lives.[7] While this term is usually used derisively, as a result of this close parenting, Millennials' relationships with their parents and families are often strong, loving, and intact. Nine out of ten Millennials report that their parents had a "positive influence" on them.[8]

That influence is not just formative, but ongoing. Eighty-seven percent of Millennials value their parents as an important source of advice and assistance.[9] Kari told the Rainers, "I call my mom about every little detail," while Mike told them he uses his parents, "as my personal consultants."[10] Twenty-something Stephanie told the Rainers, "My parents have been my champions all of my life. It's only natural for me to call on them when I need help or advice. They live in the Boston area, and I live across the country in Oregon. But that doesn't matter. We talk to each other every week, sometimes several days a week. If I have a question on almost anything, I call Mom or Dad."[11]

As Nancy Gibbs wrote for *Time*, "Kids and parents dress alike, listen to the same music, and fight less than previous generations."[12] Note that in our opening example above, Justin's mother was one of his Facebook friends—not an uncommon phenomenon for this generation. Lyra, from Gainesville, Florida, told me, "My experience of the world has been blessed because I have two loving parents and have never had to deal with financial trouble or heavy conflict at home."

This good will extends to other adults and mentors as well. Millennials view their parents as friends, and their professors and bosses as peers and coworkers. In fact, 94% of Millennials said that they greatly respect older generations.[13]

Family and an extended circle of close friends compose the center of the Millennial universe. When the Rainers asked one Millennial what was most important in life, she responded, "My parents, my husband, and friends. They are really the most important things to me in my life. I hope we all can have good health and a happy life."[14]

This sort of parenting has resulted in a generation that is profoundly *relational*. It is hard to underestimate the importance of this, as we shall see. Relationships are the one fixed point in the Millennial universe. Everything is evaluated according to how it contributes to or detracts from their ability to tend to their relationships. Jobs, for Millennials, are evaluated not so much by pay or benefits, but in terms of work-life balance—whether it will provide them sufficient time off to enjoy the relationships that they so cherish. Millennial coach Jason Dorsey told *60 Minutes*, "We definitely put lifestyle and friends above work. No question about it."[15] Alicia of Hartford, Connecticut agreed, saying, "Life is short. I am determined to enjoy the best of every relationship I can."[16]

From this insular world—almost womb-like, surrounded by love and care—Millennials were jolted awake by the events of September 11, 2001—the single most important world event in their memories. In Greenberg's research, 83% of the Millennials he interviewed rated 9/11 near the top of their list of formative events.[17] As a young man named Noel told the Rainers, "I think 9/11 will be the shaping event of our generation. It sure was for me. I have replayed the events of that day a thousand times in my mind. It really makes me focus on things that matter most, like family and friends."[18]

Ed, from San Francisco, California, told me that the 9/11 event "felt karmic for the United States. The shock was at the visceral experience of it—I was in New York, so I could smell it, you know? Those feelings permeated my body. It was an interesting combination of shock and nonsurprise."

The 9/11 event covered the Millennial world in a cloud of suspicion and overzealous caution. It made them aware of the world beyond their immediate families and friends, but left them uncertain how to respond to it. For the most part, they ignore it, but it never completely goes away. It is always a dark cloud hanging on the horizon—because Millennials are never sure if or when it may happen again. The protective bubble of their world was smashed by the terrorists every bit as much as the twin towers were.

The Boomers' response to the terror attacks was swift, however, leading to a so-called "war on terror" in Afghanistan and Iraq that utterly depleted the U.S. economy. This has also significantly impacted Millennials' world, as the bottom dropped out of the labor market just as this generation was entering it. Deni, from Addison, Texas, feels like her world is "in crisis because of the failing economy and large debt, but most people seem mostly unaware or seem to not care from my generation." This "lack of care" may simply be part of a generational tendency not to get too worked up about things they cannot change (a pragmatic trait they share with Xers). But Deirdre, from Huntington Beach, California, was less complacent: "I think overall the world is happy. How bad the economy is, though, makes everyone feel like they are deprived. I feel like a lot of people are happy with their lives but everyone wants more. Because that is human nature—to want more. But we can't get more money or better jobs with the economy the way it is."[19]

Global terrorism may be the most dramatic threat on the Millennial horizon, but global warming runs a close second on the Millennial tragedy hit parade: 65% rated it in their top formative influences.[20] Millennials are quite aware of what it means to them and their world—and they are also aware that there is little willingness among current leaders to address it. If it is going to be addressed, they know it will probably be by them.

Becca, from Oakland, California, told me, "Climate change—learning about it made me realize that the rest of the world hates America sometimes, and it prompted me to look into how America interacts with other countries politically. It has shaped my political views and my views of my personal responsibility to the world, to the environment. It got me thinking about how climate change really relates to environmental justice issues, just a kind of a widening of a worldview, how interdependent our actions are and we all are . . . . I do feel like people are good and the world is magical and great, but I also see people being careless. It's that more than a particular badness. People don't see how their actions affect others, they're not mindful of that. It isn't that the world is a bad place; it's just that people don't pay attention enough."

This conciliatory tone is typical of Millennials—they acknowledge that there is a problem, but are loathe to actually blame anyone for it. Whether or not they will take responsibility for it and create the political and economic drive needed to change things remains to be seen. Still, Millennials seem undaunted by these and other rough spots in our recent history, and seem to be sailing merrily on toward an ever-brighter future.

Experience of the World

What has shaped the Millennial experience of the world is not an event, but an evolution—specifically, the evolution of technology. The Millennial experience of the world cannot be understood apart from it, since so much of their lives actually take place in a virtual environment. The majority of their communication, socializing, entertainment, homework, and creative expression takes place online, through their computers or hand-held devices. As Lori from Encinitas, California, told me, "The invention of the Internet has had a huge impact on my life. Even the iPhone helps me with grad school. We have lots of options, you know?"

Lena from Westminster, Colorado, was more reflective: "As a whole, I feel like the world is not in a very happy place. I think it was probably a lot happier a couple of generations ago. What happiness we have now is only because we have so much technology. We're happy because we rely on things a lot. If it weren't for technology allowing us to do all of the things that we are able to do, we would be devastated. In generations before, kids would go out to hang out with their friends or to visit family. Now they just stay home and play on the computer or talk to their friends through text or on Facebook. If it weren't for those things, people just wouldn't know what to do. I think that if technology were suddenly taken away people would just lose their minds."[21]

The use of technology feeds into what is probably the most important and distinctive characteristic of this generation: connection. Their primary experience of the world is one of connection—connection to their parents, grandparents, other family members, friends, and (through online technology) the whole of the world. In fact, it is impossible to overemphasize the significance of the Internet, texting, and other technology in the lives of Millennials. According to one study, 83% of them sleep with (or beside) their cell phones,[22] not wanting to be separated from the instant access they have to an ever-widening network of friends. Researchers have determined that fully one-third of this generation's waking life is spent online or otherwise engaged with computers.[23]

While these might seem like alarming statistics to older generations, for Millennials they are just simple facts of life, no more to be analyzed or criticized than the fact that milk comes in cartons. It is important to remember that technology is not an end in itself for Millennials, but the means to an end, and that end is *interpersonal intimacy*. Again, for older generations this might seem counterintuitive, seeing technology as largely cold and impersonal—but that is not how Millennials perceive it at all. What we view as impersonal, they simply see as efficient. And necessary.

The "will to connect" is almost obsessive for Millennials (as any parent who has tried to separate his or her children from their cell phones can attest). Christian Smith, in his ongoing research on the Millennial generation, writes, "Managing personal relationships turns out for many to be not a distinct task reserved for routinely scheduled times of the day or week, but rather a ubiquitous, 24/7 life activity. Myriad friends and family members are always available at their fingertips, through cell phones, texting, IMing, blogging, and messaging."[24]

Being "trapped offline," or being for any length of time disconnected from their circle of intimates can cause significant trauma for Millennials, and can trigger severe anxiety, depression, and crises of identity. We may, in fact, be seeing before our very eyes the formation of Teilhard de Chardin's Noosphere, the "hive mind." As Teilhard described it, "The idea is that of the Earth not only covered by myriads of grains of thought, but enclosed in a single thinking envelope so as to form a single vast grain of thought on the sidereal scale, the plurality of individual reflections grouping themselves together and reinforcing one another in the act of a single unanimous reflection."[25] Teilhard thought that this was the next step in human evolution, and indeed, we may be seeing the emergence of a new kind of human being—one that does not simply *desire* to be connected, but who *must* be connected in order to function.

Older generations may view this "instant" and non-physical connection as a danger, as the desire—and perhaps ability—to interact face-to-face becomes less pronounced. Todd and Victoria Bucholz report that, "Back in the early 1980s, 80% of eighteen-year-olds proudly strutted out of the D.M.V. with newly minted licenses . . . . By 2008—even before the Great Recession—that number had dropped to 65% . . . . John Della Volpe, who directs polling at Harvard's Institute of Politics [said], 'I spoke with a kid from Columbus, Ohio, who dreamed of being a high school teacher. When he found out he'd have to move to Arizona or the Sunbelt, he took a job in a Columbus tire factory.'"[26] Why drive when one can simply hop online? Why deal with the mess and trouble of roads, paperwork, and vehicles when the information superhighway is faster, more reliable, and (in some ways) safer? Indeed, why deal with messy face-to-face interactions at all?

Xer Marie, the mother of a Millennial, echoes this concern: "My son reads Greek philosophers and other classics, learns to play musical instruments, learns languages, watches classes from many universities, interacts with people all over the world, zooms into all kinds of places with Google earth, and learns just about anything he wishes with today's technology. On the negative side, it has become very easy to socialize solely online and to miss out on physical activity and face-to-face interaction."

All the research on this generation agrees that relationship is the center of their lives, and that their happiness is dependent upon maintaining good and vigorous connections with others. Smith's research reveals something slightly more ominous, however: while the circle of their relationships is vivid and alive, the world beyond that circle seems remote and unreal.[27] As Lyra told me, "I think most of my experience of the world has been shaped by my family and friends and less by national events."

Seth, from Pasadena, California, is even more explicit about this ironic "disconnect" of the Connected Generation: "I don't see any major world events having affected my experience in a direct way. I feel like I grew up and became aware of things without that being a part of it. I think you grow and become aware of things without something like that necessarily affecting it." Thus, while Millennials are extremely—some might say obsessively— active in generating and maintaining their intimate circles in both real-world and virtual arenas (a distinction they might perceive as spurious), they are largely remote, disinterested observers of larger cultural, civic, and political life.[28]

What Are they Seeking?

The one thing that Millennials are searching for more than any-thing else is *happiness*. It is clear from their responses that for this generation, happiness is the supreme goal of life. Regardless of what question is asked, happiness is the standard against which everything else is measured. Seth told me, "We wanna be happy and have a nice life. I don't feel like there's as much of a sense of community and self-sacrifice as there was in previous generations. I mean, most people don't wanna step over other people in their own happiness, but we don't necessarily take into account doing right by the community in making decisions about our happiness. We're a bit of a 'me' generation in that way."

Derek told the British researchers, "Happiness is the ideal you aim for."[29] Likewise, when Smith asked 19-year-old June what she ultimately wanted to get out of life, she answered, "To be healthy, happy, to have a home, have my baby Ben, and for him to be healthy and happy. Have all my body parts, not be in a wheelchair, not be blind, or get any serious illnesses, anything like that. Pretty much I just want to be healthy and happy, that's really all I want to accomplish."[30]

The British researchers have identified something they call a "happy midi-narrative" that seems to be nearly universal among Millennials. They explain that while a meta-narrative is a story about how the world works on a grand scale, and a mini-narrative is a story about how an individual's life works, a midi-narrative is something in-between—it is a story about how the circle of intimates that a person knows and cares about works. Because most Millennials are cut off (or at least largely disinterested) in how the world at large works, the midi-narrative is the primary story operative in the Millennial psyche.

Anglican writer Francis Gardom, in reviewing the British research, summed up the happy midi-narrative this way: "1) the central goal in life is to be happy; 2) happiness is eminently achievable through relationships with family and close friends; 3) . . . consumption of the resources of popular culture will provide it."[31] So which is it that brings happiness, relationships or consumer culture? The answer seems to be *yes*.

For Millennials, the goal of life is to be happy; if you are doing things right, you will be happy, and if you are not happy, then you are doing something wrong. While this may smack of a blame-the-victim approach, it seems to be working for them so far—by and large, Millennials are a pretty happy lot.

Yet there is something disconcerting about the way they hold this orientation. Happiness for me and mine may not translate into happiness for others. Brad told Smith, "I'm leaning toward taking care of number one, what would make me happy, help me get ahead. You've got to do what's right for you."[32] And when Smith asked June how she tells right from wrong, she answered that she would "probably do what would make me feel happy. Whatever situation I'd be in, whatever situation that would make me happy, that's what I would go for."[33]

When I asked Natalie, from Portland, Oregon, what she was searching for, she pointed to another dominant theme for Millennials: "Validation," she said. She elaborated, "Validation from our employers, our peers, our family, most of all our government!" The Millennials' primary Achilles' heel seems to be an obsessive need for approval. They were brought up in an environment in which their self-esteem was bolstered at every turn. Consequently, they are accustomed to a constant stream of external approval, and in its absence are not good at supplying it themselves. As Jason Dorsey said, "Our parents really took from us that opportunity to fall down on our face and learn how to stand up."[34]

This has caused problems for Millennials entering the workplace, where they expected the same sort of supportive environments they have always known at home and at school. Millennial work coach Mary Crane told *60 Minutes*, "You now have a generation coming into the workplace that has grown up with the expectation that they will automatically win, and they'll always be rewarded, even for just showing up."[35] So when met with the often dog-eat-dog realities of the office, the Millennial attrition rate has been alarming—so much so that some employers have discovered that in order to retain them they have had to hire "ego-strokers" in order to bolster Millennials' self-esteem.

As Jeffrey Zaslow wrote for the *Wall Street Journal*, "Corporations including Lands' End and Bank of America are hiring consultants to teach managers how to compliment employees using email, prize packages, and public displays of appreciation. The 1,000-employee Scooter Store Inc., a power-wheelchair and scooter firm in New Braunfels, Texas, has a staff 'celebrations assistant' whose job it is to throw confetti—25 pounds a week—at employees. She also passes out 100 to 500 celebratory helium balloons a week. The Container

Store, Inc. estimates that one of its 4,000 employees receives praise every 20 seconds, through such efforts as its 'Celebration Voice Mailboxes'."[36]

Nor have the Millennials' parents stopped hovering, just because their kids are adults in the work force. Crane reports, "Career services departments are complaining about the parents who are coming to update their child's resume. And in fact, you go to employers, and they're starting to express concern now with the parents who will phone HR, saying, 'But my little Susie or little Johnny didn't get the performance evaluation that I think they deserve.'"

Of course, we all want happiness and validation, but for Millennials, the desire for these two things seem to eclipse all other concerns.

Disposition

Just like the Civic generation before them—the G.I.s—Millennials are optimists. In fact, they are almost relentless in their optimism, even when there seems to be little reason for it. Smith says that the young adults his team interviewed were "some of the most optimistic people we have ever encountered or listened to—at least when it comes to their own personal lives and futures. For the most part their eyes are firmly set on the future, and they look to it with great hope and confidence."[37] Smith also notes that those who have thus far had pretty rough-and-tumble existences, "tend nevertheless to gird themselves up with hope and confidence that things will get better, that the future will be bright."[38]

This optimism extends to their professional futures, as well as the future of the world. The Rainers' study revealed that 96% of their respondents agreed with the statement, "I can do something great."[39] Emily told them, "I really plan to make some contribution to this world in my lifetime. I don't care if I rise to the top of an organization or become a political power broker. I just want to make a contribution."[40] Ashley added, "I really see the sky as the limit for what I can do in this world. I guess some people think that being president of the United States or CEO of a big company is a super-ambitious goal. Not me. That's not how I think. I don't think in terms of positions or money; I really think about doing something to change the world for the better. You know, I really believe I can do something like that. I really believe in me.'[41]

Jess Rainer suggests that the root of this optimism is the constant bolstering of Millennial self-esteem by their parents and teachers. He writes, "Parents have instilled a belief in us that we can do anything. Teachers have taught us that we can accomplish whatever we want as long as we put our mind to it. We not only have the belief that we can make a difference; we have the desire to do so.'[42]

Becca expanded on this theme when she wrote, "Maybe a lot of us were taught in college that we need to give back, and maybe it goes back to the 'You're special' generation thing. A lot of criticism has been made of how our generation was raised, telling us that we're special and good at things and exceptional, and I think that I saw that in college. Maybe not as much of a 'You're special,' but more of a 'You've been given exceptional opportunities, not everyone has had those opportunities,' so there's a lot of pressure associated with that. A lot of people I've been talking to, they want to make a difference, make an impact, especially with their careers."

This idea of "making a difference," emerges often in conversations with Millennials. Ben, from Seffner, Florida, told me, "Seems right now that my generation is mostly seeking a way to right the wrongs and [find] balance in the world—to find our place in a society and a world that is in flux more so than previously."

But as much as Millennials express the desire to "make a difference," and believe they have the mental means to do so, they admit to cluelessness as to how to actually go about it. Becca continued, saying, "There's pressure, you know, to go out and be something really big and make a difference and use everything you've been given to make the world a better place. But then there's the realization that this is a huge task, you know? Like, which world problem should we tackle first? I think that might be why people are struggling to find their place, or try to conquer whatever problems they might want to attack."

Smith's study, while affirming Millennials' optimism and

desire to "do something big," is far less optimistic about their ability to do so. He writes that Millennials "have extremely modest to no expectations for ways society or the world can be changed for the better. Very few are idealistic or activist when it comes to their making a mark on the world . . . . Most of them are withdrawn from the public square and instead submerged in interpersonal relationships in their private worlds . . . . Almost none have any vision of a common good. Citizenship is not a word to be found on their tongues. Some even said they were not planning on voting in the upcoming election. The extent of public disengagement among the vast majority of emerging adults is astonishing."[43]

Generational Project

Given that the Millennials embody such a paradox—between an inflated opinion of their own potential on one hand and an almost non-existent ambition to actually do anything about it on the other—one wonders just what it is they are here to do.

While the Rainers' study revealed that an astonishing 77% of Millennials affirmed the statement, "I am motivated to serve others in society,"[44] only about 35% actually do so—a lower percentage than any other living generation.[45] When asked about this lack of engagement, one Millennial told Smith, "I actually don't have time for it. I feel like if I'm going to do something good for the community I might as well do something good that I get paid for too. I mean like, uh huh, but I don't have a lot of time."[46]

Nor, in fact, do Millennials generally think that people have a *responsibility* to help others. Smith writes, "The majority of those interviewed stated . . . that nobody has any natural or general responsibility or obligation to help other people . . . . If somebody wants to help, then good for that person. But nobody has to. Some simply declared, 'That's not my problem.' Others said, 'I wish people would help others', but they really have no duty to do that at all. It's up to them, their opinion."[47]

This is a long way from the mindset of the last Civic generation—the G.I.s. Or is it? The G.I. Generation were powerful advocates of self-determination, and often opposed government assistance. And yet, most G.I.s were deeply compassionate people who did not hesitate to go out of their way for another—even someone whom they did not know. What made them this way?

Crisis clearly had something to do with it—something that Millennials have little first-hand experience of. We do well to remember that when first-wave G.I.s were the same age that Millennials are at the time of this writing, the roaring twenties were only just crashing with the stock market. Up until that point, the G.I.s were a largely self-centered generation fixated upon the glamour of wealth and dissipation—as F. Scott Fitzgerald's *The Great Gatsby* depicts so painfully and exquisitely.

But great national tragedy intervened in the form of the Great Depression first, and the Second World War next, a one-two punch that knocked all that self-satisfied flapper silliness straight out of the G.I. consciousness and set them on a course toward greatness.

The last thing I am suggesting is that "what these kids need is a war," as war is always tragic and should never be wished on any, especially since it is always the worst off that suffer most. But I *am* saying that unless there is some unifying critical catalyst, one wonders in what meaningful way Millennials may be called "Civic" at all—especially since few of them can even give a cogent definition of the word.

There are two ways that I can discern to answer this question positively. One is that Millennials are a profoundly conflict-averse generation. For them, issues matter less than the civility with which they are discussed. Divisive rhetoric is a powerful turn-off for this generation. So much so that the Rainers label them "the Mediating Generation."[48] As Amy told them, "If we would just show respect toward others, this world would be a better place. It seems like all we do is argue and fight these days."[49]

Millennials could therefore become a powerful positive influence in American politics in the near future. As they gradually comprise a larger and larger percentage of the voting block (assuming they can be motivated to vote, that is), the current negativity, hateful rhetoric, and polarization that rules our political arena today will be squashed, since Millennials simply will not stand for such uncivil public ugliness. They are powerfully motivated to create harmony and good will in every arena in which they have a stake. In the event that they might begin to care about the political arena, their conciliatory natures will impact this as well.

In the meantime, Millennials are likely to make an impact in many areas in another, largely unforeseen, way. They are such masters of technology that they quite naturally see solutions that older generations cannot. Millennials are beginning to emerge—in the business world, especially—as masters of *the creative workaround*.

Unlike Boomers and Xers, Millennials are not likely to get angry or frustrated with the futile efforts of older generations. They are more likely to give us a hug, pat us on the head, say, "There there, you just keep knocking yourself out." And then, while we're arguing amongst ourselves, they quietly get online and solve the problem via their vast network of connections or some technology none of us older generations even know exists. Nor do they trumpet their achievement. They simply move on to the next thing.

This often annoying (but ultimately saving) aspect of the Millennial generation may indeed point to the way in which they will manifest the Civic role that their place in the cycle suggests. It may be that while we are arguing over our present structures, the Millennials may, quite organically (in a way that only a hive-mentality can) construct parallel civic structures much better adapted to (and indeed arising from) the present-and-coming state of all-connectedness afforded by their online culture. The "real" world as we think of it is, before our very eyes, being invaded and subsumed by virtuality, and eventually (and probably, inevitably) we may see our current civic structures simply sloughed off as a snake sheds its skin, the governance of the world having transferred when we weren't looking to an entirely new and virtual structure that we didn't even know was being built. As we shall see below, this impulse among them has serious repercussions for our spiritual communities as well.

In a Word and a Song

Among all my respondents, there was no consensus on a song that summed up the Millennial generation. I thought of defaulting to a selection of songs that were most popular, analyzing them to see if any of the lyrics matched the generational profile.[50] Ultimately I decided against it, not because there was no congruence, but because the lyrics were, frankly, unprintable in a book intended for a largely Christian readership, and also because they almost universally reflected so poorly on this generation.[51] The consistent message of these songs seems to be: live for the moment, party it up, nothing really matters. While this sentiment is as old as Ecclesiastes, Millennials seem to have embraced it with a vengeance. As Lena informed me, "We're just going to do what we want and not care a lot." Ken, from Berkeley, California, agreed, adding, "We're big on 'do your own thing,' or if it works for you, then do it. It's not motivated by a larger goal, but more of a nihilism."

One of the most surprising of the responses is also the most illuminating. When my research assistant asked Seth what song he thought summed up his generation, he said, "Can I pick something silly? I mean, this just popped into my head right now. It's [from] *Willy Wonka and the Chocolate Factory*. The girl's name is Veruca Salt, that's the character's name. She's like this spoiled little kid, she's like rich. The whole song is about, like I want immediate satisfaction. I think the song is partly called, 'Give It to Me Now.' Like she wants a goose that lays a golden egg, and her dad is like, 'I'll get it for you later,' and she's like, 'No, I want it now!'"

Since other Millennial researchers have also pointed to this song as indicative of this generation,[52] perhaps it makes sense to include it, here.

I WANT IT NOW
from *Willie Wonka and the Chocolate Factory*
by Leslie Bricusse and Anthony Newley

I want a ball
I want a party
Pink macaroons and a million balloons
And performing baboons and. . .
Give it to me
Rrhh rhhh
Now!

I want the world
I want the whole world
I want to lock it all up in my pocket
It's my bar of chocolate
Give it to me
Now!

I want today
I want tomorrow
I want to wear 'em like braids in my hair
And I don't want to share 'em
I want a party with room fulls of laughter
Ten thousand tons of ice cream
And if I don't get the things I am after
I'm going to scream!
I want the works
I want the whole works
Presents and prizes and sweets and surprises
Of all shapes and sizes
And now
Don't care how
I want it now
Don't care how
I want it now

When I asked Millennials for a motto that summed up their generational cohort, there was likewise a lack of consensus, but many answers were similar—and eerily resonant with Varuca Salt's song. Deni suggested, "I deserve it so I shall have it," while Becca said, "Everyone's a winner."

Perhaps the most telling of all the responses came from Lou, from Cleveland Heights, Ohio, who answered, "TL, DR." Being an over-the-hill Xer, I had to look this one up: it's Internet shorthand for "too long, didn't read." Lou explained, "My generation represents the divisions ingrained in our current society, and right now, we are the drivers, doers, and changers, and we are too distracted by the trinkets, gadgets, and worlds of illusion that we created." Seth sounded a similar note, suggesting, "Maybe 'information overload' . . . . We don't, like, read books, you know? If you're having a conversation [and] someone says, 'Who was the actress in . . . ?' no one really guesses because someone has already pulled out their phone to look it up on IMDb."[53]

How Millennials are Perceived vs. How They Perceive Themselves

While older generations have sometimes pegged them as shallow, they also concede that these kids are a driven lot, not afraid of hard work, but also not committed to their jobs the way some employers expect and prefer. Millennials "work to live," they do not "live to work"—a trait they share with Xers, only more so. As Marian Salzman, a manager of Millennials at J. Walter Thompson says of them, "Some of them are the greatest generation. They're more hardworking. They have these tools to get things done. They are enormously clever and resourceful. Some of the others are absolutely incorrigible. It's their way or the highway. The rest of us are old, redundant, should be retired. How dare we come in, anyone over thirty. Not only can't be trusted, can't be counted upon to be, sort of, coherent."[54]

Ken discussed his frustration with the mixed messages his generation received from their parents: "I think they think we're lazy, and I think it's their own damned fault. They raised us to believe that if we worked hard, we wouldn't end up working at Bongo Burger, and now they're pissed at us because we won't work at Bongo Burger when we can't find employment. They also told us not to work for money, but rather to work at something that will make you happy. But even those of us who have found jobs don't necessarily feel like we're happy, so we feel like we failed."

Millennial writer Paul echoes this frustration: "The recurring description of our generation is 'entitled.' I knew how we got this way. As a kid, I dropped out of the T-ball league every year . . . and they still gave me a trophy. 'You are special for just being you,' they said. And then we grew up and our parents, professors, employers, and psychologists were like, 'You all have such entitlement! You think you can just do whatever you want and get rewarded for it!' And we were like, 'That's literally what you guys have been teaching us for the past eighteen years.'"[55]

In fact, however, older generations were not as critical as Millennials' projections suggest. Xer Marie told me, "I see generations younger than mine as being more worldly, knowledgeable, and cultured than my generation was at the same age. They are definitely more technologically savvy." But when I asked Millennial Becca what she thinks older generations think of hers, her perception is harsher: "I think they see us as selfish and materialistic and focused on technology. I don't think it's a very positive image of our generation."

How Millennials feel about themselves is just as complex. Seth's rumination is lengthy, but also articulate and insightful: "We've become more about finding our own happiness or self-satisfaction, and there's less of a sense of duty or honor or 'this is the path you must follow.' Coming from my own privileged background, I can see other generations judging that. There's also a strain of people, probably like my parents, who acknowledged that, whether it's our longer life expectancies or differences within culture, they gave us the breathing room, you know, you don't have to be a full-fledged adult at twenty. My parents probably still had a sense of 'here's what you do with your life,' but they were willing to give us space to move back home after college and take time and see what we wanna do. There's room to experiment with careers and what makes you happy, whereas before there was pressure to do whatever you needed to do to support the family you already had at twenty-four. There's greater flexibility in finding your own path."

Seth continued, "The other side of that is that some members of older generations view or judge that as lacking the character to do what needs to be done. Like why are you getting a PhD in medieval literature, rather than getting a job at the factory that doesn't exist anymore? I don't think everyone in previous generations were a bunch of sourpusses who hated their lives, but I don't think life was as much a quest to make yourself happy in previous generations."

THE SPIRITUALITY
OF THE MILLENNIALS

Welcome to the world of the spiritually challenged: the vast majority of Millennials have little time or patience for anything religious. They are, in fact, the least religious generation alive today.[56] Few of them are involved in spiritual community, few pray, few are engaged in any sort of compassionate service, and few are devoted to any form of religious study.

Among Catholics and Mainline Protestants, only about 25% of Millennials have a strong affiliation with their tradition, and only 20% say that faith is important in their daily lives.[57] Even Evangelical Christians are not immune. Evangelical researcher David Kinnaman reports that "18- to 29-year-olds have fallen down a 'black hole' of church attendance. There is a 43% drop in Christian church attendance between the teen and early adult years."[58]

Kayleigh told the Rainers, "Religion? Honestly, I just don't think that much about religion. I guess it's just not on my radar screen. I guess I have too many other priorities in my life. I'm not anti-religious, and I'm not mad at churches or religious people. It's their thing and that's fine. It's just not my thing."[59] Heather told

Smith, "I don't think my faith has much of an influence on my life. Most of the kids I hang around with are, like, more not that serious."[60]

Brandon told the Rainers, "Look guys, I know religion is important to a lot of people, but I'm not really one of those people who even thinks much about religion. I'm not against religions or religious people; it's just not who I am. I call myself a Christian because that's the label my family's had for generations. But I doubt that I'm even close to being like those people who attend church a lot. Religion is just really low on my list of priorities."[61]

The desacralization of the world begun during the rise of Generation X has just kept steamrolling full speed ahead. Millennials, as a whole, have no sense of transcendent or ultimate value. Ken (who identifies as Catholic because he feels that Catholic dogma is the "least wrong") told me, "The world just *is* . . . . I think it's functionally meaningless. All these systems of people trying to ascribe meaning and significance to the world, but by and large, they're just distancing themselves from the meaninglessness in their own lives."

With no sense of transcendent hope or value, Millennials are easy prey for consumerism and nihilism. Their existence seems almost solipsistic, as there is no common ground with the greater culture or even each other to which they can cling. As Smith writes, Millennials "seem to presuppose that they are simply imprisoned in their own subjective selves, limited to their biased interpretations of their own sense perceptions, unable to know the real truth of anything beyond themselves. They are *de facto* doubtful that an identifiable, objective, shared reality might exist across and around all people that can serve as a reliable reference point for rational deliberation and argument."[62]

We should be careful not to confuse Millennial religious apathy with an aptitude for critical thinking. When Smith asked John how he might evaluate the truth claims of various religions, John responded, "I don't really evaluate it. I have my beliefs, and they're there. And that's about it."[63] Another Millennial responded, "I don't. Not at all. Honestly, I have no idea. I just believe what I believe because I was raised that way, and a lot of it, like the morals, makes sense. But besides what is right and wrong, all these other things, heaven and hell, abortion, gay marriage, political, I just don't know at all."[64]

Among those few Millennials who do practice a tradition, even fewer believe that the truth claims of their religion are absolute. Instead, they are likely to view most faiths as being valid paths to the Divine, and are open to a wide variety of ideas and influences. As one Millennial told Smith, "The line of thought that I follow is that it doesn't matter what you practice. Faith is important to everybody, and it does the same thing for everybody, no matter what your religion is."[65] As Heather put it, "There is truth in religions. More than one can be right. I feel like it's just whatever suits you. I don't see why there can't be more than one. Catholics say there is only one but I don't see what the big deal is. Institutional religion, I don't really mind it. It's kind of, whatever floats your boat. I mean, who am I to say that what someone is doing is weird or wrong?"[66] In fact, most Millennials believe that all religions teach the same basic truths: believe in God and be a good person.[67]

Smith's research revealed that, in fact, most Millennials do believe in a religion, and most of them believe in the same religion. It's not one of the main, historic traditions, but instead one that seems to have arisen organically from the mindset of this particular generational cohort. Smith calls this new faith Moralistic Therapeutic Deism (MTD).[68] Smith describes MTD as having five basic tenants:

1. A God exists who created and orders the world and watches over human life on earth.

2. God wants people to be good, nice, and fair to each other, as taught in the Bible and by most world religions.

3. The central goal of life is to be happy and to feel good about oneself.

4. God does not need to be particularly involved in one's life except when God is needed to resolve a problem

5. Good people go to heaven when they die.[69]

Smith wrote that this "de facto creed is particularly evident among mainline Protestant and Catholic youth, but is also visible among black and conservative Protestants, Jewish teens, other religious types of teenagers, and even many non-religious teenagers in the United States."[70] One seventeen-year-old Mormon told him, "I believe in, well, my whole religion is where you try to be good and, ah, if you're not good then you should just try to get better, that's all."[71]

The Spiritual Gifts of Millennials

Although few Millennials are likely to use their gifts in the service of a religious institution, those that do will bring a tempering influence. As with most of their cohort, Millennials value peace over truth. Truth is, after all, essentially unknowable, so it's hardly worth arguing over. And of arguments, they have had quite enough.

No dispute is safe with Millennials on the prowl—they'll either force everyone to sit down and discuss things until an agreement is reached, or they'll go off by themselves and concoct a solution that completely defuses either side of the issue. (The sooner they get on the Israel-Palestine situation, the better.)

When you combine this conciliatory nature with their almost total lack of confidence in exclusive truth claims, you have a generation of people who are comfortable and eager to work across interfaith boundaries. A Millennial Christian knows that her religion is no more likely to be right about everything than her co-worker's Buddhist faith is. And that's okay, because there are plenty of things the two of them can agree on, and work together towards.

There may not be much faith amongst the Millennials, but what there is will be a powerfully cooperative interfaith force. Even Millennial Evangelical Christians are jettisoning many of those items that were considered stable Evangelical platforms only twenty years ago. Millennials wave away Evangelical chestnuts like abortion and "the gay menace" with impatience, and are increasingly intolerant of puritanical finger pointing from older generations in their churches.

Partly, this is why they are leaving their churches in droves. Journalist Laura Sessions Stepp commented on this, saying, "These young dropouts value the sense of community their churches provide but are tired of being told how they should live their lives. They don't appreciate being condemned for living with a partner, straight or gay, outside of marriage or opting for abortion to terminate an unplanned pregnancy."[72] While such sentiments would have been unthinkable twenty years ago in the Evangelical Christian world, they are not only commonplace today, they are the norm.

The gift in this is that Millennials are standing up to the hypocrisy and puritanical moralism in their communities. Millennial Christians are confronting leaders with why their churches aren't outraged about issues that actually mattered to Jesus, like poverty and solidarity with the marginalized. Historic disputes over theology or methods of governance interest them not at all, and they will be eager to discard them. While Boomers and Xers may have largely neglected ecumenism, allowing the ecumenical momentum of the Silents to crawl to a complete stop decades ago, the Millennials inheriting what is left of our religious institutions are likely to pooh-pooh historic divisions and usher in a new golden age of ecumenical cooperation and unification efforts.

How Divinity Is Imaged

Most Millennials profess some kind of belief in God, but that God bears little resemblance to the deities of previous generations. They tend to see the Divine as a transcendent being who is paradoxically both distant and near. As Deirdre reported, "I feel like the Divine is close to me but it's not really intimate. I still pray every night but I am not going to church or reading a Bible or anything."

While Smith reports that 63% of Millennials see the Divine as a personal being who is involved in people's lives,[73] very few of the emerging adults I spoke to saw things that way. Many of those I spoke to simply had no use for anything spiritual at all. When my research assistant asked Lena, a Christian, about the Divine, she said, "I feel like it is not very present. In my case, if my mom were not around talking about it I would never hear anything involving spirituality. Not at school or through my friends or anything. I feel like it has gotten to be a more touchy subject. Outside of Mom, I don't feel close to it because I haven't been around it at all." Indeed, a major Australian study found that among this age group, "Religious or spiritual concerns were generally not considered important."[74]

Ben, who refers to himself as an "ardent" deist,[75] told me, "I believe there was a Divine [being] that came, created the universe, and left. It was omnipotent and omniscient, from our perspective. It could fulfill most of the classic attributes of a god but I do not believe that it requires things of people or even knows about them."

An overwhelming majority of those I spoke to imaged the Divine as "light," rather than as a person. As Iva, a Catholic from Oakland, California, told me, "When I think of God, I think of light. That light is really comforting to me. Even though it's unknown, it still feels safe, comforting." Sean, a non-practicing Christian from Brandon, FL had a similar opinion: "I believe that there is a Divine. When I imagine him, however, there is no image of it. I just imagine a white light."

I could go on and on with "light" quotations. Deni, a Presbyterian, said, "I think the Divine is both intimate and distant. He is always with you yet he is always looking after you—over you . . . . The Divine is benevolent and kind. Those images make him feel more distant more regal—less like someone who is with me all of the time. I don't necessarily like to think about God as man. I prefer to think of him as light and spirit." Tracy, a Catholic from Gainesville, Florida, answered, "Whenever I think about the Divine I think of light, a bright light—similar to when the sun shines through white billowy clouds."

Many of those who talked to me did not see the Divine in personal terms at all, but as more of an energy, or just the random unfolding of Life itself. Becca, a Catholic, told me, "I don't think I see the Divine as personal, but I think it's intimate in that it's something that can be experienced, it's accessible, but it's not like the Divine is out there loving me personally. But if I wanted to go outside and look at stars, I would feel a connection with the Divine. A lot of Divinity is just how amazing life is and how beautiful things are and how people can sometimes be great, and I think being a part of that requires you to be a certain way, to take care of each other, to contribute to that amazing-ness."

Uther, a Buddhist from Gainesville, Florida, started out by telling me, "I think [the] Divine is more personal than impersonal," but then turned around and contradicted himself in the next sentence: "I would think of [the] Divine as spiritual energy, or a strong will to achieve something, or just faith to believe in something." Ed, a Zen Buddhist, likewise sees the Divine in "ordinary" experiences: "People look for fantastical experiences because people want something else. I mean, this conversation right now, the words coming out of my mouth and yours are divine. This lunch we just shared is miraculous; we're sustained by the entire universe—the fish in the sea, the fruits of the ground. We expect that the Divine will be more of a light show. We're looking for the light show, and we miss the ride . . . . I also think of the Divine as the way it is, it's the Tao, being in accord with what is, what's ordinary. A lot of people don't see that."

Lou, a Unitarian Universalist, suggested that the Divine is a reflection of our own efforts and expectations: "The Divine is everywhere, it surrounds us, penetrates us, binds the galaxy together. It is as personal or impersonal as you are with it. The more you look, the more you see; the more you listen, the more you hear; the more you share, the more is shared with you; the more you accept, the more of you is accepted."

Seth, a lapsed Catholic, views the universe with an orientation of wonder and humility. He said, "I would consider myself an atheist, but I do . . . find myself in awe of or in respect for what the universe is . . . . I mean, life and non-life and the universe and the world—all of it—is awe-inspiring, even if not at the hand of a divine being or beings or however you wanna think about that . . . . It puts your own daily challenges and what not into a bigger context. I understand people who think there is a God who actively engages with me and makes me feel important, but on the other side of that, there's a certain release you can feel in seeing your insignificance."

When asked what the Divine requires of human beings, Sean told me: "I don't know what it wants from us. However, with the amount of suffering in this world, I don't see it doing much." No gold star for you, God. Most answers, though, reflected the Millennials' concern for harmony and kindness. Tracy said, "The Divine requires us to be the best we can be. The Divine wants us to serve one another. The Divine loves everyone." Lou's answer was similar, if a bit Bill-and-Ted-like: "Be excellent to each other and party on dudes; that is, be kind and merciful to all others, and celebrate life."

Regardless of how they image the Divine, few Millennials feel a deeply personal connection to it. Smith reports that only 29% felt "extremely or very close" to God. "Significant chunks of emerging adults state that they feel only somewhat close or distant from God," Smith wrote. "But the overall trend over the half decade between the teenage and emerging adult years is clearly away from feeling close to God and toward either feeling distant from God or not believing in God at all."[76]

Spiritual Focus

Unlike the Civic generation before them—the G.I.s—Millennials are not in any way public about their spirituality, such as it is. They are much more like Silents or Xers in this area—spirituality is a private affair. One must be fairly intimate in order to bring it up, and it is not generally considered an acceptable topic of discussion in a group. It is certainly not something to be shouted (or, perhaps, texted) from the rooftops.

In fact, few Millennials even discuss religion or spirituality with their intimates, including spouses or close friends. According to Smith, this is simply because such matters are not important enough to bring up.[77] As one Millennial told him, "You don't really want to push people away by making them feel like you're pushing your religion on them, and you don't want them to feel like ostracized for what they believe. So it's just kind of one of those things I try to like stay clear of. If they bring it up, I'm fine with talking about it, but I'm not gonna be like, 'So what do you think about . . . ?' They'll be, like, 'Wait, are we having fun here? What are we doing?'"[78]

This is an extreme spiritual introversion. Millennials are therefore likely to feel uncomfortable if spiritual issues are raised—the danger for possible conflict or disharmony is simply too high to risk it. Yet, if they feel safe, if they are certain that their opinions will be respected, and if they are sure they will not offend anyone by voicing them, they will talk about them. Those are a lot of "ifs."

And yet, even though Millennials may be loathe to talk about spirituality—even with one another—it may be that there is a common, unspoken spirituality that is emerging in their midst. As one Millennial wrote, "I find when Millennials connect, no matter the color, nationality, ethnicity, culture, language, or any other label, we tend to feel much more in touch with each other. We know that we're all experiencing a similar sense of technological spirituality in our lives, and thus feel our similarities greatly outweigh our differences. We see ourselves as global citizens above anything else and are becoming in touch with the force that connects us all."[79]

Dominant Faith Style

While very few Millennials are involved in any organized religion, 72% of them identify as "spiritual but not religious,"[80] piecing together their spirituality in an eclectic fashion, in much the same way as Boomers do. But there is a difference—while Boomers are true believers, fairly enthusiastic and extroverted about their eclectic spirituality, Millennials are actually pretty off-hand about it.

Yet even if they are lukewarm about "spirituality," they are more open to it than to "religion." When I asked Becca to describe the difference between spirituality and religion, she had a ready answer: "Spirituality is people wanting to have something bigger, wanting to connect to divine mystery, but not wanting to get tangled up in all the mistakes and bad things that religions do sometimes." Many Millennials gave me similar answers, although few were as articulate or concise as Becca. As Deirdre told me, "We don't need to have religion to prove that we love God and have people see that in us."

Millennials will certainly give lip service to spirituality—and sometimes to religion—but they are, at their core, a fairly unreligious lot. Their dominant style of faith, to the degree that they have one, is Ethical Humanism,[81] feeling a connection to others and the cosmos, but not necessarily calling what they are connecting to "God."

Ethical Humanists tend to view the Divine as Life itself, or the life force animated through nature. They are connected to this, and therefore, through it, with all things. They tend to construct meaning through compassionate action (though Millennials are far more likely to think about this than to actually act on it). Accepted sources of spiritual wisdom for Ethical Humanists are the arts, the natural world, and the scientific method. Spiritual growth is seen as the degree of one's commitment to the world-at large, especially biological sustainability. Their spiritual practices include activism, being in nature, reading, and study.

Obviously, this is not a perfect fit. My Faith Styles system was intended to map the six ways that people generally hold faith. If one does not hold faith at all, then they are simply not on the map. Millennials are more like Ethical Humanists than any other point in this assessment system, but since they are largely irreligious, one can make an excellent argument for them simply not having a faith style at all.

Prayer Style

As one might expect, with so few Millennials having any interest in spirituality or religion, few of them engage in spiritual practices, such as prayer/meditation or attending worship services (65% say they do neither[82])—fewer than any other living generation.

This research is congruent with what I heard in my interviews. When asked about prayer, Ken said, "I don't have an active prayer life." Lena told me that she does pray, but not very often. She said, "When I pray I do it in my head. There is no ritual or anything like that. I have prayed for family members during hard times. The last time that I prayed was about a month ago." Sean figures that God simply has better things to do than to listen to him: "I don't really pray much," he says. "I figure there are people who need to be heard much more than me out there in the world, and I hope it increases their chance of getting heard."[83]

Regarding meditation practice, most Millennials are similarly uncommitted. Seth told me, "I don't pray. And depending on how you define 'meditate,' there are moments and times when I'm deeply . . . reflective." For Ben, meditation is practical, not religious. He said, "Meditation for me is merely a calming thing. It's something I do when I'm annoyed, angered, or frustrated. It's a way to ground myself and bring myself back to focus. I don't pray, I don't seek guidance or ask for things that I know won't happen from a god."

The percentage of those who are committed to a spiritual practice is, as one might expect, higher among Millennials who strongly identify with a religious tradition. While only 30% of Millennials at large pray daily, among Catholic and mainline Protestant Christian Millennials that number bumps up to 40%; conservative Christian Millennials come in at 42%, while Mormon Millennials score highest, with 54% of them praying daily.[84]

As Iva told me, "When I pray, I spend time saying the Our Father and Hail Mary . . . going through a list of people in my life that I want to support, and I thank God for supporting them. I do something similar at church, too. Also, just throughout my day, I pray in situations that need it." Nick, a Christian from Florida said that when he prays, "Mostly it's just at times throughout the day without doing anything special. I pray for safety for my family and for others. Also I pray for guidance." Tracy answered similarly: "When I pray, I say it in my head or quietly out loud. I kind of think of it as a conversation with God. I usually pray for other people and very rarely for myself. I don't feel comfortable praying for myself. Some of the things I pray for include health, happiness, and safety."

Deni was a rarity among her cohort, in that she felt kind of guilty for not practicing more. "I don't practice enough," she said. "I rarely go to church, read the Bible or pray. If I have been away too long, I feel the need to go back to church to recenter myself . . . . I will sit down and say 'Dear God . . . .' I pray for guidance, for direction, to help heal others. I am bad about praying because I still feel like I am supposed to do for myself. God doesn't fix, I fix and he helps . . . . I wish I could give it over to him more often—[but it's] not my nature."

I only spoke to one person for whom prayer was not practical, but intimate and relational. Lyra, a Christian, said, "I imagine God being in front of me or sitting on his lap talking to him. If I am praying for someone, I often imagine that person standing in front of God and me talking to God on their behalf. I pray for guidance and that God will show the people I love how much he loves them and cares for them. I pray that God will use me in big ways to further his kingdom and that he will make my boyfriend and friends more like him. I pray for things I want, like good grades or success. I pray for forgiveness when I feel I have been unfaithful. I thank God when I am in low points because it helps me remember it all belongs to him anyway. Everything here is temporary. I pray for courage to do the right thing and wisdom to know what the right thing is. I often pray for the Holy Spirit to speak loud to me because often times I am too busy and miss it."

Only one other respondent was deeply committed to a practice. Ed was deeply insightful as he considered his generation and their spiritual practices. He said, "The biggest challenge of our generation is to learn to sit still. When you look at the high price of advertising, text messaging, we're inattentive. If paying attention helps us access the Divine, and I see our generation as inattentive, it saddens my heart. But a heart can change very quickly . . . someone can change their life in a moment. I mean, if I can change my life, then other people can change, the planet can change; it can happen. I just hope it happens sooner rather than later. We have a mentality of a quick fix—we can fix what's broken or buy a new one. That attitude is detrimental to our well-being and that of the planet. If we break it, that's it—there's no other place to move to."

For even the most religious Millennials, there is little emphasis on traditional forms of discipline. Lyra, for instance, says, "When I feel desperate or ashamed sometimes I will kneel but usually I pray while driving or walking to class or laying in bed or in the shower." But Ed, again, proves there are exceptions to the rule. He considers the traditional posture in Zen meditation of utmost importance, saying that it is "a metaphor for your experience of reality. You're either reaching out for something that you want, or running away from someone you don't want to be with, or avoiding a memory of something painful, but when you're sitting upright, you know, can you find that sense of uprightness? It's a physical expression of ethics, and that mirrors the mind. What you do with your mind, you don't want to lean, you don't wanna move away from anything, you want to be in proper relationship with everything. You don't wanna kill or steal or cause harm . . . so I think that meditation is crucial. It's the one thing that I've found that can transform suffering. The only thing to transform suffering is to witness it and not try to manipulate it."

But Ed is unusual among his cohort. Other Millennials are finding meaning in non-traditional practices. Natalie, a Catholic, told me, "I am very spiritual. I find my spirituality in my crafts. Particularly in my knitting and fiber arts. It is the one thing that brings me peace, something I use to meditate and to pray." Becca said, "I spend a lot of time alone and thinking, just being present and walking around and looking at things, and I try to let go of things. I definitely do that more than the traditional, 'Dear God' kind of praying. I also write in a journal a lot, which I consider a form of prayer, and I address it to God, which is kind of interesting because I don't have a sort of solid God view."

It is not surprising that few Millennials have a disciplined spiritual practice, since they are disinterested in spiritual matters generally. Among those who do pray, their motivations are congruent with the fourth tenet of Smith's Moral Therapeutic Deism, "God does not need to be particularly involved in one's life except when God is needed to resolve a problem." Prayer is generally practical—likewise meditation. For such a relational generation, it seems strange that real, intimate relationship with the Divine has such a low priority. But, as we have seen, for most Millennials, the Divine is a distant, largely absent being. In large part, Millennials and their God seem mutually disinterested in one another.

Millennials in Community

It is also ironic that for such a deeply relational generation, spiritual community—gathering with others for a sacred intention— seems to hold such little appeal. Yet, this is undeniably the case:

only 13.5% of Millennials attend a religious service on a weekly basis.[85]

Even among those who do attend, few see that community as "their" community—their place of "real social belonging." That distinction properly belongs to their circle of friends, their families, or even co-workers.[86] As one Millennial told Smith, "I wouldn't say *belonging* in the church I'm in now. I mean they're Southern Baptist, but it's run basically by really old people, basically conservative, wear a dress, wear a suit to church every Sunday kind of thing" [emphasis mine].[87]

As a Christian, Lori thought that going to church was definitely a good thing. She said, "I think you have to keep yourself accountable, and going to church is a place in which you can grow in your faith through others, through meeting others." But in the next breath she qualified that, adding, "I think of religion as a good thing, [but] our relationship with God is what really matters." Sean agreed, saying, "I don't go to church. I believe that one's relationship with a greater being can only be known between the individual and said being."

Unlike some Xers, Millennials aren't actually hostile to religion—they're just terminally indifferent. As Presbyterian mission developer Adam J. Copeland wrote regarding his ministry with Millennials, "The young adults I've come to know are not antagonistic toward the church. They convey not an aversion to historic congregations but a collective indifference, a 'whatever.'"[88]

Millennials see congregations as flawed, human institutions that nevertheless do a lot of good in the world. They're just . . . not for *them*. When I asked Becca about her religious affiliation, she said that she was "Catholic. It's a love-hate kind of thing . . . . It's hard to be associated with a religion that messes up a lot, but it's human, but I don't fault it too much because it's a human-run religion." But it was Seth's answer that really pegged the overall attitude of the generation. He told me, "The majority of religions that I have experience with—read about, experienced, whatever—they *want* to be good. I don't think religion is an inherently bad thing like some activist-y atheist person might think. Like, it's not an evil tool to scam people to get money or whatever. But at the same time, overly religious people make me uncomfortable, and I do find them to be, on a lot of levels, irrational. If we were to do a word association, and you said, 'religion,' I would say, 'unnecessary.'"

In part, it is clear that Millennials' antipathy toward organized religion was instilled in them by Boomer and Xer parents of the same opinion. But the Rainers' research uncovered a significant and poignant insight that just may be a large, missing piece of the puzzle. They believe that Millennials' lack of interest in spiritual communities is directly tied to their allergy to conflict. They write that Millennials view organized religion as "just another divisive force in the world . . . . The Millennials are the mediating generation and, from the perspective of many, organized religion leads to negativity and conflict."[89]

Tabitha told them, "I'm just not too interested in organized religion . . . . I did attend church for several months about three years ago. But the more I got to know people in the church, the more I heard about infighting and fussing. That made me notice how negative church people and preachers are in general. You know, it seems like every time I read about a Christian leader, he's telling people what he's against. It just all seems so negative."[90]

The Millennials are not only not interested in the culture wars that have so consumed churches on both the right and the left over the past thirty-five years—they are actively repelled by them. So long as society insists on pushing mean-spirited polarizing agendas, Millennials are simply going to say, "I'm out of here." That goes for spiritual communities as well.

Some religious leaders are hopeful that this will change. Copeland says that the emerging adults he works with "don't know their life goals. They hope to move soon, and they work three part-time jobs, which they hate. They live with roommates, are 'freaked out' by the idea of having children and, as one young adult said, they 'live in constant flux.' These people don't fit in with the population of most mainline churches in town."[91] The hope of many church leaders is that once Millennials finally emerge from their extended adolescences and start acting like responsible adults (in other words, like *them*) they'll come back to church. I say: "Don't hold your breath."

Spiritual Growth Continuum

Many Millennials agree that spiritual growth is important, but are not able to articulate what it actually *is*, what it looks like, or how it is achieved. Iva is sure it is important, but still doesn't know what "it" is: "I think the interesting thing is that all people need to develop spiritually. I know I need that, and even my priest talks about going on retreats and coming back and having grown spiritually. He shares the techniques that he's learned and stuff like that. It makes me feel like I have a lot of work to do, too. But I don't know how I'd judge it or be able to see it in someone else."

Lena likewise has no theories about what spiritual growth is, but thinks it must be tied to being involved with a spiritual community. She said, "I feel like becoming involved and stuff like that would probably influence it. Mostly because I never have been before. I think it is important, but I don't feel like it affects someone's life although it could affect how someone is and how they think. It gives people more insight more than anything. I don't really feel like I care right now. I don't know if that will change."

Several of the young adults I spoke to did have theories about spiritual growth—but there was little consistency among them. Becca told me that spiritual growth was about an awareness of interconnection—an insightful and uniquely Millennial response. She said, "A spiritually developed person would be compassionate, would have a good grasp of the importance of serving others and their role as an interdependent member of society, and they'd feel that way with other people and with the environment, so I guess I'd say a developed person is someone who sees themselves as connected to the world and has obligations toward that, be loving toward people. An underdeveloped person would be someone who is just independent and doesn't care about people and thinks that what they do doesn't really matter."

For Ed, however, spiritual growth is measured by an individual's willingness to be transformed. He told me, "I think it's simple. Change. Being willing to change is a really developed spiritual being, and being rigid against change is immature. Transformation. That's the key word. When I look at some of my most respected and wisest and oldest teachers, they don't know what's going to happen in their lives. They're totally successful, established, realized people, and they're in the throes of uncertainty. Transformation."

Seth's ideas are clearly in conflict. On the one hand, he acknowledges that several traditions value submission to the deity (the only theory that had more than one taker among my respondents, by the way), but he himself does not see that as a virtue. As Seth expressed it, "Depending on your religious tradition, spiritual growth, if it's coming closer to God, in a lot of respects, it might be submitting more and accepting more and letting go of control more, which for me obviously is getting further away from my ideal. So I think for a lot of people, the continuum is on one side pure rationality and the other side is letting go and letting God and having total faith that God is in control."

Although none of my respondents generated this answer themselves, I believe they do have a unified notion of spiritual growth, and that it is tied to the midi-happy narrative articulated by the British researchers. The fact that no Millennials actually named this is not surprising, as the midi-narrative is invisible to Millennials, in the same way as water is invisible to fish. The narrative is so much a part of their world that gaining enough objective distance to reflect upon it is difficult. As the British researchers wrote regarding their own discussions with Millennials, "There was no need to explain why happiness is the goal of life—this was self-evident to our young people."[92]

Very simply, I believe that Millennials intrinsically see spiritual growth as a continuum from unhappiness on one side (spiritual immaturity) to happiness on the other (spiritual maturity). Therefore, the degree to which spiritual guides can assist Millennials in being happy—by finding satisfying and rewarding connections to family, friends, the Divine, their own souls, and the world—is the degree to which their ministry among this generation will be deemed successful, at least by Millennials themselves.

MINISTERING
TO MILLENNIALS

Few Millennials are likely to seek out spiritual direction anytime soon, but for those that do, a non-directive modality is imperative. Millennials do not see elders as authority figures to be challenged (as Boomers and Xers did in their youth) but friends and partners who are there to help and collaborate. This fits in well with current thinking in spiritual guidance, but Millennials are less likely to come for one-to-one direction than they are to find (or more likely, form) discernment groups online—although they would certainly not call them that!

Guides who are comfortable with technology may find ample opportunity to connect with friendly, cooperative Millennials, who will want to have creative input in shaping the future of online guidance. There is no way to predict the future of this ministry, but it isn't something we need to worry about—they're just going to do it, with or without our participation. In our opening vignette, Justin and his peers weren't waiting around for older mentors to "get something going" online. Millennials are just forming their own groups and sharing, like the Sexuality and Spirit Facebook page. At the same time, spiritual guides of older generations who are able to meet Millennials on their (online) turf and on their generational terms will find plenty of opportunities to mentor and guide them.

Thus far, this book has been descriptive, not prescriptive. I have simply described what *is* (albeit with the occasional snarky editorial comment, I'll grant you) but nowhere have I suggested that something about a generation ought to change. Yet, if you have been concerned by the findings of this chapter (as I have— my hair stood on end at several points as I did my research), you will perhaps agree with me that mentoring and guidance for this generation is both appropriate, necessary, and even urgent. Millennials sense this, I believe, and will not resent honest, vulnerable, and collaborative mentoring.

Specifically, I believe that guidance is needed regarding the central place of happiness in their worldview. I am in complete agreement with the British researchers when they say, "The desire for happiness is entirely valid. Who wants to be unhappy?" but I also agree when they say that the Millennial Happy midi-narrative must be challenged.[93] The midi-narrative needs to become a meta-narrative. Helping Millennials broaden their happy midi-narrative (happiness for me and mine) to a happy meta-narrative (the greatest happiness for the greatest number of people) will be transformative, and salvation itself for this generation (and, quite possibly, the world).[94]

I'm not recommending some kind of Utilitarian renaissance, but something much more creative—an investment in a larger myth or story that enlarges their circle of concern. As the British researchers wrote, "The Happy midi-narrative foreshortens hope, forgoing a vision of a better future for the world, for a better short-term future for ourselves as individual or families . . . . The Happy midi narrative settles for too small a set of questions."[95] Instead, they say, "Authentic happiness requires a meta-narrative, a full story which offers long-term hope, not a midi one focused on the immediate."[96]

This will happen not through shaming or "should-ing," however, but through deeply authentic and emotional storytelling—through literature, movies, and other works of art—in which Millennials find themselves connected beyond their bubble of concern. Examples of past shifts in concern can be illustrative and helpful—such as in the case of the Buddha. According to Mahayana Buddhist teachings, the Buddha rejected the "liberation for me alone" model of the yogis under which he studied, and after his enlightenment refused to enter into his own bliss until all beings could be likewise liberated. Such an enlightening shift in perspective is clearly needed here, as well.

Concern-widening can also happen through international travel and online communities (where distance is irrelevant). Millennials are relational, so building relationships between them and those most unlike them will create networks of concern that will enlarge and transform their circle of care.

G.I.s Ministering to Millennials

Millennials are naturally open and friendly to older generations. They are respectful and will value your time and attention. They may not respect you for the reasons you believe you deserve respect, but here is something you might learn from them—they are not going to admire you for things you have done, but because of who you are; truly a gift from one (allegedly) Civic generation to another. This is because, as we have seen, Millennials are a deeply relational generation. They want harmony and interaction and friendship with people who are like them as well as people who are not. If you can embrace them, they will embrace you. To do this, you may have to set aside your judgments and evaluations of them and how they live. Remember how the Boomers used to trigger you? The Boomers were tame in comparison to Millennials, especially when it comes to lifestyle choices and values. The difference is that the Boomers were rebelling (against you, naturally), while Millennials are simply trying to navigate their worlds in as conflict-avoiding way as possible. So while you might be tempted to treat them like Boomers, please resist this temptation. Their motivations are completely different, as indeed, are their worlds.

The fact is that, no matter how computer savvy you might be, Millennials actually do live in a different universe—they see technology and the Internet in terms of possibility and with a creative plasticity that will be hard for you to imagine. For older generations, adapting to computer technology requires porting things we know how to do in the "normal" world to the online environment via metaphor. We can put things on a "desktop," we can keep things in "folders," and so forth. But Millennials have a native comfort with technology that is less reliant on tactile metaphors, and they are able to see creative possibilities that are simply invisible to the rest of us.

There's no need to compete with them or try to meet with them on their own turf—that is impossible. *The best thing you can do for them is to invite them into your space, and love them.* They will respect and appreciate that, and your love will be returned.

Ideas that have guided your life, like "responsibility" and "duty" are just abstract notions to Millennials, not realities, and appealing to them will afford you little. They are not likely to be interested in hearing war stories or about life on the farm during the Great Depression. If you must go there, go sparingly. Notice when the eyes glaze over and shift gears quickly. Also, Millennials are not going to be the salvation of the institutions you built and love, any more than Xers are. They simply don't see the value in them that you do. Their communities are constructed differently—remember that *different* is not *wrong*.

But take heart, because they *do* understand other concepts important to you, like "love" and "caring" and "family." Quality time inquiring into what matters most to them will be gratefully received. Millennials have few people in their lives that they can talk about spiritual matters with—their peers are largely uninterested, and their parents often have agendas around these things. A great gift you can give to Millennials is interested, open-ended questioning, inviting them to articulate (and thereby discover) how they feel about spiritual matters.

Again, a non-directive approach is key, here. Invite their questions, but avoid giving them pat answers. Affirming their questioning, and exploring the possibilities will help them feel out their own resolutions. One thing Millennials are poor at is critical thinking—a skilled spiritual guide can help Millennials tease out the critical implications of their positions. This can lead to deep and fruitful inquiry that invites self-sufficiency and ownership of their spiritual lives.

They will be grateful for mentoring—providing an example of how to live with spiritual integrity—but they will be less open to advice or correction or sermonizing. Millennials can benefit tremendously from being in spiritual community with older generations that treat them as co-workers and peers. You have already established your greatness—you now have the opportunity to help the Millennials discover theirs.

Silents Ministering to Millennials

My advice to most other generations regarding Millennials is "don't expect them to care about what you care about," but in this case, just the opposite is true. Silents and Millennials have many common goals—chief among them is a preference for peace over ideology. I'm not saying that Silents or Millennials don't believe in anything—certainly Silents have deeply held convictions, and the same could be said for some Millennials. But for both these generations, their convictions are not as dear as peacemaking, which emerges as the primary value to which all others must bow.

There is a strong Utilitarian streak in both generations—which is partly why I suspect that both are actually Adaptive in nature. Division and rancor causes distress and unhappiness (Millennial bogie-men), which in turn leads to oppression and violence (Silent bogie-men). The answer for both generations is mediation, conciliation, and the smoothing over of differences, even when those differences are real and mutually exclusive.

Thus, Silents will find allies in Millennials when it comes to peacemaking, which has great implications for social justice work. The problem is making peacemaking at this meta-level matter to them. Silents are naturally empathetic, and are focused on creating peace and justice (and thus the possibility of happiness, although they would not be likely to think of it this way) for *others*. Millennials, on the other hand, are focused on happiness for "*me and mine.*" Guiding Millennials to broaden the "mine" to include progressively larger chunks of humanity is an enormously important goal for Silent mentors.

Yet Silents will become frustrated trying to involve Millennials in peace and justice work through persuasion—they'll be met with an infuriating yawn, a wave of the hand, and a bored, "yeah, yeah, where's the Xbox controller?" The solution to this apathetic impasse is relationship and connection. Don't just tell Millennials about poverty, take them to live with impoverished people for a week, put them in situations where they make affective connections with these people—friendships, puppy-love romances, loyalties. When they return home, those connections will not be broken—they will sustain them through cell phones, texting, and Facebook.

But they will see and care, their circle of concern will widen to include an economic diversity they had not embraced before. These are the seeds of real ministry, transformation, and may blossom into salvation, not just for the oppressed, but for Millennials themselves.

Silents make up the majority of people involved in religious institutions today. These institutions matter greatly to them, and while they have been able to attract some Boomers to work beside them (largely due to ideological affinity), there are only a smattering of Xers or Millennials. This is not likely to change. The great crisis in church work is how to make congregational involvement attractive to Millennials. I believe this is a Quixotic task. The "sea of blue" (hair, that is) that make up the majority of our mainline congregations today is not likely to change. Silents may pay lip service to changing their worship in order to attract Millennials and Xers, but in fact they do not want to change enough—the service that Millennials themselves might construct would simply not feel like "church" to Silents.

Boomers will have an easier time of it, in that they enjoy many worship elements that appeal to Millennials. Boomers can bend enough, but Silents will break. Silents must face the fact that their way of worship will likely die when they do. Ministering to Millennials simply will not—in the real world—include them joining Silents for worship, standing for prayers and sharing a hymnal. Sorry, Silents. It's not going to happen. Millennials are not going to save your churches or synagogues.

Instead, they are going to create new ways of being church—indeed, they already are. Xers who pioneered the Emerging Church movement are creating flexible structures that Millennials can mine and adapt for their own use. The best you can do for these emerging adults is to form relationships with them, mentoring them by being living examples of faith that point to a believer's responsibility beyond his or her immediate circle of concern. If this is the one legacy Silents leave to Millennials, it will be profound and salvific.

Boomers Ministering to Millennials

Younger Boomers and first-wave Xers are the parents of the Millennials, and the ones that Millennials feel closest to, respect most, and are most open to learning from. Boomers and Millennials often have a lot of music in common that they enjoy. The Boomer-forged praise style of worship is more appealing to Millennials than older forms, especially in its edgier, poppier incarnations. But the Boomer phenomenon in which this style of worship prevails, the mega-church, often leaves Millennials cold because of its size and impersonality.

When megachurches work well, it's because of attention to forming and maintaining small cell groups that provide house-church intimacy alongside stadium-size worship experiences. The both/and approach works, and can work for Millennials, too, if they find social connections in their cell groups. Millennials are all about friendships and personal connection, and if that connection can happen in a spiritual community, then that community has their complete loyalty. As we have seen above, however, this is rare.

Small spiritual communities will have an even harder time attracting them because of the inflexibility of older members when it comes to worship styles. Again, as with my advice to the Silents, you simply cannot look to Millennials to refresh and enliven current spiritual communities. The mega-churches have the edge, here, but I suspect that their impact is already on the wane.

Boomers have an excellent opportunity to reach out to Millennials through campus ministries, if you can devise programs that will appeal to them. Such programs will need to be deeply relational, focused on forming friendships rather than on addressing issues. Relax, Boomers, I know issues are important to you. Putting them on the back burner is not the same as taking them off the stove. Different generations have a different hierarchy of needs (nods to Maslow), and for Millennials, relationship needs are primary. Once those are established, they may be able to discern together other needs to be addressed.

Your frustration with Xers regarding their apparent apathy and disinterest in those things that matter most to you has only amplified in the Millennials. What you didn't understand about Xers is that they actually *do* care about many of these things, they simply don't want to waste energy on inefficient, ineffectual, or unrealistic methods. In some ways the Millennials are your worst nightmare, because unlike Xers, this younger generation really *doesn't* care about most of these things. If it doesn't affect them or their immediate circle of intimates, it doesn't exist.

Most Boomer parents are on friendly terms with their Millennial children, and still have opportunities to influence them. Other Millennials are open to Boomer mentorship, so there are numerous possibilities there. The problem is finding opportunities to connect with Millennials who are not part of your family or spiritual community in ways that are organic. Boomers have enough overlap with Millennials in terms of enjoyment of popular culture, sports, dance, and enthusiast groups to make these connections. In later life, some Boomers have become more introverted and withdrawn, but those who are not will find lots of opportunities to connect.

In some ways, Millennial attitudes model good dating advice: friendship first, commitment later. This is wisdom, Boomers. Millennials want friendship above and beyond all else. And from elders they want encouragement, they want to be seen, they want approval—you know how to provide that. But you can also provide an example that reveals to Millennials the concerns of a wider world. The British researchers are adamant that the happy midinarrative must be challenged if Millennials are to be saved from their own solipsistic impulses. This borders on a judgmental attitude that may not fully understand or appreciate the Millennial worldview, yet I am in sympathy with their conclusion. Boomers can affirm the importance of happiness, while at the same time questioning whether it really is the most important thing in life. Is it? Is it *really*?

Perhaps some Millennials will make a surprising case for this position, in which case we may all learn and benefit. But we may find that they benefit as well from considering other possibilities.

Boomers (and first wave Xers) are responsible for forming Millennials, and the failure to teach even the most basic critical thinking skills to young people must be laid at their feet. I contend that it is not too late to teach younger Millennials or to mentor older Millennials in this area. Boomers, you have your work cut out for you. This is especially true in matters of religion and spirituality. Ironically, both Boomers and Xers have excelled in this very area—both generations are masters of ideological deconstruction and reconstruction. How so little of it has gotten passed on to the next generation is a mystery.

Finally, Boomers, Millennials have something valuable to teach about *method*. The old adage, "you attract more flies with honey than with vinegar," is true. Many Boomers are still fighting the good fight like it's 1969, with their passion, polarization tactics, and vitriol undiminished. This kind of approach is not effective now (if it ever was), and certainly not among Millennials.

This is going to be a hard thing for Boomer religious ideologues on both sides of the spectrum to hear, since these agendas have largely driven their faith approaches for the majority of their adult lives. But for good or ill, Millennials care not a whit for your agendas. Go ahead, spit, bluster, and rant to your therapist, but please, get over it.[97] If you want to help form Millennials spiritually, start where they are at. Make friends. Help them nurture their friendships. Then help them expand those friendships into larger and larger areas of concern (see my advice to Silents, above, for more on this). You need to work *with* the flow of this generation, rather than *against* it. You can't stop their boat, but you might be able to help steer it. After all, they value your advice. Play your cards right and they might just take it.

Xers Ministering to Millennials

Xers emerge as the most likely candidates for spiritual leadership among Millennials. While there are significant differences between the two generations, they have much in common, specifically a post-modern sensibility that eschews certainty and exclusive claims, values difference and diversity, and honors the intimacy and privacy of individual faith.

While Millennials will be open to mentorship from any generation, with Xers they share much pop culture and comfort with technology. The Gen X-driven Emerging Church movement is pioneering new structures and models of "church" that may prove to have some appeal to Millennials. Certainly it has more of a chance than any of the models of spiritual community favored by previous generations. Emerging Church models are deeply relational, putting friendship and fellowship front and center.

Further, the theological models emerging from this movement speak to issues deeply resonant for Millennials. Emerging Church pioneers view the goal of the Christian faith as the restoration of broken relationships in four directions: between humans and God, between people and people (both individuals and communities), between humans and the earth, and between individuals and their own souls (the ability to love oneself).[98] While I am most familiar with what is being done along these lines in Christian circles, I believe that the same will be true among Xers and Millennials of other confessions as well, especially in developed nations where we have a shared and largely homogenous culture.

Another important way that Xers can provide effective leadership for Millennials is in terms of praxis. While Xers are plenty interested in theory, few Millennials are. Where Xers excel, however, is in the nitty gritty, let's-get-our-hands-dirty kind of ministry. Boomer and first-wave Xer parents instilled in Millennials the nearly universal belief that they were special, that they were destined for greatness, that they as individuals would achieve great things. However, since most Millennials have absolutely no idea what those great things might be or how to go about them, Xers can take them by the hand and invite Millennials into hands-on ministries that make a real difference in people's lives while remaining practical and manageable. Xers can affirm Millennials' belief that they can do great things, and can lead them in acts of greatness. More than any other generation, Xers can help Millennials make their fantasies of greatness realities.

A further way that Xers can assist Millennials has to do with Xers' comfort with questions, deconstruction, and ambiguity. Xers understand that spirituality is much more about living the questions than having the answers. Mountains existed for Victorians to climb, answers exist for Xers to deconstruct and demolish. To sit in the not-knowing and still be faithful is a powerful form of faith, and one that will speak to Millennials. As Xer minister Adam Copeland wrote of his ministry among Millennials, "One essential aspect of this ministry is space for young people to address questions of faith, life, and ethics in public settings. We've real-ized that our forums—and this is key—should not focus on deliv-ering an 'expert answer' from some theologically trained stranger. Instead, they must allow participants to listen to one another, to form friendships, and to relax in the beauty of holy conversation."[99]

. . . AND THE NEXT GENERATION?

SO WHAT ABOUT the people born after 2001? What are they called and what are they like? It's too early to tell, but most likely they will either be an Adaptive generation (humanizing and tweaking what the Millennials are building now), or an Idealistic generation (raging against the Millennials' excess and ineptitude), depending on whether the Millennials turn out to be Civic or Adaptive.

It is certain, however, that this new generation will be just as unique as the generations that came before, worthy of our time and patience in understanding their perspective and needs. Only time will tell, however, how they will unfold, and how their uniqueness and spirituality will manifest.

NOTES

INTRODUCTION

1. Popular movies at the time included *The Matrix, The Truman Show,* and *Dark City,* all of which are retellings of the Gnostic myth.

2. *Presence*, Vol. 5, no. 2, May 1999.

3. John R. Mabry, *The Way of Thomas* (United Kingdom: O Books, 2006).

4. Metaphor, "Starfooted," (Switzerland, Galileo Records, 1999).

5. William Strauss, and Neil Howe. *Generations: The History of America's Future, 1584–2069* (New York: Wm. Morrow and Co., 1991).

6. Okay, what I *actually* say to them is, "Everything I'm about to say is bullshit." I just don't think I can get that past my editor. God bless endnotes.

7. Thom S. Rainer and Jess W. Rainer, *The Millennials: Connecting to America's Largest Generation* (Nashville: B & H Books, 2011).

8. This cycle is also detectable in other first-world countries.

9. Strauss and Howe summarize the generations this way: "Idealist generations tend to live what we might label a *prophetic* lifecycle of vision and values; Reactives a *picaresque* lifecycle of survival and adventure; Civics a *heroic* lifecycle of secular achievement and reward; and Adaptives a *genteel* lifecycle of expertise and amelioration," 74.

10. Now, you're thinking, "A clever ruse to get me to read the endnotes!" Is that so wrong?

CHAPTER ONE ■

1. Strauss and Howe, 263–4.

2. Strauss and Howe, 18.

3. Tom Brokaw, *The Greatest Generation* (New York: Random House, 1998), xxviii.

4. Strauss and Howe, 267.

5. Strauss and Howe, 265.

6. Brokaw, 37.

7. Brokaw, 44.

8. Brokaw, xxxviii.

9. We are, after all, still here.

10. Strauss and Howe, 269.

11. Strauss and Howe, 265.

12. Quoted from http://en.wikipedia.org/wiki/My_Way_(song)#cite_note-8

13. David Ward and Lucy Ward, "My Way Tops Funeral Charts," *The Guardian,* Wednesday 16 November, 2005.

14. Strauss and Howe, 268.

15. Brokaw, 39.

16. Quoted in Tom Brokaw, *The Greatest Generation Speaks* (New York: Random House, 1999), 73.

17. "A Conversation with Howard Rice: Aging and Loss, Generational Issues, and the Pastor as Spiritual Guide," *Presence,* January 1998.

18. Brokaw 33.

19. For a detailed description of Traditional Believers, see my book *FaithStyles: Ways People Believe* (Morehouse Publishing, 2006), 1–12.

20. Hebrews 10:25.

21. This partly explains their extreme reaction to their children—G.I.s viewed Boomer rebellion as a form of spiritual immaturity.

22. It seems that theodicy is as much a bitch for the Greatest Generation as for the rest of us.

23. But usually without the apocalyptic hysteria that can accompany G.I. despair.

24. Note I am not talking about nursing homes, which can be depressing places indeed, but facilities where elders "own" their own apartments, but are tended to by medical and recreational professionals working in the same building.

25. For instance, if you are a Christian minister on Sunday mornings, how about going to that great Jewish Renewal Synagogue on Friday nights? You may need to get creative, but it will be worth it.

26. Which they undoubtedly are, when served by Xers. Xers are not being intentionally disrespectful, but simply cannot help their own reactions, and cannot resist a well-timed pot shot.

27. Not to be confused with "manatee," an aquatic mammal.

CHAPTER TWO ■■

1. Strauss and Howe, 279.

2. Strauss and Howe, 262, 300.

3. Strauss and Howe, 74.

4. An authority that Boomer political leaders have largely squandered.

5. Unlike the G.I.s with their twitchy fingers on the button.

6. Strauss and Howe, 281.

7. To appropriate a phrase from John 16:13.

8. Strauss and Howe also note the importance of this song, 282.

9. Strauss and Howe, 281.

10. Strauss and Howe, 282.

11. Strauss and Howe, 282.

12. Strauss and Howe, 281.

13. Strauss and Howe, 285.

14. Strauss and Howe, 285.

15. They don't actually use this word, but it comes through loud and clear in their description, 279–294.

16. See my chapter on Liberal Believers in *Faith Styles,* 49–64.

17. *Asanas* are yoga postures.

18. http://www.gallup.com/poll/117382/church-going-among-catholics-slides-tie-protestants.aspx

19. "Know the active, the masculine, yet keep to the passive, the feminine," *Tao Te Ching, A New Translation*, John R. Mabry, trans. (Rockport, MA: Element Books, 1994), poem 28.

CHAPTER THREE ■■■

1. Strauss and Howe, 74.

2. This phrase derives from the series of television interviews Bill Moyers conducted with Joseph Campbell, titled *The Power of Myth*, very popular among Boomers in the late 1980s.

3. Strauss and Howe, 299.

4. Acts 2:17, rephrasing Joel 2:28.

5. See my chapter on Spiritual Eclectics in *Faith Styles,* 13–30.

6. *The Secret* is a 2006 film (adapted into a book by Rhonda Byrne) describing the New Thought-derived teaching called "The Law of Attraction," which holds that one's interior thoughts and attitudes influence exterior events in one's life.

7. There have been many high-profile books and memoirs documenting such abuse. See, for instance, Michael Downing's *Shoes Outside the Door* (Berkeley: Counterpoint, 2002), Jayanti

Tamm's *Cartwheels in a Sari* (NY: Three Rivers Press, 2010), or John Hubner and Lindsey Gruson's *Monkey On a Stick* (NY: Onyx Books, 1990), among many others.

8. Matthew 5:15.

9. *Faith Styles*, 29.

10. A "directee" is a spiritual direction client.

11. A minister friend told me once of her experience in Japan, where women were eager to join her Christian church because it would mean freedom from the oppressive patriarchal demands of their Buddhist families.

12. http://www.religioustolerance.org/chr_tren.htm

13. Garfield, Charles, Cindy Spring and Sedonia Cahill, *Wisdom Circles: A Guide to Self-Discovery and Community Building in Small Groups* (New York: Hyperion, 1999).

14. So long as they admitted G.I. dominance, rolled over, and showed their bellies.

15. When did the new Boomer motto become "Never trust anyone under 50?"

CHAPTER FOUR ■■■■

1. Some researchers have created a separate category for the 1960–1965 crowd, labeled "Generation Jones." While there are some distinctions shared by this group, they are definitely a sub-group of Xers and not deserving of a separate category in this book.

2. Holtz, Geoffrey T. *Welcome to the Jungle: the Why Behind Generation X* (New York: Macmillan, 1995), 15

3. Strauss and Howe, 328.

4. "GenX: A Prescription for Despair. Tricycle Talks with Twentysomethings" *Tricycle*, Spring, 1997, 71.

5. Ronald J. Allen, "Preaching to Different Generations" *Encounter*, Autumn 1997, 393.

6. For more on the sociological forces which shaped Generation X, see my article "Rebels without Applause" at http://www.apocryphile.org/jrm/articles/rebels.html

7. You can find a link to the lyrics to "Smells Like Teen Spirit" at www.apocryphile.org/gen/

8. Christian Smith with Patricia Snell, *Souls in Transition* (New York: Oxford University Press, 2009), 93.

9. "Independent Sacramental Movement" is a phrase used by Dr. John P. Plummer to describe any of the small, independent Catholic, Orthodox, or Anglican movements often referred to as "independent catholic" churches. Most of these jurisdictions derive their orders from the Old Catholic Church of Utrecht, among other sources. See *The Many Paths of the Independent Sacramental Movement* (Berkeley: Apocryphile Press, 2006).

10. Rob Bell, *Love Wins: A Book About Heaven, Hell, and the Fate of Every Person Who Ever Lived* (HarperOne, 2011).

11. Which, I guess, would make Starbuck's the largest denomination.

12. James Fowler, *Stages of Faith* (San Francisco: Harper & Row, 1987).

13. 1979 *Book of Common Prayer* (ECUSA), "Collect for Purity," 355.

14. See my article "The Gnostic Generation: Understanding and Ministering to Generation X" for more on this, published in *Presence: The Journal of Spiritual Directors International,* May 1999.

15. See Charles Garfield, Cindy Spring, and Sedonia Cahill, *Wisdom Circles: A Guide to Self Discovery and Community Building in Small Groups* (New York: Hyperion, 1999).

16. Mark 2:27.

CHAPTER FIVE ■ ■ ■ ■ ■

1. Thomas S. Rainer and Jess W. Rainer, *The Millennials: Connecting to America's Largest Generation* (Nashville: B & H, 2011), 8.

2. Eric Greenberg with Karl Weber, *Generation We* (Emeryville, California: Pachatusan, 2008), 20.

3. Christian Smith with Patricia Snell, *Souls In Transition* (New York: Oxford University Press, 2009), 48.

4. This chapter is based on my own observations and interviews, but also on extensive research done by sociologists of religion studying this particular age group. Christian Smith has been following a group of over 3,000 young people for the past ten years, conducting personal interviews with 230 of them from forty-five states for his latest project (Christian Smith with Patricia Snell, *Souls In Transition* [New York: Oxford University Press, 2009], 3–4). Father and son team Thom Rainer and Jess Rainer studied 1,200 young adults for their research. Finally, a fascinating study done on behalf of the Church of England by Graham Cray, Sylvia Collins-Mayo, Bob Mayo, and Sara Savage was also very helpful—although their study was done on Millennials in the United Kingdom, there is sufficient consistency among so-called "first-world" Millennials to make their findings relevant for us here, as well (Graham Cray, Sylvia Collins-Mayo, Bob Mayo and Sara Savage, *Making Sense of Generation Y* [London: Church House Publishing, 2006]). While there were minor differences in these studies—the Rainer's findings present a consistently rosier view than Smith's, for instance— overall, the portrait that emerges of this enigmatic generation is congruent. I will be quoting from these researchers—and from the Millennials they interviewed— liberally in this chapter.

5. According to Strauss and Howe, there is precedent for this: During the Civil War, the Reactive Gilded generation (1822–1842) was followed by the Adaptive Progressive generation (1843–1859), skipping over a Civic generation. So it *can* happen—the question is, has it happened here?

6. Smith, 49.

7. The term was invented by Foster W. Cline and Jim Fay, and first used in their book, *Parenting with Love and Logic: Teaching Children Responsibility* (Colorado Springs: Pinon Press, 1990), 23–25.

8. Rainer and Rainer, 19.

9. Rainer and Rainer, 56.

10. Rainer and Rainer, 57.

11. Rainer and Rainer, 120.

12. Gibbs, Nancy. "Generation Next," *Time* (www.time.com/time/magazine/article/0,9171,1971433,00.html).

13. Rainer and Rainer, 59.

14. Rainer and Rainer, 75.

15. You can see his *60 Minutes* interview at http://www.cbsnews.com/stories/2007/11/08/60minutes/main3475200.shtml.

16. Rainer and Rainer, 161.

17. Greenberg, 24.

18. Rainer and Rainer, 133.

19. Note Deirdre's use of the word "happy," here—it will become more and more pronounced in our profile as we continue.

20. Greenberg, 24.

21. Note again the importance of "happiness" in Lena's response—more on this later.

22. Pew Research Center, "Millennials: A Portrait of Generation Next" (February 2010), 32.

23. Rainer and Rainer, 198.

24. Smith, 74.

25. Blanche Gallagher. *Meditations with Teilhard de Chardin* (Santa Fe: Bear & Co., 1988), 40.

26. Todd G. Buchholz and Victoria Buchholz, "The Go-Nowhere Generation," *New York Times*, March 10, 2012.

27. Smith, 73.

28. Smith, 73.

29. Graham Cray, Sylvia Collins-Mayo, Bob Mayo and Sara Savage, *Making Sense of Generation Y* (London: Church House Publishing, 2006), 35.

30. Smith, 25.

31. http://www.trushare.com/0134JLY06/06GenerationYNot.htm

32. Smith, 13.

33. Smith, 20.

34. http://www.cbsnews.com/stories/2007/11/08/60minutes/main3475200.shtml

35. http://www.cbsnews.com/stories/2007/11/08/60minutes/main3475200.shtml

36. http://richardsinstitute.org/UserFiles/Most-Praised%20Generation.pdf

37. Smith, 36.

38. Smith, 37.

39. Rainer and Rainer, 16.

40. Rainer and Rainer, 7.

41. Rainer and Rainer, 117.

42. Rainer and Rainer, 37.

43. Smith, 72–73.

44. Rainer and Rainer, 117.

45. Smith, 93.

46. Smith, 71.

47. Smith, 68.

48. Rainer and Rainer, 151.

49. Rainer and Rainer, 158.

50. See, for instance, Ke$ha's "Tik Tok."

51. Feel free to Google them yourself, however: Deirdre suggested "Lose Yourself," by Eminem, Lena nominated "Young, Wild and Free" by Wiz Khalifa, Deni pointed me to "It's All About the Benjamins" by Puff Daddy, while Kyle suggested "Too Much, Too Young, Too Fast" by Airborne.

52. See Paul Carr, "NSFW: Generation Whine—Why I'm Relieved not to be a Millennial," http://techcrunch.com/2010/10/10/dont-care-how-i-want-it-now/

53. Internet Movie Database: http://www.imdb.com

54. http://www.cbsnews.com/stories/2007/11/08/60minutes/main3475200.shtml

55. Paul Downs Coliazo, *Entertainment Weekly*, March 9, 2012, 23.

56. Rainer and Rainer, 47.

57. Smith, 92, 112.

58. Reported in Laura Sessions Stepp, "Why Young Evangelicals are Leaving Church," CNN, December 16, 2011.

59. Rainer and Rainer, 112.

60. Smith, 200.

61. Rainer and Rainer, 230.

62. Smith, 45.

63. Smith, 202.

64. Smith, 164.

65. Smith, 146.

66. Smith, 200.

67. Smith, 145.

68. Smith is quick to point out that no actual Millennials describe him- or herself as MTD—that's the name invented by him and his colleagues to describe the cluster of beliefs that they kept seeing among those they were studying.

69. Christian Smith with Melinda Lundquist Denton, *Soul Searching: The Religious and Spiritual Lives of American Teenagers* (New York: Oxford, 2005), 162–163.

70. Smith, *Soul Searching,* 163.

71. Smith, *Soul Searching,* 163.

72. Laura Sessions Stepp, CNN Opinion, "Why Young Evangelicals are Leaving Church," Friday December 16, 2011. http://www.cnn.com/2011/12/16/opinion/stepp-millennials-church/index.html

73. Smith, 119.

74. Michael Mason, Andrew Singleton, and Ruth Webber. *The Spirit of Generation Y: Young People's Spirituality in a Changing Australia* (Australia: John Garratt Publishing, 2008).

75. Which may, upon reflection, be oxymoronic.

76. Smith, 121.

77. Smith, 153.

78. Smith, 153.

79. Greg, posting on http://www.grapethinking.com/millennial-generation-spirituality

80. Cathy Lynn Grossman, *USA Today*, 4/27/2010.

81. See my chapter on Ethical Humanists in *Faith Styles,* 31–47.

82. *USA Today,* April 27, 2010.

83. It takes considerable creativity to frame the neglect of spiritual practice as altruism.

84. Smith, 116.

85. Smith, 112.

86. Smith, 152.

87. Smith, 152.

88. Adam J. Copeland, "No Need for Church," *Christian Century*, February 8, 2012, 13.

89. Rainer and Rainer, 171.

90. Rainer and Rainer, 171.

91. Copeland, 13.

92. Mayo, et al., 38.

93. Mayo, et al., 164.

94. Although I know I say that at the risk of sounding Boomerish.

95. Mayo, et al., 164–5.

96. Mayo, et al., 170.

97. And while you're at it, apologize to your Xer friends, who really *did* care about these things, even if they declined to participate in your cockamamie schemes.

98. Scott McKnight, *A Community Called Atonement* (Nashville: Abingdon, 2007), 36.

99. Copeland, 13.

ABOUT THE AUTHOR

REV. JOHN R. MABRY holds a Master's degree from Holy Names College and a doctorate in Philosophy and Religion from the California Institute of Integral Studies. He has served as editor for *Creation Spirituality* magazine as well as *Presence: An International Journal of Spiritual Direction.* A United Church of Christ minister, he currently serves as pastor of Grace North Church in Berkeley, California (an Anglican-rite Congregational parish), and as Director of the Interfaith Spiritual Direction Certificate Program at the Chaplaincy Institute. He is the author of *FaithStyles: Ways People Hold Faith* and *Noticing the Divine: An Introduction to Interfaith Spiritual Guidance,* among many other books on spirituality and religion.